Marx's Social Critique of Culture

LOUIS DUPRÉ

Yale University Press

New Haven and London

Designed by Nancy Ovedovitz and set in VIP Baskerville type.
Printed in the United States of America by Halliday Lithograph,
West Hanover, Mass.

Library of Congress Cataloging in Publication Data

Dupré, Louis K.
   Marx's critique of modern culture.
   Includes bibliographical references and index.
   1. Communism and culture. 2. Communism and society.
3. Marxian school of sociology. 4. Marxian economics.
5. Historical materialism. 6. Marx, Karl, 1818–1883.
I. Title.
HX523.D86   1983   301   83-42871
ISBN 0-300-03082-7
ISBN 0-300-03475-X (pbk.)

3   5   7   9   10   8   6   4   2

Marx's Social Critique of Culture

Contents

Foreword

The writing of this study passed through a considerable evolution. What started as an attempt to correct and further explore certain theses I proposed in an earlier publication eventually led to a wholly new assessment of Marx's significance in the history of Western consciousness. He had been, I was forced to conclude, the first major critic of a process of cultural disintegration that began with the modern age and has continued unabated down to our own time. The various names emerging in our new awareness of what has now become a crisis—objectivism, subjectivism, dualism—describe singular aspects of a phenomenon that Marx precociously, though perhaps one-sidedly, perceived. To evaluate his unique contribution in analyzing this process of cultural disintegration and in proposing measures to remedy it is the purpose of my study.

I owe debts to many, not only for my understanding of Marx, but even more so for that of the underlying conception of cultural development. To name them all would be impossible. Yet one name must be mentioned. Over the years my friend and assistant, Roger Kimball, patiently read and edited successive versions of the present text. Without his help this book might never have seen the light.

Portions of chapters 1, 2, 3, and 5 have previously appeared in the following journals: *Man and World* (chap. 1), *Tijdschrift voor Filosofie* (chap. 2), and *Review of Metaphysics* (chaps. 3, 5).

Note on Sources

References to Marx and Engels first give the German text and then the English translation. For the early works, I have used the *MEGA* edition (*Marx Engels Gesamtausgabe*, 11 vols., Berlin and Moscow, 1927–35), which remains incomplete but was resumed for the Manuscripts of 1871–73. For the later works, I refer to the *Werke* (*Marx Engels Werke*, 39 vols, Berlin: Dietz, 1957–72); for *Grundrisse*, to the Dietz edition (Berlin, 1953).

Translations of the early writings, unless otherwise indicated, are taken from the still incomplete *Collected Works* (New York: International Publishers, 1974–). Translations of *Capital* are taken from the three-volume edition published by International Publishers, 1967; those of *Grundrisse* (abbreviated as *GR*), from Martin Nicolaus, *Grundrisse* (Baltimore: Pelican Books, 1973; abbreviated as NIC), and occasionally from David McLellan's partial translation published by Harper & Row in 1971 (abbreviated as McLellan). Other translations have been taken from *Engels Marx Selected Works*, vols. 1–2 (Moscow, 1955; numerous reprintings).

The notes published by Karl Kautsky as the fourth volume of *Capital* appear as vols. $26^{1,2,3}$ of the *Werke* and have been translated as *Theories of Surplus Value* by Emile Burns (Moscow: Progress Publishers, 1963), vols. 1–3 (abbreviated as *TSV*).

Introduction
The Reintegration of Culture

How do we define culture? As a process of "cultivating" a given nature or as one of creating a new, second nature? The answer to that question divides the ancients from the moderns. Neither the Greeks nor the Romans recognized the opposition between nature and culture that lies at the basis of the modern concept. They thought of humanization as the organic development of a *given* nature. The Greek *paideia*, as well as the Latin *cultus animi* and *cultura animi* (derived from the agricultural *colere*), stress the need to harmonize erudition and education with the demands of an established, social nature.

It was, I believe, in the early Italian Renaissance that the task of fostering and developing an existing potential started giving way to the desire for unlimited self-assertion. From that point on, man began to regard the entire socialization process as a construction of his own free will and insight. Only by surpassing his given humanity would he grow fully "human." In *De vulgari eloquentia* Dante attributes the origin of vernacular languages, the source of national cultures, to a technical enterprise undertaken in defiance of a divinely established order. The construction of the Tower of Babel made the assigned tasks so specialized that the workers ceased to know the names of each other's tools. Thus an act of rebellion, a decision to surpass one's allotted nature, stands at the birth of the new concept of culture. We shall not dwell on Dante's remarkable anticipation of the link, established by Marx, between division of labor and cultural diversity, but merely note the autonomous character which the idea of culture here suddenly acquires.[1] Increasingly in the fol-

---

1. Dante remains, of course, a transitional figure, in many respects loyal to the medieval world. His *De monarchia* continues to order even "secular" society by

lowing centuries culture came to consist of a refusal to accept
nature as *given*. The term *humanitas* itself articulated an ideal, an
invitation to lift oneself above ordinary mankind. What had
once been a means of accomplishing one's assigned task now
became an independent end in itself, an ideology.[2] In acquiring
humanitas, man as the new creator of his nature rivals his divine
Maker. Henceforth the rebel Prometheus, the thief of heaven's
fire, replaced the loyal Hercules as principal hero in the myth of
culture. The unpleasant final episode of Pandora's box, in which
the Greeks expressed their deep suspicion of god-daring exploits, was prudently omitted.

The idea underwent a final, somewhat ambiguous development when, in the eighteenth century, the meaning of *culture*
(now used as an independent term) changed from an individual
creation—*cultura animi*—into the objective expression of the
spirit of a whole nation. Did the change mark a further stage in
the Promethean development of modern culture, with the national genius fulfilling individual aspirations of divine creativity?
Or should we regard the romantic concept of organic growth
rather as a return to the classical idea of a harmonious development of an existing nature? Probably both. But since a similar
ambiguity appears in Marx's thought, we had better directly
consider his own position.

---

divine ordinance. Only with Machiavelli did the modern view extend to unrestricted human control over civil government. Of course, the question concerning the natural φύγει or conventional νόμῳ origin of culture had already arisen
among the Sophists. Yet Plato's vigorous criticism seems to have defused this
explosive issue. At any rate, whenever Aristotle discusses it in the matter of
language and ethics, *physis* and *nomos* no longer appear as alternatives: diverse
customs are grafted onto a common, given nature. Thus, in *On Interpretation* he
writes: "Just as all men have not the same writing, so all men have not the same
speech sounds, but the mental experiences which these directly symbolize are the
same for all, as also are those things of which our experiences are the images"
(16[a]5). The same conception returns in Horace *Ars Poetica* 2. 60–62, in Dante's
Paradiso 26 (where Adam reiterates Horace's image of the falling leaves), in
Rabelais ("les langues sont par institutions arbitraires," 3:19), and in du Bellay.

2. Cf. Joseph Niedermann, *Kultur, Werden und Wandlungen des Begriffs und
seiner Ersatzbegriffe von Cicero bis Herder* (Florence: Biblioteca dell'Archivum Ro-
manicum, 1941), 28:31, 77–78.

In one sense the modern Promethean tradition culminates in Marx's vision of man as the sole shaper of his destiny. Intolerant of any divine interference, the young graduate in philosophy prefaced his doctoral dissertation with a phrase taken from Aeschylus's rebellious Prometheus: "In one word I hate all the gods." An eager reader of the Greek tragedians, the young Marx found much inspiration in the mythical hero, and his friends were undoubtedly right in feeling that he strongly identified with him. One of them drew a caricature of a half-naked Marx chained to a printing press with the royal eagle of Prussian censorship picking at his liver. The drawing may have been in dubious taste, but the model appropriately symbolizes a life devoted to the emancipation of culture from reputed powers of oppression—both celestial and terrestrial. We shall find this Promethean streak in Marx's thought confirmed by his faith in the unlimited possibilities of technology.

And yet there is a sense in which Marx challenged the pretensions of the modern age, criticizing any view that would detach socialization from its natural basis. This naturalistic strand in Marx's thought turned him into the first radical critic of the very cultural development that culminated in his work. From the beginning to the end of his career, explicitly and implicitly, the great critic exposed the spurious claims of a culture which had erected itself into an independent, quasi-religious reality, a dehumanized, denaturalized fetish. The putative "disinterestedness" of such a culture maintains a secret but solid collusion with the acquisitive mentality. The bourgeois world "collects" art and erudition, shackles science to an economically dominated technology, "invests" in paintings and in learning as in stocks and bonds. Marx attempted to reverse this tide and to reintegrate culture with the totality of human activity, starting from the elementary relation with nature. His radical interpretation of the modern view unexpectedly rejoins the naturalist, holistic tradition of the ancients. Not, to be sure, that Marx advocated a romantic return to nature, only that he demanded the firm link with nature characteristic of the ancient ideal.

Critique of culture has never been wanting in the West. But not even the vocal iconoclasts of the eighteenth century or the revolutionaries who succeeded them had attacked the foundational structures of society, much less the relations between these structures and culture as a whole. Anxious to integrate all facets of socialization within one tightly woven complex, Marx focuses his attention on the base as it affects the whole, rather than on the legitimacy of isolated phenomena or cultural attitudes. Not surprisingly, many have attacked the intimate link he forged between the selfless quest for theoretical knowledge or pure beauty and social-economic structures. But often they do so because they view culture as an artificial, secondary environment superimposed on a sphere of natural, vital activity. The inadequacy of this view shows itself in the profoundly schizoid attitude typical of the modern tradition, which inconsistently alternates between a daily pursuit of economic interests and an intermittent escape into the ethereal realm of "culture." Marx rejects any such arbitrary separation between a purely theoretical and a wholly practical realm of activity.

If Marx's critics have failed to appreciate the holistic quality of his approach, so, unfortunately, have many of his followers. Where he stressed social coherence, they defended causal determinism. Thus culture became demoted to a byproduct of economic production. Organic wholeness and mutual determination were shunned in favor of rigid stratifications and linear causalities. Indeed, the very equation of culture with the intellectual and imaginative products of society current among Marxists conflicts with Marx's views. As Raymond Williams observes, "Marxists should logically use 'culture' in the sense of a whole way of life, a general social process."[3] Did Marx himself succeed in reuniting what centuries had separated? At this point the answer to that question must remain uncertain. The principle that social-economic relations, themselves determined by the "forces of production," form the "base" of the cultural process, naturally instills some doubt about this success. But the titanic scope of Marx's enterprise and its significance at a critical juncture of our culture merits, in any event, the effort of a serious investigation of his critique.

3. Raymond Williams, *Culture and Society* (New York: Harper & Row, 1966), p. 282.

It is worth reminding ourselves that while Marx's critique of capitalist society and its system of production contains a judgment on bourgeois culture as a whole, he never developed a systematic *theory* of culture. Nevertheless, this study assumes that Marx's critical analysis of the intricate web of interdependence between production relations and all other social and cultural expressions also *implies* a theory about culture in general. To find it, however, we must look beyond the superficial and oft vetted structure–superstructure dialectic. Marx's original contribution consists not in having shown the impact of the social-economic sphere upon all others, but in having shown this impact to be a mutual one. Ideas and works of art exercise as direct an influence upon production and consumption as changes in the production affect all other facets of culture. Marx's critique focuses primarily on the negative character of the existing relation, the basic alienation that separates consciousness from life, theory from practice, productive activity from produced objects. Though the term *alienation* virtually disappears from the later writings, the idea of an objective separation between man and his self-realizing activity inspires his critique to the end. The fundamental estrangement occurs, not in subjective states of awareness, but in the basic productive attitudes of society. Hence, after an introductory chapter on cultural alienation we must pursue Marx's critique within the concrete, historical dialectic of social development and, ultimately, of economic production.

Marx never justified his dialectical method of interpretation. After his death it became the center of controversies that continue to divide various groups of Marxists and Marxologists. For some, dialectic is no more than a remnant of Marx's philosophical youth, at best a heuristic device that occasionally interferes with a basically empirical analysis of society. They choose to interpret the critic as a social scientist who operates with permanent social structures rather than with dynamic, ever-changing concepts. Such a view conflicts with Marx's clearly expressed intentions. Without the dialectic his critique loses its logical power. But this dialectic does not allow itself to be formulated in a set of a priori principles: it emerges from praxis itself in its concrete historical developments. Hence the dialectic must be studied where Marx applied it most consistently, in his critique of economics. The third chapter will deal with this concrete structural dialectic of the economic base.

Is a technical discussion of the dialectic, particularly the dialectic of the social-economic base, necessary in a study of Marx's theory of culture? The answer is that those cultural achievements which the Marxist tradition considers part of the superstructure cannot be understood independently of their relation to the base and its internal dialectic. It was precisely against the separation of the two spheres of activity that Marx directed his sharpest critique. In this respect his conception of culture differs from that of the modern era, but also from that of those "dialectical materialists" who, in the communication between base and superstructure, gave an absolute primacy to the influence of the base and thereby reopened the gap between "culture" and social-economic activity which Marx intended to close. Once again, then, culture begins after the serious business of economics has been taken care of: it may still feed back into that business, but its causality remains strictly secondary.

On the other side, if Marx conceives social-economic activity itself as an integral part of the cultural process, it should not be allowed to detach itself from all other activity. For Marx, economic activity functions as the vital catalyst of the process of socialization, not as a privileged pursuit of narrowly economic ends. The so-called contradictions in capitalist practice and theory are less flaws in logic than in integrative praxis.

Only after having thoroughly explored the nature of the dialectic will we be able to tackle what within the traditional conception of culture would have been the sole subject of this study—namely, that particular part of a society's intellectual and aesthetic achievements which has, since the beginning of the modern age, become isolated from all others. In referring to it as ideological or superstructural, Marx denies its self-proclaimed sufficiency. No other part of his critique more radically differs from the traditional view. Nor has any other part been more criticized. If culture is indeed rooted in social-economic activity, how does it succeed in transcending this activity? Marx has left the clarification of this intricate problem mostly to his successors. Yet on one point he is unambiguous, and on that ultimately depends the acceptability of his hypothesis. The primacy of theory which had dominated ancient, medieval, and most of modern thought must give way to a primacy of praxis. On this issue Marx took his stand against the *entire* Western tradition and marked a wholly new beginning.

The principle that man must fundamentally express his humanity in *praxis* rather than in *theoria* so basically conflicts with the constant assumptions of our intellectual tradition that, until the eighteenth century, hardly anyone would have seriously entertained it.[4] Nevertheless, here also Marx follows a strand that reaches back to the beginnings of Greek philosophy—the characteristically Western belief in the rationality of the real. But Marx brought that tradition to an unexpected conclusion. For the Greeks a rational Logos animated all natural phenomena and endowed them with a meaning discernable to methodic reflection. This healthy rationalism, to which we owe the unique quality of *objectivity,* connects the dawn of Western civilization with modern thought. Yet a basic difference in the conception of the rational separates the ancient from the modern interpretation. For the Greeks it was an objective quality inherent in the given, objective nature of things. It definitely did not emerge from a human mind imposing its own categories upon a world devoid of immanent reason. The turn toward the subject as the sole source of rationality did not occur until the beginning of the modern age. This is clearly not the place to discuss the circumstances that occasioned it: the disintegration of the intrinsically rational world order in the nominalism of the late Middle Ages and the discovery (Galileo, Descartes) that the logical processes of the mind apply equally to the outside world. The move resulted in a rising oppositon between an imperious subject and an amorphous world which it informed with its own rationality. The rational subject's mastery of this newly forged scientific

4. Giordano Bruno may have hinted at such a reversal when one of the characters in his dialogue, *Spaccio,* declares that the gods have given man intelligence and hands in order to transcend the laws of the existing nature and to create another nature.

method inaugurated an unprecedented upsurge of the physical sciences. It also reduced the real to what the subject can analyze and control. This subjectification of the rational culminated, of course, in Kant. With him thought ceased to be intuitive contemplation altogether and became entirely controlling action. We cannot imagine the Greeks, the medieval scholastics, or even the rationalists of the modern age describing the cognitive attitude as that of "a judge compelling a witness to answer" (Kant). The change reflects the momentous impact of the experimental method of science upon the very concept of reason.

The immediate effect was that the "real" became reduced to the *ob-jective,* that is, what was constituted by an autonomous subject. While the Greek *theoria* had required the soul to be purified from its passions before being lifted up to the divine act of contemplation, the subject now adopted an attitude of domination toward its object. Its supremacy culminated in the idea "that only what I am going to make will be real."[5] Overall reason acquired a practical orientation, even in its theoretical activity. Its task now became to bestow form upon a formless world. The ideas of constituted objectivity and practical control entirely replaced the conception of meaning and value *inherent* in a given reality. They ended the rule of contemplation and introduced that of fabrication which, as Hannah Arendt has argued, resulted in an unlimited instrumentalization of the world: confidence in tools, supremacy of the principle of utility, reduction of

5. Habermas considers the Greek ideal to be directly responsible for the technocracy of the modern age (*Knowledge and Human Interests,* p. 304). The Greek emphasis upon the object's independence from the knower's immediate interests did indeed create the *possibility* of a value-free science, a necessary precondition for such a technocracy, but only after late medieval nominalism had eroded the axiological dimension of thought.

Marxists are by no means alone in their criticism of pure theory. Thus Rudolf Boehm also holds the Greek ideal of "superhuman," purely theoretical knowledge responsible for the inhuman technology and technologized pace of life in our age. According to him, Descartes's separation of the *res extensa* from the *res cogitans* which reduced the self to the status of an empty subject and the world to a mechanistic object, merely drew the conclusions already contained in the ancient notion of theory. Rudolf Boehm, *Kritik der Grundlagen des Zeitalters* (The Hague: Martinus Nijhoff, 1976), especially chap. 4.

nature to a workshop for human tinkering.[6] But even more significant in this process was the instrumentalization of reason itself. What began as a radical subjectification of the real, ended by reducing the subject itself to the mere function of *constituting objectivity* in the theoretical and the practical order. Max Horkheimer has shown how this instrumentalization of reason eventually deprives it of all content of its own.

> The more all nature is looked upon . . . as mere objects in relation to human subjects, the more is the once supposedly autonomous subject emptied of any content, until it finally becomes a mere name with nothing to denominate. The total transformation of each and every realm of being into a field of means leads to the liquidation of the subject who is supposed to use them. This gives modern industrialist society its nihilistic aspect. Subjectivization, which exalts the subject, also dooms him.[7]

The instrumentalization of reason made industrial capitalization possible. Yet capitalism, in turn, transformed all human achievements into "commodities" and thus subjected all aspects of culture to a more thorough objectivism.

It is against the backdrop of this all-encompassing objectivism that we must understand Marx's attack upon the "fetishism of commodities" and the fetishist mentality. Marx fully shared the traditional belief in rationality, especially the rationality of history. Few ideas are more basic to his thought than that man's development through the ages, after all aberrations and perversities, in the end must come out right. Marx never abandoned Hegel's principle that the real ultimately coincides with the rational. Indeed, he strengthened "the portentous power of the negative" by carrying it to the depths of industrial dehumanization and thereby giving the dialectic of history a tragic dimension which Hegel's social philosophy did not possess.

In another respect, however, Marx transformed the modern understanding of the rational precisely by following it to its ulti-

6. Hannah Arendt, *The Human Condition* (Chicago: The University of Chicago Press, 1958), p. 305.

7. Max Horkheimer, *The Eclipse of Reason*, (New York: Seabury, 1974), p. 93; also pp. 107–08, 124.

mate consequences. Before him, especially in idealist philosophy, the subject had been the sole source of meaning and value.
Marx took the principle of creativity still further by including
the subject itself in the productive act. For him, the subject no
longer *precedes* that act but results from it. Goethe's phrase, "Im
Anfang war die Tat," became the starting point of a new conception of subjectivity. Through his productive activity man creates
both *himself* and his world. In thus converting the idealist philosophy of knowledge into a theory of action, Marx absolutized its
fundamental principle that meaning and value are not *given*
with the nature of things, but *constituted* by the living deed. Here
the Promethean quality of Marx's thinking clearly gains the upper hand. Paradoxically, guided by the Greek belief in rationality (in its subjective interpretation), Marx toppled the ideal of
contemplation with which that belief began. Here we confront
the questions: Is such a primacy of praxis still compatible with
his overall attempt, likewise of classical origin, to reintegrate the
entire socialization process on a natural basis? Does the "practical" character of his rationality not stand in the way of his fundamental "naturalism"? Certainly, praxis tolerates no preestablished position within an eternal cosmos, as in the Greek model
of culture. It reduces nature itself to a subsidiary element of the
socializing act. Still, in rejecting the contemplative ideal (including the idea of a normative cosmos) Marx did not betray his
overall attempt to unify all social activity. He never tried to reintegrate *man with nature,* after the Greek model. His vision,
though reminiscent of a Greek ideal of harmonious, total expression in unison with nature, is unprecedentedly new: to unify
all stages of the socialization process in a *dialectic with nature.*
Whether a culture based on the foundation of praxis can remain
fully human is a question we must not raise until the end. For
now it suffices to point out the dynamics of Marx's thought and
to ascertain the basic compatibility of the various tendencies.

Before concluding this introduction, a word must be said
about the methodological consequences of approaching Marx's
theory as a critique. Marx's theory is only part of an intellectual
activity that also included revolutionary propaganda, blueprints
for concrete political action, responses to practical problems of

various kinds, and even plain journalistic hackwork. The following pages deal exclusively with the theory. They assume throughout that the theory is in the first place an *interpretation*, not only of the social-economic conditions of capitalism, but of the entire bourgeois culture. Since this interpretation views its subject as being *in transition*—that is, as being the *necessary* result of an earlier state and as *necessarily* preparing an entirely different one—it is by its very nature critical. This means that, while interpreting the present, it already views it as *passing away*. To view a mode of consciousness in its dependence on practical conditions is to understand it as part of an overarching process rather than as a self-contained structure of permanent meaning. It is, in fact, as Habermas has argued, to change hermeneutics into a critique of ideology. Marx himself regarded his work as primarily critical. From his earliest to his latest writings the term *critique* appears in titles and subtitles. First, ironically, in his controversies with the Young Hegelians *(The Holy Family, Critique of the Critical Critique);* later with a new, practical meaning (as in the title of *A Contribution to the Critique of Political Economy* or in the subtitle of *Capital: A Critique of Political Economy*). This places Marx within the intellectual tradition initiated by Kant and continued by Hegel and his followers. But Marx radically transformed this tradition. In his view, the epistemological critique of Kant and the Hegelians had halted well before the critical task was completed. Thought itself, according to Marx, plunges its roots in the deeper soil of the practical consciousness. A fundamental critique, then, must trace all theory back to its "practical" source.

Yet a critique undertaken from a radically historical perspective must, at least in principle, extend to its own judgments. Recognizing its own historical situation, it must also recognize the need for critical investigation beyond its own position. Even in his own time the critic can claim no absolute authority over the "ideologies" of his contemporaries, for he also argues from a historical position. To acknowledge the historical conditioning of all thought is not to become infallible oneself, but rather to submit all modes of consciousness, including the critique, to the test of fallibility.

Unfortunately, Marx's followers have commonly refused to subject their master's theory to the same kind of questioning to which he submitted all other theories. When Karl Korsch proclaimed that the materialist conception of history must also be applied to the materialist conception of history, his message met with fierce resistance and eventually led to his expulsion from the Communist party. All too often Marxists refuse to be measured by the same yardstick by which they measure others. Yet a social critique as fundamental as Marx's demands more than lip service to "changing historical circumstances." Instead of using social critique as a tool for interpreting a culture through its unique social conditions, many have frozen it into a ready-made set of principles indiscriminately applicable to every age and civilization. Such an ahistorical interpretation falls into the very error which Marx most consistently denounced in his predecessors—the assumption of an unchangeable social basis. Had Marx's disciples possessed his historical awareness, they would not have simply reapplied the principles he used for the analysis of *his* society. Marx formulated a *method of interpretation;* he did not leave us a master key that automatically opens the door to every culture.

Many of the problems that beset the bourgeois societies of the middle of the nineteenth century no longer exist; others, unforeseen by Marx, have taken their place. Our interpretation of the current global struggle over the distribution of dwindling resources can profit but little from a direct transposition of the Marxist theory of class antagonisms. Traditional class distinctions still exist and even continue to dominate the social life of some societies. But their importance is much diminished in modernized ones. The struggle for the redistribution of power and resources is no longer dominated by the antagonism between different groups within a society: it has developed into an explosive opposition between entire societies. The "communications revolution," accomplished largely through radio and television, has made this opposition tangible to the populations of all societies. Today virtually every inhabitant of an economically underdeveloped country has come to recognize himself as living under severe yet contingent restrictions. The intimate connection between economic realities, social structures, and cultural patterns has more than ever become a matter of general concern.

This study, then, posits the following thesis. Marx perceptively criticized the fragmented character of modern culture and forcefully argued for reintegrating all facets of human activity (theoretical as well as practical) on the basis of man's productive relation to nature. To this end he shifted the center of meaning from the thinking subject to *social praxis*. However radical, Marx's critique and his attempt at cultural reintegration remain partly *within the ideological horizon of the modern age*. Sharing a common assumption of the early nineteenth century, he attributed a unique priority to social-economic activity in the overall process of culture. At the same time, in contrast to the modern emphasis on the subject as sole source of meaning, he asserted the primacy of social praxis over theory. Both positions affected the success of his project. The former unduly narrowed it. The latter, if consistently maintained (which it was not), would abolish the very possibility of disengaged reflection indispensable for the pursuit of wisdom and the good life.

My critical reading of Marx does not intend to be a *critique* of Marx. Its primary purpose is to *interpret* the message, not to criticize it. But the lasting effectiveness of Marx's analysis invites us to an active dialogue. This distinguishes him from past figures whose impact has long been absorbed by our culture. Descartes steered modern thought in a new direction, but he has ceased to inspire cultural innovation. Marx's critique continues to challenge our attitudes today. He remains a living partner in the sociocultural discussion. But precisely on that ground he demands to be treated as a contemporary—that is, critically rather than deferentially. The very nature of Marx's undertaking excludes uncritical acceptance. To interpret a living critique is to investigate its supporting arguments. One hardly serves the interests of an oeuvre written against the uncritical use of authority by taking its own authority for granted. In Marx's case, because of the historical distance, an additional demand must be met. A cultural hermeneutic must be read in the light of those later developments which it initiated. Hence we must press our critical questions beyond Marx's recorded answers and consider conclusions far surpassing his stated intentions.

The dialectic between interpretation and critique is difficult to follow consistently, and I am not altogether confident that I have always succeeded in avoiding the two extremes of an uncritical presentation or an external critique. Yet I have tried to resist the temptation to go beyond Marx's text or its implications. Even this conservative policy has forced me to make hazardous choices in a corpus of writings that, constantly interrupted, include much development, occasional juxtapositions of incompatible theories, and a few plain contradictions. By claiming Marx's authority for any single one of them, one inevitably imposes one's own interpretation on the reader. As far as possible I have at least tried to indicate my preferences. In no case can this study claim to be more than an essay in hermeneutics—of Marx's critique of culture, obviously, but perhaps indirectly and in a modest degree also of the earlier roots and present ramifications of *what* he criticized in that culture.

1
Cultural and Social Alienation

THE HEGELIAN ORIGINS OF MARX'S CRITIQUE

It is rather unfortunate that this study must begin by analyzing a concept that in our time has become virtually empty of specific content. The term *alienation* has been applied to every conceivable form of malaise, individual or social, such as distrust of authority, the feeling of powerlessness, dissatisfaction with one's occupation or one's social relations, meaninglessness, lack of solidarity, political apathy, loneliness, a feeling of isolation from the culture of one's society, or lack of control over one's work. In the case of Marx, this is doubly unfortunate because the concept of alienation has at once been the principal source of the enormous revival of philosophical interest in his work and the main cause of its misinterpretation. What French existentialist philosophers after the war presented as Marx's key concept amounts in fact to little more than a secularized version of Feuerbach's theory of religious alienation. The critical reader, then, should be excused for feeling a natural aversion toward reopening a discussion of a term that by now has become virtually depleted of meaning. And yet a study on Marx's critique of culture has no alternative but to discuss first what for him served as the foundational concept of that critique.

In a very real sense this entire study deals with the estrangement between those activities by which man satisfies his biological needs and his attempts to develop his sociocultural potential. We naturally assume both to occur simultaneously, and to some extent they do, even under the worst of circumstances. Yet Marx more clearly than anyone before him (with the possible exception of Rousseau) has shown how small this "extent" may be. As he interpreted the social condition of his age, providing for their

15

elementary needs had, for the vast majority of his contemporaries, become an alternative to true humanization. As a result of, and partly in compensation for, this painful disjunction, the ideal of a "pure culture," that is, a culture detached from elementary social and biological liens, gained ever more ground. This detached purity hid the crude reality of its solid roots in some basic economic conditions. The culture of luxury was, in fact, the culture of privilege. Now every cultured contemporary of Marx would proudly have conceded his exceptional status; but few realized the inherent and fatal discrepancy between this status of privilege and cultural vitality. Marx's perception of this fatal separation is hard to overestimate. Personally steeped in literature, he nevertheless paid little attention to the cultural problem as such. Instead he concentrated on the more fundamental separation between man's endeavor for physical survival and his self-fulfilling sociocultural activity. His insight becomes apparent in the transformation whereby he turned the religious and cultural idea of alienation into a social-economic one.

Everyone knows the Hegelian origins of this idea, and there would be no need to go into this matter again if Hegel's conception had been correctly presented. Yet this is far from being the case with Marx's interpreters. On the whole, they have given a simplistic and largely distorted picture of Hegel's position. At least some of the responsibility must be laid at Marx's own doorstep. Having taken from Hegel what he needed, he appears to have delighted in reducing the philosopher's contribution to such popular simplicities as "setting Hegel on his head." Hegel scholars know better, of course, and so did Marx—but they do not write the commentaries on Marx's theory. Hence the need for describing, at least briefly, the historical background.

Marx's social critique started from what Hegel had described as the mind's inability to recognize itself in its objective creations. Yet this "alienation," which for Hegel had been a primarily "cultural" phenomenon, became for Marx an all-comprehensive social one. Not that Marx simply "socialized" Hegel's idea of culture. But he incorporated its entire content (including the spheres of Hegel's Absolute Spirit: art, religion, philosophy) into the wider realm of social expression. Hegel himself, in *The Phenomenology of Mind,* had attributed the causes of cultural es-

trangement to social-political degeneration. Moreover, his later
theory of the Objective Spirit was entirely devoted to social and
legal institutions (with morality as the reflective moment that
interiorizes the legal realm into the ethical one). Yet Hegel never
fully clarified the relation between this social objectification and
the Absolute Spirit in which much of what we call "culture" finds
its place. Marx resolutely united one with the other. *Bildung*
came down from its lofty heights into the hustle-bustle of social
strife and economic struggle. Yet Marx never drowned "culture"
in social-economic problems. The present popularity of his early
critique of social alienation is due to the fact that, beyond capitalist economy, it took on the entire value system of bourgeois
society.

Granting the correctness of the preceding interpretation,
however, we may wonder whether Marx's sociocultural approach extends to his later writings, where he dealt exclusively
with economic matters and (except in his personal notes)
avoided even the term *alienation*. We must postpone our answer
to the later chapters of this book. Yet in considering the question
we must remember what Marx's position was from the start—
namely, that culture becomes marginal to the serious concerns
of life unless it integrates all forms of social expression, the
economic as well as the narrowly cultural. Modern society has
reduced culture to a recreational activity to be indulged in by
those who are able to count on the economic services of others.
Next to it functions a wholly noncultural activity. Marx wants to
reintegrate this activity with the totality of sociocultural objectification. On the basis of a more comprehensive social vision, he
questions the assumptions of capitalist economy and of its theoretical proponents. All aspects of productive activity must be
reunited into an organic totality. To achieve this Marx had to
criticize economic activity, the dominant one in a capitalist society, on its own terms rather than through some extrinsic authority. This is the opposite of the *economism* with which Marx's later
writings have been so often charged. But neither does the term
humanism appropriately describe the early ones. From the beginning Marx *criticizes* the purely economic, and he criticizes it
through itself.

To be sure, the Paris Manuscripts bear traces of the humanist critique of economy of Sismondi and Buret. In *De la misère des classes laborieuses en Angleterre et en France* Buret had written: "All the trouble derives from the fact that a moral science has become a mathematical science and, especially that one has violently separated what should have remained united."[1] In the same vein, Marx refers to the "cynicism" of the classical economists, but he attributes this cynicism to the situation itself which they describe, rather than to their personal attitudes. Indeed, Marx defends Ricardo against Michel Chevalier's charge that he has left morals out of account: "M. Chevalier takes no account of political economy insofar as he moralizes, but he really and necessarily ignores ethics insofar as he practices political economy" (*MEGA* 1³: 132; *Coll. Works* 3: 311). If, as Engels had shown in his "Outline of Political Economy" (1844), no human interference can deflect the course of the ruling economic system, all attempts at moral and political reform must remain inadequate for remedying economically induced misery. Only by studying the self-destructive tendencies in the present system can we effectively prepare the next one. To Marx the human abuse of the capitalist economy reflects its internal incoherence. The so-called social-economic contradictions described in the three volumes of *Capital* consist mainly, and sometimes exclusively, of situations not so much self-contradictory as conflicting with the fundamental (i.e., human) nature of economic activity. In this sense the idea of alienation goes to the heart of Marx's thought, and its recent rediscovery, however one-sided its interpretation, has substantially contributed to our understanding of that thought.

Before it reached Marx, the term *alienation* had passed through a complex history that it would be tedious to review here.[2] Yet a word must be said about Hegel's use of the term, so crucial for a proper understanding of Marx's interpretation and so often misrepresented. Before Hegel, *Entfremdung* had exclusively held a theological and psychological meaning. Following

---

1. (Paris, 1849), 1:115.
2. Most of this prehistory has been covered by Istvan Meszaros, in *Marx's Theory of Alienation* (London: Merlin Press, 1970).

Fichte, Hegel used *Entäusserung* for the mind's objectification of itself, through knowledge and action, in the external realm of culture.[3] Alienation *(Entfremdung)* for him consists of that form of objectification *(Entäusserung)* in which the mind no longer recognizes itself in its own objective creations. Once a culture has been established, it largely escapes the control of those who belong to it and they inevitably become estranged from it. For such a cultural "alienation" to occur the mind must have attained that level of consciousness where it is "consciously aware of itself as its own world and of the world as itself"—that is, the level of Spirit.[4]

The alienation of the Spirit may adopt a positive or a negative form: either the Spirit fails to recognize its essence in its self-created culture *or* it seeks its essence in the projections of faith beyond the reality of the present. The two are, of course, connected. After the Spirit has abandoned its natural self and fails to recognize itself in its self-constituted objectivity, it tends to withdraw into the ideal sphere of pure "belief": "This second world, being constructed in opposition and contrast to the es-

3. This appears perhaps most clearly in the following sentence taken from Hegel's second *Realphilosophie* (1806): "I have externalized *(entäussert)* myself; this negation is positive; externalization *(Entäusserung)* is appropriation" *(Jenaer Realphilosophie*, p. 218).

4. *Phänomenologie des Geistes*, ed. J. Hoffmeister (Hamburg: Felix Meiner, 1952), p. 313. *The Phenomenology of Mind*, trans. J. B. Baillie (New York: Macmillan, 1949), p. 457. On the distinction between the two terms, one may consult: Joseph Gauvin, "Entfremdung et Entäusserung dans la Phénoménologie de l'Esprit de Hegel," *Archives de Philosophie* 25 (1962): 555–71; Albert Chapelle, *Hegel et la religion* (Paris: Annexes, 1967), pp. 101–25; Koenraad Boey, *L'Aliénation dans la Phénoménologie de l'Esprit* (Paris, 1970).

Since *Entfremdung* is a particular mode of *Enträusserung* on the level of Spirit, the two terms are occasionally interchanged. Yet Hegel never equates the two. In the second series of Jena lectures (1805) he applies *Entäusserung* to the Greek culture, which he never would have termed *"entfremdet."* The very passage of the *Phenomenology* which has frequently caused the confusion of the terms clearly implies their distinction: "On the one hand, actual self-consciousness passes through its *self-externalization* in the real world and the latter returns into the former. On the other hand, this very actuality, person as well as objectivity, is sublated; they are purely universal. Thus their *alienation* is pure consciousness or essence" *(Phänomenologie*, p. 348, my translation). In an article on "Hegel's Concept of Alienation and Marx's Reinterpretation of It" *(Hegel-Studien* 7 [1972]: 217–33), I have attempted to establish and to justify Hegel's use of the term.

trangement [*Entfremdung*], is just on that account not free from it; on the contrary, it is only the other form of that very estrangement, which consists precisely in having a conscious existence in two sorts of worlds, and embraces both."[5] Unfortunately Hegel complicates this relatively simple picture by referring to the process of culture itself (and not merely to culture gone astray) as alienating man from his original "natural" state. Man is not *by nature* what he must be if he is to be fully human. To break away from his animal state of nature requires *Bildung*, that is, a deliberate attempt on his part to acquire novelty in knowledge, maturity in judgment, composure in attitude, moderation in passion and wants.[6] The very process, then, through which the person divests himself of his limiting particularities and acquires "substantiality" is also said to alienate him:[7] "The means whereby an individual gets objective validity and concrete actuality here is the formative process of culture *(Bildung)*. The estrangement on the part of Spirit from its natural existence is here the individual's true and original nature, his very substance. The relinquishment of this natural state is, therefore, both his purpose and his mode of existence."[8] Clearly the *Entfremdung* involved in the creation of culture is a positive act, related to the "divestment" required by the social contract according to Grotius, Locke, and Rousseau.[9] However, while the traditional divestment was exclusively social, Hegel's is primarily cultural. *Bildung* consists above all in a conscious effort to shed "natural" idiosyn-

5. *Phänomenologie*, p. 350; *Phenomenology*, p. 513.
6. This description of *Bildung* appears in Hegel's earlier *Propädeutik* written for his Nürnberg "gymnasium" students. *Sämtliche Werke* (Jubiläumsausgabe) 3 (Stuttgart, 1949), pp. 82–83.
7. *Phänomenologie*, p. 348; *Phenomenology*, p. 510. As early as the *Differenz des Fichteschen und Schellingschen Systems der Philosophie* (1801) Hegel had referred to the *Bildung* of a particular epoch as its *"unfreie gegebene Seite."*
8. *Phänomenologie*, p. 351; *Phenomenology*, p. 515.
9. In Hobbes's *Leviathan*, the "divestment" needed for social cooperation and the estrangement from nature appear connected as the two presuppositions of culture. The condition of war that precedes the social state parallels the war with nature, the first requisite for any human culture. Cf. Gary Herbert, "Hobbes' Dialectic of Desire," in *The New Scholasticism* (1976), pp. 143–46. Richard Schacht, *Alienation* (New York: Doubleday, 1970), pp. 55–56, has rightly drawn attention

cracies and to attain "universal" personhood. It is an attempt at objective self-awareness that requires a great deal of struggle and often results in failure. The discrepancy between the two meanings—the painful but successful effort to give consciousness objective "substance," and the ultimate inadequacy of the cultural enterprise as a whole, accompanied by a flight into an idea beyond—is never resolved.[10]

The description that follows Hegel's general discussion introduces yet a third kind of alienation, negative as is the second, but more social than *cultural:* the deterioration of social attitudes during the absolute monarchy just prior to the French Revolution. Here we detect most clearly the impact of Rousseau's idea that the transfer *(aliénation)* of sovereignty from the people is an abuse of power.[11] The increasing exploitation of state power for

---

to the connection between social "divestment" in Locke and Rousseau and the notion of estrangement.

10. Despite a text in which the two appear organically united: "This world, although it has come into being by means of individuality, is in the eyes of self-consciousness something that is directly and primarily estranged, and, for self-consciousness, takes on the form of a fixed, undisturbed reality. But at the same time self-consciousness is sure this is its own substance and proceeds to take it under control. This power over its substance it acquires by culture, which, looked at from this aspect, appears as self-consciousness making itself conform to reality, and doing so to the extent permitted by the energy of its original character and talents" (*Phänomenologie*, p. 352; *Phenomonology*, p. 516).

11. It is this abuse which Hegel must have had in mind when he borrowed the neologism *entfremdet* from Goethe's translation of Diderot's *Le neveu de Rameau.* The main character of this strange novel incarnates the total decadence of social life at the end of the absolute monarchy. Though the term *aliéné* (Goethe: *entfremdet*) in Diderot's text refers exclusively to a psychological state of derangement, Hegel seems to have transferred it to the prevailing climate of social depravity in which the story takes place (Diderot, *Selected Writings*, ed. Lester Crocker [New York: Macmillian, 1966], pp. 234–35). It is not inappropriate to connect Diderot's *Supplement to Bougainville's Voyage* with Hegel's usage of the term, as Meszaros does (*Marx's Theory of Alienation*, pp. 46–48, 319a). For here Diderot shows us the full impact of Rousseau's unlawful alienation. A direct line could be drawn from Rousseau to Diderot to Marx, for which Hegel merely provided the term *Entfremdung.* The obvious influence of Rousseau's *ideas* has led some to read in Hegel's *Entfremdung* a direct translation of Rousseau's *aliénation* (Jean Hyppolite, *Genèse et structure de la Phénoménologie de l'Esprit de Hegel* [Paris, 1946], pp. 375–76). Yet in *Du contrat social, aliéner* means only "to trans-

private purposes resulted in an evergrowing disaffection between individuals and the common weal. The disintegration was
not primarily the result of the "base" attitude that seeks private
advantage through public functions. The self-sacrificing, "noble" consciousness, by identifying private honor with the common good, is first responsible for deflecting that good toward its
particular interests. Thus it inevitably turns into a base consciousness. More deeply alienated than the noble one which
takes a positive attitude toward the State and its wealth, the base
consciousness, as the negative element in the dialectic, is the one
that moves history. The base consciousness acts essentially as a
revolutionary consciousness. "It looks upon the authoritative
power of the State as a chain, as something suppressing its separate existence for its own sake and hence hates the ruler, obeys
only with secret malice and stands ever ready to burst out into
rebellion."[12] Wealth is considered with contempt and accepted
without gratitude. The French Revolution, in which the base
consciousness triumphed over the noble one, concludes Hegel's
discussion of the alienated mind.

Not a word about the social-economic conditions which, according to Marx, constitute the true alienation of man. Indeed,
in Hegel's mature theory of society, the *Philosophy of Right,* the
concept of alienation no longer appears. The ultimate social
synthesis of the state is presented as resolving all social tensions
created by citizens working only for their particular interests.
Hegel now optimistically holds that the pursuit of private profit
under the high but benevolent supervision of the state inevitably
contributes to the general well-being. Yet such had not always
been his position. In his earliest projection for a philosophical

mit," specifically, the transmission of certain rights whereby the individual becomes a member of society. Hegel translated this kind of *aliénation* by *Veräusserung.* (*Hegels theologische Jugendschriften,* ed. Hermann Nohl [Tübingen, 1907],
pp. 212, 213. In the *Philosophy of Right* [para. 67], *Veräusserung* describes a legal
transfer of ownership.) A direct connection between *Entfremdung* and Rousseau's
aliénation cannot be supported. Nevertheless, Rousseau's description of the
present state of society as one of contradiction has clearly influenced Hegel's
usage of *Entfremdung.*

12. *Phänomenologie,* p. 359; *Phenomenology,* p. 525.

system (Jena, 1803–04), Hegel had taken a dim view of such independently operating social systems as the capitalist economy. His critique, although not phrased in the language of alienation, anticipates much of what Marx wrote under that title. Specifically he exposes the baneful separation between the worker and his product. "The individual satisfies his needs by his labor, but not by the particular product on which he has worked; to satisfy his needs the product must become something else than what it is."[13] As Marx was to point out later, the total separation between use and exchange inevitably subordinates the worker to the product. Hegel also foresaw that a market based upon abstract labor drives up the production at the expense of the worker. Mechanization, instead of liberating the worker from heavy labor, merely increases the working hours and decreases the value of the products. "The need to work diminishes only for the whole; not for the individual. On the contrary, for him it increases. The more labor becomes mechanized, the less value it has and the more he must work."[14] "The value of labor decreases in the same proportion as the production of labor increases."[15] Hegel's pessimistic description of industrialized capitalism differs from Marx's only in the optimistic note on which it ends: a strong state power can still keep the system in control. But the terms of his description convey as strongly the negative meaning of alienation as Marx's social protest. A remnant of this social criticism may still be found in the *Phenomenology*'s analysis of state wealth and state power. Yet here the critical impact is already weakened by the impression of logical inevitability.[16]

13. *Jenenser Realphilosophie*, vol. 1, ed. J. Hoffmeister (Leipzig, 1932), p. 238.
14. Ibid., p. 237.
15. Ibid., p. 239.
16. It is, of course, tempting to draw an analogy between Hegel's theory of cultural alienation and that of modern sociologists. In some cases, such as Georg Simmel's, the resemblance is due to a direct influence. In other cases, the analogy is all the more striking because the influence is indirect or nonexistent. Robert Merton's alienation from the norms of society, Talcott Parson's failure in the process of value acquisition, Peter Berger's inability to share in a particular, given culture no longer supported by the socializing power of religion—all develop aspects of Hegel's social critique.

THE PROPER CONTENT OF THE SOCIAL AND ITS FALSIFICATION

It would be tedious to retell the well-known story of the idea of *Entfremdung* from Hegel via Feuerbach to Marx. Yet it may be worth noting that Feuerbach's religious interpretation of it (as a projection of man's infinite potential into an autonomous, superhuman realm) deprives the concept of its characteristic sociocultural meaning. Even when Feuerbach in his "Provisional Theses for the Reform of Philosophy" (1843) included all philosophy in this "alienation" as being the secularized stronghold of religious mystification, his allegedly concrete "anthropology" remained a purely speculative construction, indeed far more so than Hegel's social philosophy. Marx must have felt this, for he never accepted Feuerbach's interpretation, even though he himself had begun with a critique of religion. Nevertheless, Feuerbach alerted him to the possibility of liberating Hegel's dynamic philosophy (which he needed for his own social critique) from its inherent idealism. Feuerbach had attempted to exorcize Hegel's "religious" idealism. Yet Marx detected a more fundamental idealism in the implied independence of the conscious sphere of culture with respect to social-economic activity.

First Marx restricted his critique to Hegel's political idealism. The state and its subaltern institutions, rather than being the basis, as Hegel claimed, were no more than an ideal, quasi-religious projection of the real, social-economic basis of society. Reinterpreting Feuerbach's "Theses" in a political sense, Marx proceeded to apply the idea of alienation to what he now came to view as the political projection of the modern state with respect to the underlying social-economic basis.

Hegel's *Philosophy of Right* not only described the "religious" projection of the modern state, but in addition it "justified" this projection through a theory that was itself a religious alienation in disguise. The state, Hegel claims, subordinates the selfish individualism of the civil society to its own spiritual aims. In reality, however, the state serves the existing economic relations by providing them with a legal sanction. Empirical reality and logical projection have been reversed in this "logical, pantheistic mysticism" (*MEGA* 1¹: 406; *Coll. Works* 3: 7). While mixing religious metaphors with social criticism, Marx does, in fact, more than *apply* Feuerbach's religious notion of alienation: he transfers the entire discussion to a social-economic ground. The state which, according to Hegel, constitutes the substance of man's social existence, is in fact a *social* illusion which merely lends social respectability and legal protection to the economic interests of its citizens. Man's alienation, then, according to Marx's earliest interpretation, consists not in a religious projection but in the estrangement of his social nature.

In an article written for the *German-French Yearbooks* in reply to Bruno Bauer's defense of the political emancipation of the Jews, Marx brought these reflections to a conclusion. Attacking Bauer's proposal of total secularization as the solution of the Jewish problem in Germany, Marx claimed that the secular, democratic state is *the* modern version of the religious illusion. It maintains the same relation of *apparent* dominance and *real* subservience to civil society which exists between the religious sphere and the profane world. The state expresses the religious relation in political terms. The more the modern state is emancipated from religion, the more religious it becomes itself, for the secular state alone fully absorbs an alienation which first appears in religion. Religion is an inverted world consciousness produced by an inverted world. To wake up from the religious consciousness man must first rid himself of the inverted world structure.[17] This is the task to which Marx addresses himself in the Paris Manuscripts of 1844.

17. At the end of the article on the Jewish Question, Marx refers to a text in which Rousseau describes the social contract as "taking from a man his own powers and giving him in exchange alien powers" (*MEGA* 1¹: 599; *Coll. Works* 3:167). Now obviously Rousseau's term *aliénation* differs substantially from Hegel's *Entfremdung;* yet Marx here connects the term *Entfremdung* with Rousseau's theory. To understand it, however, we should think more of the descriptions of the abstract and self-estranged state of modern society in *Du contrat social,* and even of the situation of man who has left the natural state in *Emile* (book 4), than of Rousseau's usage of the term *aliénation.*

Cf. Hans Barth, "Über die Idee der Selbstentfremdung des Menschen bei Rousseau," *Zeitschrift für philosophische Forschung* 13 (1959): 16 ff. Friedrich Müller, *Entfremdung. Zur anthropologischen Begrundung der Staatstheorie bei Rousseau,*

Almost imperceptibly, Marx had transformed Feuerbach's abstract anthropology into a concrete one of needs and production. He had understood the *social* inadequacy of Feuerbach's theory from the start. A close reading of Hegel's *Philosophy of Right* had drawn his attention to the intimate connection between political institutions and economic production. Hegel had granted a priority to political life. But after having read Engels's "Outline of Political Economy" (1844), Marx understood that the priority belonged to the economic sphere. He began to study the classical economists and reformulated his theory. In the process of doing so, he rediscovered Hegel. Feuerbach had in fact sacrificed the dynamic relation between the dialectical moments in favor of a mechanical schema imposed upon a static, humanist theory. Even Marx's early efforts to replace Feuerbach's abstract "man of flesh and blood" by a concrete center of social relations had not succeeded in restoring the *driving force* to the concept of alienation. It had remained an undesirable condition. For Hegel, he now understood, "alienation" referred to a forward-moving impulse that negates and, with the same necessity, overcomes the negation.

In his analysis of Hegel's *Phenomenology* at the end of the Manuscripts, Marx clearly moves beyond Feuerbach's critique of religious idealism. Not the idea of Spirit or of God is the problem, but the assumption (also prevalent in Feuerbach) of an autonomous realm of consciousness. Alienation is *not* a state of mind: it consists in an objective social condition. For Hegel, Marx claims, each time the mind objectifies itself in the real world it becomes estranged from itself. This is a puzzling statement. Even a superficial reading of Hegel's text shows clearly that he distinguishes alienation from objectification. Nor does he dissolve the real world into consciousness, since consciousness itself becomes "real" only in its objective, sociocultural expression. Consciousness does not overcome alienation by abolishing its dialectical opposition to the real world, but by abolishing that particular

---

Hegel, Marx (Berlin, 1970), esp. pp. 26–27, 34, 56, 60–61. Müller rightly stresses the identical emphasis on the historical character of what Marx calls *Entfremdung* in both authors.

opposition which prevents it from *recognizing* itself in its cultural expression. How could Marx have come up with an interpretation that so obviously conflicts with Hegel's text? The answer, I believe, lies in the different problematic of the two thinkers. Hegel's problem is a purely theoretical one: how can *consciousness* (the subject of the *Phenomenology!*) come to terms with an actual tension between the self and the nonself? Marx raises a practical issue: how must the tension between the individual and society in their common conquest of the world *practically* be resolved? He rejects Hegel's reappropriation, because he interprets it as the solution of a practical problem—which it is not. Yet beyond this erroneous interpretation lies Marx's own insight that any theory isolated from praxis distorts reality. To explain cultural alienation as the mind's inability *to recognize itself* in its objective structures is to remain within an alienating perspective. Marx's questionable exegesis, then, should be read in view of his own position.

Here the difficult question of which norm he measures man's condition by awaits us. To conceive of the present condition of society as alienating presupposes a positive state to which the present one is related. Is it a historical phase or a normative ideal that has never existed in history? Marx, of course, ruled out the wholly unsubstantiated assumption of a "state of nature" such as the natural law philosophers of the seventeenth and eighteenth centuries had postulated.

> Do not let us go back to a fictitious primordial condition as the political economist does, when he tried to explain. Such a primordial condition explains nothing; it merely pushes the question away into a grey, nebulous distance. . . . We proceed from an *actual* economic fact. The worker becomes all the poorer the more wealth he produces, the more his production increases in power and size. [*MEGA* 1³: 82; *Coll. Works* 3: 271–72]

Yet, at least in the Paris Manuscripts, the internal contradictions of this "actual economic fact" appear to have been conceived against a normative ideal of human nature. "Normative" must not be understood as if the ideal of human nature had ever been fully actualized. What man can do *ideally* may be gathered from the dynamics of the existing society, not from present or past achievements.[18]

Nevertheless, the frequent appearance of the terms *nature* and *natural* indicates the presence of a cultural apriority, a concern on Marx's part to keep all human activity well within a "given" relation. Thus he refers to man as a "natural" and "objective" being (*MEGA* 1³: 150–51; *Coll. Works* 3: 336) that remains intrinsically dependent on physical nature and constitutes, in fact, an integral unity with it. "To say that man *lives* from nature means that nature is his *body* with which he must remain in a continuous interchange in order not to die" (*MEGA* 1³: 87; *Coll. Works* 3: 275). As an *objective* being man finds the satisfaction of his needs as well as the exercise of his powers outside himself. He must "objectify" himself: he must create objects because he himself is established by objects (*MEGA* 1³: 160; *Coll. Works* 3: 336). Yet objectivity does not suffice. If he were only objective, man would be satisfied to produce for the satisfaction of his private needs, but he would never raise himself to cultural activity. In fact, man "adopts the species as his object . . . [acting] as a universal and consequently free being" (*MEGA* 1³: 87; *Coll. Works* 3:275). "The object of labor is, therefore, the *objectification of man's species-life;* for he no longer reproduces himself merely intellectually, as in consciousness, but actively and in a real sense, and he sees his own reflection in a world which he has constructed" (*MEGA* 1³: 89; *Coll. Works* 3:277). Only the distance from nature established by a production exceeding man's immediate needs effects "the accomplished naturalism of man and the accomplished humanism of nature" (*MEGA* 1³: 116; *Coll. Works* 3: 298). But it does so only as long as the individual retains a direct contact with the nature he transforms through his productive activity. Industrial capitalism has broken this natural link. The worker no longer identifies with the hundreds of iden-

18. With William L. McBride, we assume that as a moral ideal, human nature for Marx does not yet exist but will exist in the future. William L. McBride, "Marxism and Natural Law," in *The American Journal of Jurisprudence* 15 (1970): 127–40.

tical products he has brief contact with on the assembly line and to which he contributes only a minimal share.[19] Thus he loses the control over his environment at the very moment when society has gained an unparalleled dominion over nature. Capitalism has driven a wedge between man and his needs by directing its production to ends entirely alien to those needs. By the same token, it has caused a breach between his work and the satisfaction of his needs. Work becomes exclusively a matter of physical necessity, unrelated to desire. It "is not the satisfaction of a need [self-realization through work], but only a means for satisfying other needs [elementary, physical]" (*MEGA* 1³: 86; *Coll. Works* 3: 274). With his work the worker sells his own self. He *himself* has become an exchange commodity dependent for his very identity upon the purchasing power of others.[20]

Somewhat intriguingly, Marx adds that capitalist production also estranges man from his species. It deprives his work of that social and universal quality that enables him to produce for the sustenance and development of the entire species beyond that of the single individual (*MEGA* 1³: 86; *Coll. Works* 3: 276). In the capitalist production process, the worker's activity regresses to a more primitive satisfaction of individual needs (*MEGA* 1³: 88; *Coll. Works* 3: 276). Capitalist production is, of course, heavily socialized in its methods, but these methods of production fundamentally conflict with its strictly individualist appropriation. Bourgeois society sanctions this individualist appropriation by giving absolute legal priority to the right of private ownership, which thereby becomes the "summary expression of alienated labour" (*MEGA* 1³: 94; *Coll. Works* 3: 281). Religion, the state, bourgeois morality, and culture merely manifest what private

19. On the separation of the worker from his material and thereby from his environment, cf. Georges Friedmann, *Problèmes humains du machinisme* (Paris: Gallimard, 1946).

20. Erich Fromm paraphrases Marx's idea: "The 'feeling of self' is merely an indication of what others think of the person. It is not *he* who is convinced of his value regardless of popularity and his success on the market. If he is sought after, he is somebody; if he is not popular, he is simply nobody." Erich Fromm, *Escape from Freedom* (New York: Avon Books, 1966), p. 180.

property institutionalizes: that man has become an object to himself, a commodity (*MEGA* 1³: 115; *Coll. Works* 3: 297).

The most significant feature of the Paris Manuscripts, the novelty of which we might easily overlook because of its familiarity today, is the idea that man realizes himself through his work. Greek philosophy had imprinted upon the Western mind an ideal of leisure and contemplation. The Christian interpretation of work as the curse of Paradise, as well as the vision of an eternity of contemplation had enriched this ideal with aesthetic glamor. Even the cultural revolution of the Renaissance or the anti-Christian reaction of the Enlightenment did not challenge it. Work was praised often enough, but more for its effects than for its intrinsic worth. Leisure for contemplation had remained the norm of the good life in which, ideally, work provided only the contrast needed for greater harmony. To this model Marx opposed his own, of the *homo faber,* discarding any connotations of punishment and sacrifice which had been connected with the hardship of work. The ideal of man's self-creation through the once despised activity of labor constituted a total reversal of Western humanist ideas. According to the new ideal, humanity is not a *given,* but an acquired attribute, the result of productive activity. Not man's theoretical reason, but his *labor* distinguishes him from the animal.

Yet, for all their innovative power, the Manuscripts abound in ambiguities and contraditions. Marx does not consistently apply his new theory of man. On the one hand, he defines the humanizing process exclusively through a social-economic activity that accepts no norms other than its own and is subject only to internal criticism (the position more or less consistently taken in *Capital*). On the other hand, Marx continues to measure all social, moral, and cultural characteristics of bourgeois society by the model of an *ideal Gattungswesen* endowed with all the qualities of a humanist model. This humanist ideal, occasionally expressed in the traditional form of *leisure,* does not rest comfortably on its social-economic console. Even the critique remains obscure. What carries the social alienation? Is it the highly specialized, machine-directed, commodity-oriented mode of production? Or an appropriation exclusively aimed at the accumulation of private property? The two are related, but Marx fails to clarify how.[21]

Much of this ambiguity is cleared up in *The German Ideology*. Here Marx sets out to do what he had announced but never accomplished in the Paris Manuscripts: he shows the historical conditioning of allegedly timeless economic concepts. Private property thereby appears to be a particular stage in a process of ownership basically determined by the division of labor. What the Manuscripts had generally referred to as the worker's alienation from his producing activity is now traced back to a division of labor soley based upon the principle of maximum productivity. Marx again insists on the damage done to the individual by such a system. But, more importantly, he shows how the consequent separation of workers and instruments of work creates a socially explosive division of classes.

Human production has always been social and, hence, systematically divided. In primitive societies, the division of tasks "develops spontaneously or 'naturally' by virtue of natural disposition (e.g. physical strength), needs, accidents, etc." (*MEGA* 1[5]: 21; *Coll. Works* 5: 44). This inevitably creates inequality, for even the most primitive system regulates tasks according to social, rather than individual, needs. Only an economically advanced society could afford to pay as much attention to the individual's well-being as to that of the group. In fact, however, industrial capitalism, with its separation between labor and its instruments, allows its distribution of labor to be entirely determined by the most productive use of the instruments. This, in turn, leads to an ever greater separation of labor and capital and to increasing tensions between the mode of production and social relations. "The more the division of labor develops and accumulation grows, the sharper are the forms that this process of differentiation assumes" (*MEGA* 1[5]: 56; *Coll. Works* 5: 86).

The negative connotation of the terms *nature* and *natural* as Marx applies them to the divison of labor confirms that he did

---

21. Maurice Dobb has drawn attention to this ambivalence in his introduction to *A Contribution to the Critique of Political Economy* (New York: International Publishers, [1970] 1976).

not set up primitive society as an ideal. The alienating process of capitalism follows directly from conditions already present in such a society.[22] Indeed, in the discussion of the "natural" division of labor he erases the last traces of the romantic ideal of a unity with nature that still colored the Paris Manuscripts. It was capitalism that first enabled man to subjugate nature and to submit it to his own purposes. This position cannot be reversed. Only the act of negating a *given* nature launches man on his historical course.[23] Yet, in the process of negating nature, man risks enslaving himself to a new objectivity even less authentically human than his original "unity" with nature was.

The German Ideology deals not only with social-economic relations. Its primary subject is, of course, the rise and significance of ideologies. We shall devote an entire chapter to this question. Yet we must note even now how in *The German Ideology* Marx extends the impact of alienation from the social-economic field to the entire realm of culture. Capitalist production has spawned particular moral values and the spiritual ideals necessary to support them. Generally speaking, Marx concentrates more on the causal link between the social-economic and the cultural (which we shall analyze in the fifth chapter) than upon the distorting, alienating effect the capitalist system has upon bourgeois cul-

22. Some present-day Marxists, e.g., George Lefebvre in his *Critique de la vie quotidienne,* idealize the primitive village community. This is certainly not Marx's view. (Cf. Ernest Mandel's critique of Lefebvre in *The Formation of the Economic Thought of Karl Marx,* trans. Brian Pearce [New York: Monthly Review Press, 1971], pp. 180–83.) To consider the alienation of capitalism as merely a transient result of contingent factors, as T. A. Oiserman does, implies an equally optimistic view of "nature." (Cf. Oiserman, "Alienation and the Individual," in *Marxism and Alienation,* ed. Herbert Aptheker [New York: Humanities Press, 1965], pp. 146–48.) Of course, it is no less incorrect to assume, as Jacob Hommes does (*Der Technische Eros* [Freiburg, 1955], p. 45), that for Marx the "natural" was simply the "inauthentic" in man, a position close to Hobbes's state of nature as a state of general warfare. The passage on which this interpretation is based (*MEGA* 1[5], 22; *Coll. Works* 5:45) does not truly support it. In our discussion of the Paris Manuscripts we saw that the ambiguous term *nature* refers to the historical and therefore ever-changing quality of human existence, or to a lasting, though as yet not realized, ideal.

23. Gayo Petrovic, "Histoire et nature," in *Praxis* (Belgrade, 1966), p. 75. See also, Leszek Kolakowski, *Main Currents of Marxism,* 1:267.

ture. But in a passage of the much neglected second part of *The German Ideology* he shows this alienating effect in the one instance of moral utilitarianism. In the *Phenomenology* Hegel had interpreted the absolutization of the category of usefulness as the final result of the Enlightenment. For Marx, the entire capitalist economy is no more than an application of a theory that subordinates all relations to that of utility. In Bentham's work, the perfect expression of the utilitarian mind, "the bourgeoisie no longer appears as a special class, but as the class whose conditions of existence are those of the whole society" (*MEGA* 1⁵: 391; *Coll. Works* 5: 413). Mutual exploitation becomes the basis of personal relations, even when they are swathed in a veil of philanthropy. Utilitarianism, like all ideologies, is illusory insofar as it fails to recognize its real motives; but as it reflects the real state of society, it is a "historically justified philosophical illusion about the bourgeoisie" (*MEGA* 1⁵: 389; *Coll. Works* 5: 410).

In *The Holy Family,* written a few months earlier, Marx made it clear that more than a single class is alienated by the capitalist system. Society as a whole suffers. Mindful of Hegel's dialectic of the noble and the base consciousness in the chapter on cultural alienation, he shows how both the capitalists' and the workers' mentalities become warped through the class system, even though the groups react in opposite ways.

> The propertied class and the class of the proletariat present the same human self-estrangement. But the former class feels at ease and strengthened in this self-estrangement; it recognizes estrangement as its *own power* and has in it the *semblance* of a human existence. The latter feels annihilated in estrangement; it sees in it its own powerlessness and the reality of an inhuman existence. It is, to use an expression of Hegel, in its abasement the *indignation* at that abasement, an indignation to which it is necessarily driven by the contradiction between its human *nature* and its condition of life. [*MEGA* 1³: 206; *Coll. Works* 4: 36]

The German Ideology enunciates the basic principle of Marx's critique of culture: What determines the economy of a society determines all other aspects of its culture. His later, almost exclusive concentration upon social-economic problems should never make us lose sight of the full scope of Marx's critique. In the *Grundrisse*, the preparatory notes for *Capital*, the link between the economic and all other spheres of life remains clear. Perhaps more than any of his other writings, it conveys the full import of the Marxist theory of alienation.

GRUNDRISSE: ECONOMY AS ALIENATION

During the period intervening between the early writings and the publication of *Capital*, Marx increasingly focused his critique of bourgeois society on the economic system as being solely responsible for all its ills. In the following section we shall consider only those factors in that system which directly affect the *entire* cultural process. Three stand out: society's loss of control over the conditions of its production; the overriding impact of an object-directed technology upon the method of producing; the dissolution of traditional social bonds and their replacement by the abstract socialization of an advanced economic-exchange web. Those factors radically transformed life during the bourgeois epoch. Not only did they change the nature of social relations, but they revolutionized the entire process of social expression. The perspective of the *Grundrisse* has shifted from that of the early writings. The theme is the nature of economic production under capitalism. Nevertheless, throughout his analysis Marx keeps referring to the sociocultural effects of the economic system. In this respect the *Grundrisse* differs from *Capital* (and the preparatory drafts of 1861–62), where Marx concentrates on the internal conflict within the economic system. Here Marx misses no opportunity to show the full social effects of economic policy.

Even the economic discussion differs from that of the early writings. Economic categories in the *Grundrisse* are more radically historicized. Thus, the concept of property no longer refers to the mere possession of material objects (particularly, then, objects detached from the living act of labor), but to the producer's *control over the conditions* of his productive activity as defined through law and custom.[24] Hence, what alienates man

24. *Grundrisse der Kritik der politischen Oekonomie (Rohentwurf)* (Berlin: Dietz Verlag, 1953). Henceforth, I shall refer first to the German edition as *GR* fol-

from his economic activity in the capitalist system is now a *lack of ownership*. Marx has shifted, not from a subjective, humanist position to an objective, economic one, as existentialist writers used to present it, but from a nonhistorical position to a thoroughly historical one. In the *Grundrisse* he concretely applied the theory of human development in and through economic activity which he had initially formulated in *The German Ideology* but had inadequately integrated with his critique of society.

Capital's tendency to bring all forces to their full productive capacity demands an increasing production "where advance beyond the point of departure is the only presupposition" (*GR* 438; NIC 540). Only a wage system allows the economy to build up such a necessary surplus. The value produced by the worker in addition to his remuneration Marx terms "surplus value."[25] Capital converts this added value into an objectified, ever-increasing labor power, while living labor allows the conditions of labor "to assume an ever more colossal independence" that confront it as "an alien and dominant power" (*GR* 715; NIC 831). Marx describes the opposition between capital and living labor in terms reminiscent of the one between the product and the producer in the Paris Manuscripts.

> The independent and autonomous *(Fürsichsein)* existence of value as against living labor power . . . —the objective self-sufficient indifference, the alien nature of the objective conditions of labor as against living labor power, reaching the point that these conditions confront the person of the worker in the person of the capitalist . . . (and) are opposed to the worker as alien property . . . —and that labor hence appears as alien labor opposed to the value personi-

---

lowed by the first page number and second to the English translation, also followed by the first page number (*GR* 393; NIC 493). I have most often used Martin Nicolaus's translation and refer to it as NIC (*Grundrisse*, trans. Martin Nicolaus [Baltimore: Penguin Books, 1973]). Wherever I have used David McLellan's partial translation (Harper & Row, 1971), I refer to it as McLellan.

25. "The worker begins by adding so many new forms to the value of the raw material and the instrument, through the utilization of the instrument as an instrument and the transformation of raw material, as would equal the working time that is contained in his own wages. Anything more that he adds is surplus working time, surplus value" (*GR* 265; McLellan 88).

fied in the capitalist or to the conditions of labor—this absolute divorce between property and labor, between living labor power and the conditions of its realization, between objectified and living labor . . . this separation now also appears as the product of labor itself, as an objectification of its own elements. [*GR* 356; McLellan 98—(slightly altered)]

Interrupting "the organic cycle" of work, instruments, and material, capitalist production can only result in the producer's impoverishment. It proclaims the liberation of property through a "free labor market," yet in depriving the worker of the control over the conditions of his work it takes away his real property. Objectified labor is "posited as the worker's *non-objectivity*, as the objectivity of a subjectivity antithetical to the worker, as *property* of a will alien to him" (*GR* 412; NIC 512).

When products are reduced to commodities, namely, to mere moments in the process of exchange, they take on a being independent of use and intrinsic quality. Their abstract being is symbolized in the medium of pure exchange.

Because money is the *general equivalent*, the *general power of purchasing*, everything can be bought, everything may be transformed into money. But it can be transformed into money only by being alienated [*alieniert*], by its owner divesting himself of it. Everything is therefore alienable, or indifferent for the individual. [*GR* 722; NIC 838]

Reintroducing Feuerbach's religious imagery, Marx refers to money as "the heavenly existence of commodities" while the commodities themselves present the earthly reality (*GR* 134; NIC 221). Alienation, in the early writings the *result* of private property, now reappears as the worker's loss of control over the conditions of his productive activity—that is, as a loss of property. Capitalist labor, then, is "negated property or property as negation of the alien quality of alien labor" (*GR* 373; NIC 470).

Hence, just as the worker relates to the product of his labor as an alien thing, so does he relate to the combination of labor as an alien combination, as well as to his own labor as an expression of his life, which, although it belongs to him, is alien to him, and which A. Smith therefore conceives as a burden, sacrifice, etc. [*GR* 374; NIC 470]

Alienation has now come to mean loss of property. Has Marx reversed his position? No, his concern now goes beyond the institution of private property to the more fundamental right to control the conditions of one's own production. In a capitalist system the producer loses that of which the right of property is merely an imperfect, historical form—namely, the control over his objective expression, the very basis of culture. Without a fundamental concordance between the needs of the producing society and the nature of its objective accomplishments, a culture must collapse. Undoubtedly there has always existed a discrepancy between the desires of the few and their fulfillment by the many. Ancient cultures depended largely on slave labor. Even in the Middle Ages high cultural projects were executed by uninformed masses. In contrast to them, bourgeois society has enormously extended the range of active cultural cooperation. Marx deeply admired this class, which "during its rule of scarce one hundred years, has created more massive and more colossal productive forces than all generations together" (*Werke* 4: 467; *Coll. Works* 6: 489). Then why should a civilization endowed with such titanic powers be doomed? At stake is not the empirical conflict between the desires of the few and the many, but the contradiction between society's objective needs and potential, and its system of fulfilling them.

In a similar way Marx has deepened his conception of the division of labor. In *The German Ideology* he had shown how this division aims not at increasing humanization but merely the production of commodities. In the *Grundrisse* he more specifically attributes the antisocial quality of this division to the dominance of technology over human activity. Of course, in the early writings he had often criticized the worker's enslavement to an unlimited production. But it is in the *Grundrisse* that he first presents technology as an independent middle term between the producer and the process of production. As we shall see later, Marx does not attack technology as such—at times he appears to have based exceedingly high hopes for social reform on it—but he criticizes the role of technology within the capitalist economy. Given its premises, technology is bound to escape all other control but that of the most profitable production. In the capitalist economy technology acquires a wholly new function: it transfers the reins of production from subjective praxis to the realm of objective science. The machine no longer serves as a tool that transmits the worker's activity to the object; now the worker merely transmits the machine's power to the material. His intervention requires little skill and no initiative. The machine is the real virtuoso in the performance of industrial capitalism. Knowledge, skill, and all the subjective qualities required by the production process have been successfully transformed into objective attributes of capital. "Machinery then appears as the most adequate form of capital as such" (*GR* 586; NIC 694). Even the subjective act of *inventing* new technology comes to depend more and more upon already existing technical equipment. Industry in a developed stage no longer depends on good luck and personal genius. It mobilizes science itself into the service of industrial technology. "Invention then becomes a business, and the application of science to direct production itself becomes a prospect which determines and solicits it" (*GR* 591; NIC 704).

Labor becomes totally integrated with a collective enterprise over which the individual worker retains no control at all. The machine guides the process; he merely produces the man power (*GR* 374, 587–89; NIC 470, 699–701). Under those conditions Adam Smith's axiom that humans will sacrifice the state of rest only when forced by necessity becomes fully vindicated. But this alienation of the worker's subjectivity is due not to his involvement in a process of objectification, but in his enslavement to a technology that has been severed from its subjective sources.

> The emphasis comes to be placed not on the state of being *objectified*, but on the state of being *alienated*, dispossessed, sold [*das Entfremdet, Entäussert-, Veräussertsein*]; on the condition that the monstrous objective power which social labor itself erected opposite itself as one of its moments belongs not to the worker. [*GR* 715; NIC 831]

It is important to keep in mind that Marx does not attribute the problem to the rise of technology as such, but to its particular function in the capitalist mode of production. To the extent that bourgeois society has promoted the development of technology and the methods of industrial production, it has, in fact rendered a unique service to the emancipation of human culture. Yet industrial capitalism itself never used its advanced technology in the service of cultural creativity. Although it created the *possibility* of leisure for self-fulfilling activity, it in fact prolonged the working day and dehumanized working conditions.[26] The reason is that the capitalist system itself requires an ever-increased production and this, in turn, demands ever more surplus labor.

> What is new in capital is that it also increases the surplus labor time of the masses by all artistic and scientific means possible, since its wealth consists directly in the appropriation of surplus labor time, since its direct aim is value, not use value. Thus, despite itself, it is instrumental in creating the means of social disposable time, and so in reducing work time for the whole of society to a minimum and thus making everyone's time free for their own development. But although its tendency is always to create disposable time, it also converts it into surplus labor. [*GR* 595–96; McLellan 44 (slightly changed)][27]

The detachment of technology from the objectification process is not the only problem at the root of what Marx earlier referred to as the worker's alienation through the division of labor. Even more important is the subordination of all aspects of

26. Needless to say, Marx's predictions about future developments of the capitalist economy must be read as hypothetical statements pointing toward tendencies which, *if unchecked,* will result in the predicted effect.

27. Marx here is not advocating free time as an end in itself. Leisure merely allows time for more creative forms of activity which, in the end, improve the production process itself. "Free time—which includes leisure time as well as time for higher activities—naturally transforms anyone who enjoys it into a different person, and it is this different person who then enters the direct process of production" (*GR* 599; McLellan 148; NIC 712). Does Marx mean that the cultured person finds relatively more fulfillment in the same type of work than does the uneducated one, or does he expect the production process to change so radically that drudgery has no more place in it? The truth of the former interpretation appears questionable in light of our present experience with a more educated labor force: menial work is resented and carelessly performed by "educated" workers. As for the second alternative, it is doubtful whether any future production system will ever succeed in dispensing with tedious work altogether.

the production process to the exclusive goal of creating economic exchange. Thus labor becomes divided not according to the interests of the workers but exclusively according to the requirements of exchange.

> Exchange and division of labor reciprocally condition one another. Since everyone works for himself but his product is nothing for him, each must of course exchange, not only in order to take part in the general productive capacity, but also in order to transform his own product into his own subsistence. Exchange when mediated by exchange value and money, presupposes the all-round dependence of the producers on one another, together with the total isolation of their private interests from one another, as well as a division of social labor. . . . [GR 76; NIC 158]

In this passage Marx succinctly formulates the two factors that condition the universal exchange of capitalist society: the transformation of all labor into exchange value and the universal convertibility of the entire labor output, as well as of labor itself, into money. Both factors have intensified social contact to an unprecedented degree, but by restricting the process to the requirements of exchange, they prevent the more basic socialization needed for full human emancipation. Let us first consider, then, the fundamental social role of money.

In a capitalist society, money becomes the concrete bond that ties its members together. It differs from such earlier social ties as the group, the city-state, or the social hierarchy of a feudal society, in that it remains wholly extrinsic to its possessors and admits no limits but those of the universe of capitalist exchange (which is, potentially, the whole world). However, this social bond dissolves all existing groups or reduces them to secondary status. Hence, "socialization" resulting from exchange plays a decisive role in what Marx calls the historical process of individualization.

> Exchange itself is a chief means of this individuation (Vereinzelung). It makes the herd-like subsistence superfluous and dissolves it. Soon the matter [has] turned in such a way that as an individual he relates himself only to himself, while the means with which he posits himself as individual have become the making of his gener-

ality and commonness. In this community, the objective being of
the individual as proprietor, say proprietor of land, is presupposed, and presupposed moreover under certain conditions
which chain him to the community, or rather form a link in his
chain. In bourgeois society the worker, e.g., stands there purely
without objectivity, subjectivity; but the thing which *stands opposite*
him has now become the *true community* [*Gemeinwesen*] which he
tries to make a meal of, and which makes a meal of him. [*GR* 395–
96; NIC 496]

This objective social bond seemingly born out of private interests is nothing like Adam Smith's "invisible hand" that mysteriously directs the pursuit of particular interests toward further-
ing the common good. It is, in fact, from the start, a "socially
determined interest which can be obtained only within the conditions laid down by society and with the means provided by
society" (*GR* 74; NIC 156). Though the interests are privately
chosen, their content and means of realization are intrinsically
social. A money economy allows no entirely private transactions.
Classical economists failed to see the full social significance of
the capitalist system of exchange—not surprisingly, because its
social bond differed from any social connection in the past. To
members of the ancient society, at least before the Roman Empire, the common good *was* the good of the individual. This
situation continued to exist in a different way through most of
the Middle Ages. Capitalism destroyed this subjective link with
the common good. But it intensively socialized the production
process, primarily by removing that process from the immediate
satisfaction of the producer's particular needs. In producing
primarily for the satisfaction of the needs of others, the capitalist
economy has paved the way toward a general and practical recognition of a common human species beyond the boundaries of
family, tribe, or nation (*GR* 154; NIC 243. Also *GR* 88; NIC
171). The capitalist mode of production, for the first time in
history, treats all human beings as equal partners.

Each has the same social relation towards the other that the other
has towards him. As subjects of exchange, their relation is therefore that of *equality*. It is impossible to find any trace of distinction,
not to speak of contradiction, between them; not even a differ-

ence. Furthermore, the commodities which they exchange are, as exchange values, equivalent, or at least they count as such. . . . [*GR* 153; NIC 241]

The capitalist rightly claims that each "arrives at his end only insofar as he serves the other as means" and that each "becomes means for the other (being for another) only as end in himself (being for self)" (*GR* 155; NIC 243).

But this unprecedented socialization does not take place through the voluntary interaction of free individuals: it consists rather in a common subjection to a single, objective exchange system. "Money—becomes the *real community (Gemeinwesen)*, since it is the general substance of survival for all, and at the same time the social product of all" (*GR* 137; NIC 226). The worker is tied to his economic "community" by his physical dependence, by being "a virtual pauper" (*GR* 498; NIC 604). He finds himself caught in a network of impersonal, mostly antagonistic relations, resulting from "the collision of different individuals with each other" (*GR* 75; NIC 157). "Their own collisions with one another produce an *alien* social power standing above them, produce their mutual interaction as a process and power independent of them" (*GR* 111; NIC 192). Thus social life turns into an autonomous power that rules the individuals by sheer physical necessity. Man's social relations have become reified. Money, "the objective entity which can be re-exchanged for everything *without distinction*" (*GR* 80; NIC 163), seals this reification. It dissolves all relations that are not reducible to the one form of material exchange.

> In money relationships, in the developed exchange system—the ties of personal dependence are in fact broken, torn asunder, as also differences of blood, educational differences, etc. (the personal ties all appear at least to be *personal* relationships). Thus the individuals appear to be independent—. [*GR* 72; NIC 164]

The money economy requires this break-up of existing relations in order to impose its own social structure geared entirely toward the creation of surplus value.

From the preceding discussion of property, technology, and exchange it appears that the idea of alienation, far from vanishing from Marx's thought, had in fact deepened during the period when he was preparing his decisive work. Even the terms *Entfremdung* and *Entäusserung* (now used less discriminately than in the Paris Manuscripts, cf. *GR* 716; NIC 831 and *GR* 440; NIC 541) frequently return in the *Grundrisse*. If in *Capital*, the mature expression of the reflections here initiated, the language of alienation recedes, this change is certainly not the result of a reversal in Marx's position. Some of Marx's reasons were purely strategic: only a critique of economy written entirely in the language of classical economy could effectively refute the classical positions. But as we shall see in the next section, the intrinsic development of the concept of alienation itself played an even more decisive role. However the recession may be justified, in *Capital* the idea of alienation remains the unspoken theme that guides the entire argument.

CAPITAL: ALIENATION AS ECONOMIC CONTRADICTION

In the preface to the new edition of his *Studies in the Labor Theory of Value* Ronald Meek claims: "*Capital*, in a very real and important sense, is in fact a book about alienation."[28] Indeed. The issue is not whether the idea of alienation appears in *Capital*—it obviously does—but how its appearance differs from earlier ones. As economic production ceased to be an integral part of the cultural process as a whole, economy itself became a self-contradicting practice. The alienation now appears in the very functioning of the economic system—specifically, in the conflict between the socializing forces of that system and the tendency inherent in the capitalist structure to restrict these forces to private utilization.

What thus presents itself as an inner conflict corresponds in essence to what Marx earlier described as man's estrangement from his own nature. Though there may be little left of the early humanistic expression, Marx's critique remains fundamentally the same. Since human nature concretely actualizes itself in social-economic praxis, the economic "contradictions" indicate, in

28. Ronald Meek, *Studies in the Labor Theory of Value* (New York: Monthly Review Press, [1956] 1975), p. xii.

fact, the discrepancy between what man does and what he aims at, between his behavior and the intrinsic intentionality of that behavior. The idea of alienation, then, remains dominant in Marx's thought, despite a sharply decreased use of the term and a clear change in perspective.[29] Actually, the term does not disappear from *Capital*. Considering the nature of the change, it even appears a surprising number of times.

Since *Capital* formalizes ideas conceived at the time when Marx wrote the *Grundrisse,* one might expect the critique to agree with that of the preparatory notes. Yet a careful look reveals a considerable shift in emphasis. The notion of surplus value which had held the center stage in the *Grundrisse* now becomes part of a larger complex determined by other factors. The exploitation of surplus value, Marx more clearly realized, is not a distinctive trait of the capitalist economy: it appears in all systems that precede it, even in the cruder forms of slavery or serfdom. Nor will the production of surplus value end with the capitalist system. The socialist community of the future will still need labor reserves for future expansion that it does not directly compensate. The critical difference consists in the facts that surplus labor in capitalism is performed for the sole purpose of creating immediate exchange value and, even more importantly, that to fulfill this purpose *labor power itself must be objectified into an exchange commodity.* The worker sells the living power which to him has no useful value to an employer for whom its productive value exceeds its exchange value (expressed in wages). Now such an objectification *(Entäusserung)* of the worker's subjective power is the very essence of alienation *(Entfremdung).* Within this new perspective Marx, quite naturally, ignores the distinction between *Entäusserung* and *Entfremdung* to which he had attached so much importance in his earlier polemics with Hegel. Thus money, which objectifies everything including labor power, becomes the symbol of general alienation.[30]

---

29. Michel Henry, *Marx* (Paris, 1976) 2:134.

30. To refer to the dehumanizing effects of this illegitimate objectification, however, Marx continues to use the term *Entfremdung* pretty consistently. Thus he writes that the means for the development of capitalist production "estrange

In *Capital* Marx's critique focuses on the alienation of labor power resulting from its reduction to a trade commodity. The difference between the *Grundrisse* and *Capital* should not be interpreted, however, as if Marx had essentially changed his theory. I know of no thesis in the *Grundrisse* that he abandoned in *Capital.* The difference, as I see it, lies exclusively in the emphasis, and hence the perspective. It can be traced to the 1861–63 manuscripts which Marx wrote in preparing the voluminous work he intended to publish (of which he completed only *Capital* 1). He writes:

> The value, the objectified labor existing in the form of money, could increase only through exchange with a commodity the use value of which would consist in increasing exchange value, and the consumption of which would equate the creation of value or the objectification of labor. . . . Only living labor power has such a use value. The value, money can only through exchange with living labor power be converted into capital. Its conversion into capital requires on the one hand its exchange for labor power and, on the other, for the material conditions presupposed by the objectification of labor power. [*MEGA* 2³: 31–32]

This statement introduces no new thesis, but it opens a new perspective—the perspective of *Capital.*

Marx does not claim, as earlier socialists had done, that labor is not equitably remunerated. Instead of attacking wages Marx attacks the wage system, the far more fundamental abuse whereby the source of all exchange value is itself converted into an exchange commodity. To secure a "living" for himself and his family, the worker must divest himself of the fruit of his work.

> Since before entering on the process, his own labor has already been alienated from himself by the sale of his labor power, has been appropriated by the capitalist and incorporated with capital, it must, during the process, be realized in a product that does not belong to him. . . . The laborer therefore constantly produces material, objective wealth, but in the form of capital, of an alien

---

[the worker] from the intellectual potentialities of the labor process . . ." (*Werke* 23; *Cap.* 1:708. Also *Cap.* 1:571 and 3:85–86).

power that dominates and exploits him. [*Werke* 23: 596; *Cap*. 1: 571]

Thus Marx provides a foundation for the idea of alienation as he had first formulated it in the Paris Manuscripts: the capitalist mode of production estranges the worker from his own labor and sets the fruits of his labor up as an independent, hostile force. The descriptions in *Capital* of factory workers slaving for interminable days at stultifying tasks complete the picture of the alienated worker in the 1844 Manuscripts. The mechanization of labor has extended the working day to an unprecedented length; for the sooner surplus labor reproduces the value of the machine, the more surplus value that machine yields (*Werke* 23:425; *Cap*. 1:403–09). Similarly, the division of labor, which seems to be eliminated by machines that are able to perform a multiplicity of tasks in one operation, actually becomes intensified when the specialized handling of one tool makes room for the even more monotonous serving of one machine or the accomplishing of one simple movement at the assembly line (*Werke* 23:445; *Cap*. 1:422).

All this merely seems to amplify and document what Marx had denounced in the Manuscripts as the alienation of the worker from his own activity. Yet the perspective has changed. For in *Capital* the primary issue is no longer the "wrong" kind of objectification: it is the objectification itself of what should not be objectified, namely, subjective labor power. It is not the division of labor *as such* that alienates man from his activity. All modes of production in an advanced economy, including a socialist one, require some distribution of productive tasks. But only in a commodity-oriented economy does such a distribution estrange the worker from his productive power. Abandoning the simplistic criticism of *The German Ideology*, Marx in the fourteenth chapter of *Capital* 1 shows how the dehumanizing effects of the division of labor are themselves an effect of the commodity orientation of capitalist production. The "necessary" division of labor differs from the one that originated with the capitalist manufacturing system.

"While division of labor in society at large, whether such division be brought about or not by exchange of commodities, is common to economic formations of society the most diverse, division of labor in the workshop, as practiced by manufacture, is a special creation of the capitalist mode of production alone" (*Werke* 23: 380; *Cap.* 1: 359). Even "some crippling of mind and body" may be inevitable. But only the capitalist system of production has entirely sacrificed human development to operational effectiveness. Once labor power itself must compete as an exchange commodity with the very products it produced, it forfeits all human privileges. "The connection between the detail operations in a workshop is due to the sale of labor power of several workmen to one capitalist, who applies it as combined labor power" (*Werke* 23: 376; *Cap.* 1: 355). Inhuman division of labor directly follows from itself only after absolute priority of exchange value over use: "It is not merely the products of laborers turned into independent powers, products as rulers and buyers of their producers, but also the social forces and the future form of this labor, which confront the laborers as properties of their products" (*Werke* 25: 823; *Cap.* 3: 815). Capital is a social power, but it is a social power of domination whereby relations among commodities come to determine all other relations: "The labor of the individual asserts itself as a part of the labor of society only by means of the relations which the act of exchange establishes directly between the products, and indirectly, through them, between the products" (*Werke* 23: 87; *Cap.* 1: 73). The social quality of production becomes entirely determined by the impersonal social nature of capital. "It (capital) becomes an alienated *(entfremdete),* independent, social power which stands opposed to society as an object, and as an object that is the capitalist's source of power" (*Werke* 25: 274; *Cap.* 3: 264). Thus originates the "fetishism of commodities."

It is often claimed that the "alienation" of the early writings became the fetishism of commodities in *Capital.* Certainly, the reduction of all value, as well as of its subjective source, to exchange value results in a fetishist reification. Nor can there be any doubt that the various phenomena earlier described as "alienating" lead to such a reification. Nevertheless, commodity fetishism is a relatively late phenomenon, while capitalism has been oriented toward the creation of exchange value, regardless of use, since the beginning.[31] This alienating tendency turned into a real fetishism of commodities only when the production of exchange value pervading all of modern culture converted every aspect of it into a commodity. For such a total reification of life to take place, the commodity economy first had to gain control over the entire production process and to transform mental attitudes as well as methods of production and distribution. In earlier stages of capitalism this "economic mystification" existed only with respect to money and interest bearing. Thus Marx had referred to mercantilist economists who equated national wealth with the possession of gold and silver as "fetishist." Modern capitalism has abandoned this fetishization of a particular substance in favor of the abstract category of exchange value. In elevating exchangeability into the sole standard of economic profit, it has universalized the fetishist attitude that once was limited to a single aspect of the production system. Not until every transaction and every product had been endowed with potential exchange value did the entire culture become reified. In his still unsurpassed essay on "Reification and the Consciousness of the Proletariat," Lukacs regards this transition as a qualitative leap to an entirely different form of society.

> The qualitative difference between the commodity as one form among many regulating the metabolism of human society and the commodity as the universal structuring principle has effects over and above the fact that the commodity relation as an isolated phenomenon exerts a negative influence at most on the structure and organization of society.—And *this* development of the commodity to the point where it becomes the dominant form in society did not take place until the advent of modern capitalism.[32]

The reification of all aspects of man's productive activity has caused a rift between the subjective agent and his products com-

---

31. Ernest Mandel has shown how Marx spoke of alienation even in precapitalist societies, which are definitely not "commodity fetishist" (*The Formation of the Economic Thought of Karl Marx*, p. 184).

32. Georg Lukacs, *History and Class Consciousness* (Cambridge: MIT Press, 1971), pp. 85–86.

parable to the religious separation between man's terrestrial and celestial existence. Marx now resumes the religious language in which he had formulated his earliest critique of alienation.

> [In] the mist-enveloped regions of the religious world . . . . the productions of the human brain appear as independent beings endowed with life, and entering into relation both with one another and the human race. So it is in the world of commodities with the products of men's hands. This I call the Fetishism which attaches itself to the products of labor, so soon as they are produced as commodities, and which is therefore inseparable from the production of commodities. [*Werke* 23: 86–87; *Cap.* 1: 72]

In declaring the generation of exchange value as the single objective of production, the bourgeois economist speaks as the theologian of this new religion. Like theologians of old, he projects an abstract and ideal realm entirely beyond the real sphere of human existence: "In material production, therefore, we have exactly the same relationship that obtains, in the domain of ideology, with religion: the subject transformed into object and vice versa."[33]

Marx's religious metaphor may have had an unintended effect upon the further development of his idea. Gradually, the term *fetishism* has come to stand for a particular *ideology*. More and more the emphasis has shifted from a particular mode of economic production to a particular way of looking at the world. This expanded meaning undoubtedly follows from Marx's economic theory, but only as a secondary effect. Marx never conceived of fetishism, or even of alienation, as being primarily an attitude or a feeling. This is precisely what distinguishes his concept of cultural alienation from Hegel's. For Hegel also the living bond between the human subject and its objective expression has been severed. Instead of a vital exchange with a self-constituted world, man finds himself left with a mere "given" over which he exercises no more control. But this cultural event by no means results from an economic production process. The

33. This text, written for *Capital* but withdrawn from the printer's copy, is now in the Marx Engels's Archives in Moscow. Translated by David McLellan in *The Thought of K. Marx*, p. 118.

usage of the term *alienation* in the social sciences today owes
more to this Hegelian concept of cultural frustration than to
Marx's critique of a particular mode of production. Marx always
connects the reified state of mind with a social-economic basis.
Even the founders of the Frankfurt School, who among Marxists went furthest in their independent critique of culture, occasionally felt it necessary to stress the priority of the economic
condition. Thus Theodor Adorno wrote to Walter Benjamin:
"The fetish character of commodities is not a fact of consciousness, but dialectic in the eminent state that it produces consciousness."[34]

The point deserves emphasis, for with the considerable
changes that have revolutionized production methods since
Marx's day, Western Marxists tend to turn their interest from
the critique of social-economic conditions to that of the cultural
inadequacy of contemporary society, thus converting the critique of alienation into a critique of ideology. To some extent
this move compensates for the one-sidedness of the position of
Marx and Engels who, by their own admission, were so occupied
with the critique of the economic structure that they spent little
attention on the superstructure. Yet, the name "Marxist" loses all
precise meaning when applied to an all-comprehensive indict-
ment of modern culture which, despite such Marxist terminology as *fetishism* and *alienation,* fails to take seriously the very real
dependence of this ideological superstructure upon its social-
economic basis. Quite possibly, as our own conclusion will suggest, Marx's basis is too narrow for such a general critique of
culture. Much even of what he himself attributes to an economic
system may stem from tendencies that long antedate this system
and of which the capitalist structure itself is only a uniquely
powerful manifestation. Yet we should be aware that in explor-
ing this possibility we have left the area of Marxist hermeneutics
for what is in fact a critique of Marx. In the following pages we
restrict ourselves to a critique of those aspects of culture which
are directly connected with a particular mode of production.

34. Walter Benjamin, *Briefe,* ed. Gershom Sholem and Theodor Adorno
(Frankfurt, 1966), 3:672.

A PROVISIONAL CONCLUSION

From his earliest writings on, Marx has consistently charged the capitalist system with fostering, and indeed requiring, the reifying mentality to which *Capital* refers as fetishist. We should not take this critique to express Marx's entire position on bourgeois culture. The following chapters, especially the concluding one on bourgeois ideology, will present entirely different facets of his thought. Nevertheless, the recent extension of the capitalist principle to all spheres of existence has unquestionably been a major factor in the reification of modern culture. It is directly responsible for the commercial character and concomitant vulgarization of culture, as well as for the reaction of cultural elitism and the increasing isolation of a realm of allegedly "pure" culture. This has become even more the case today than in Marx's time.

The conversion of what once barely provided its "producers" with a modest livelihood into a major source of exchange value has, of course, directly affected the methods of production. Those who "produce" education, art, and entertainment for mass consumption well know that standardization, a requirement of mass production, must operate at the lowest common intellectual denominator. Of course, for a long time popular literature and kitsch art have comfortably existed side by side with genuine aesthetic or scientific creations. Nor is there anything "fetishist" in this phenomenon. However, our present powers of marketing and reproduction have given rise to a veritable "culture industry."[35] The familiar case is commercial television, where the high production expenses rarely tolerate less than a mass audience. Yet television seldom claims to be more than mass entertainment. It shamefully sacrifices a unique educational opportunity to commercial interests. But it rarely deceives its viewers. A more subtle danger lurks in the commodity status of genuine works of art and literature. Not only are they increasingly appreciated according to their market value, but the possibility of an unrestricted reproduction has lowered the

35. Cf., Max Horkheimer and Theodor Adorno, "The Culture Industry," in *The Dialectic of Enlightenment* (New York: Herder and Herder, 1972), pp. 120–68.

requirements for their proper aesthetic appreciation. To be sure, new techniques of production and distribution have made generally available what formerly was reserved to a privileged few. Excellent reproductions and recordings, inexpensive editions have, with admirable effectiveness, brought art and letters within the reach of virtually every inhabitant of a fully industrialized country. But the same mass production has played a considerable part in the lowering of culture to a level of casual entertainment. Respect for a creation uniquely bound to a particular context, space, and time has made room for the desire to have it "at hand," to "use" it at random as a pleasure commodity.[36] An object for which the buyer has paid a certain price should meet certain expectations, mostly recreational, occasionally instructional, but always defined by his own immediate needs. This attitude has, of course, considerably promoted the concept of art as amusement and has degraded it to a source of "pleasure."

A commercialization that so obviously conflicts with the very nature of culture could not but provoke a reaction. Resentful of the cheapening of taste, the educated have turned their backs on this vulgar commodity culture and have withdrawn into elitist cenacles of their own. A chasm separates their "high-brow" system of values from that of the masses. This unprecedented, deep-running antagonism in which each bitterly resents the other's attempts to impose its own standards may appear to be merely the newest manifestation of that inability to recognize oneself in the dominant culture which Hegel in the *Phenomenology* defined as the essence of alienation. But Marxists interpret it as a symptom of a more fundamental social malaise, in which the masses' daily occupation of uninspiring toil has forced "culture" to withdraw into an independent realm of its own. While the uneducated fill their leisure with undemanding spectator sports or emotionally overcharged cinematographic or musical productions, the elite retires to an ethereal world of "pure" art or literature. One stands as far from the vital source of culture as

---

36. Cf. Walter Benjamin's memorable essay, "The Work of Art in the Age of Mechanical Reproduction," in *Illuminations* (New York: Schocken Books, 1969).

the other. Separated from life, culture turns into a cult object. The emergence of the principle "l'art pour l'art," as well as that of the concept of "the intellectual," signals creative decline. The term *culture* itself, bandied around as if it were an independent entity, fetishizes what should be an integral part of all human activity. "To speak of culture was always contrary to culture. Culture as a common denominator already contains in embryo that schematization and process of cataloguing and classification which bring culture within the sphere of administration."[37] The detachment of culture from the mainstream of man's productive activity is responsible for the characteristically modern response of total passivity. Lukacs explains this contemplative stance "through the worker's role in a production process that mechanically conforms to fixed laws and is enacted independently of human awareness of intervention."[38] Yet the phenomenon appears even more among intellectuals. I doubt whether it allows itself to be exhaustively explained by social-economic factors. But it is unquestionably related to the commodity production. The "cultural" products of this industry leave virtually no creative role to the hearer or spectator. Television has of course long earned the reputation of inviting this sort of passivity. The fleeting parade of images and voices, directed at a fourth-grader's mind, requires no serious intellectual involvement. Its casual chatter and broken images may be picked up and abandoned at random, as the constant interruptions for commercial announcements vividly illustrate. This undemanding kind of entertainment reduced to a constant stream of images may appear to merit no mention in a general critique of a commodity culture. In its constant production of detached images, however, it typically corresponds to a mentality satisifed with a detached perception of objects.

Easily tired of its observation of an indifferent reality, the

37. Horkheimer and Adorno, *Dialectic of Enlightenment*, p. 131. In an early article on "The Affirmative Character of Culture," Herbert Marcuse exposes the schizoid nature of such an escapist culture. "Humanity becomes an inner state.— It thus exalts the individual without freeing him from his factual debasement" (*Negations*, trans. Jeremy J. Shapiro [Boston: Beacon Press, 1968], pp. 88–132).

38. Georg Lukacs, *History and Class Consciousness*, p. 89.

fetishist mind constantly demands a new input of images to compensate for a decreased perceptual involvement. Yet the continuous flow of new images intensifies the fetishist's problem. As Susan Sontag has observed, the attempt to bolster up a depleted sense of reality contributes to the depletion. "We consume images at an ever faster rate and . . . images consume reality."[39] As the sense of reality diminishes, any desire to become morally involved recedes. Only neutral impressions remain, neither real nor unreal, good nor bad. Even actual experiences must first be reduced to images in order to gain full acceptance. An eye-witnessed event does not become wholly "real" until it has appeared on the evening news or in the morning paper. Our most intimate relations are defined through public images. Generally speaking, we adopt a purely observational attitude toward reality. Even a violent crime committed before their eyes elicits but little response from people who have gradually lost the capacity to perceive reality and who have been daily exposed to images of violence. The symptomatic detachment of many criminals from their situation, both their own and that of their victim, betrays an inability to penetrate through the universal, objective image to the individual, responsible deed. But we all have learned to enjoy our evening meal while keeping a distracted eye on televised film clips of war atrocities. Far from conveying an enhanced "sense" of reality, our continuous exposure to such images emotionally screens us from their real content. More than any other factor, the commodity-oriented production has contributed to this reduction of reality to its imagistic appearance.

If we assume, then, that the early concept of alienation continues in a general way to determine also the later critique, then how can we give it some conceptual precision? Clearly *alienation* does not refer to an objective state of affairs in the manner of scientific concepts. But neither does it express a general awareness of inadequate social integration, as the term does in much modern sociology. Against such a subjective position Marxists insist on the priority of a social condition which may affect a person all the more as he is less aware of it, being, as it were, "swallowed up by [his] alienated existence."[40] Marx's early de-

39. *On Photography* (New York: Farrar, Strauss and Giroux, 1977), p. 179.

scriptions combined with his mostly implicit, later use of the concept leads us to conceive of alienation as a particular mode of active involvement with the world that determines economic methods and social institutions as well as subjective states of awareness. It affects human praxis, the very source of socialization and cultural consciousness. One would be tempted to describe it as a fundamental mode of being-in-the-world—what Heidegger termed an *existential*—if such a description did not eclipse the primarily active character of praxis. Alienation appears only to the extent that man grasps his existence as *active project in the world* (Sartre). Moreover, that active involvement with the world must be understood as *intrinsically* social. Only from a social perspective does it appear how a culture as a whole can be alienated.

Yet Marx, perhaps suspicious of an idea so comprehensive as to defy precise definition and to elude empirical verification, chose to restrict his scientific critique of society to more definable social factors. Thus he came to concentrate primarily on the capitalist mode of production and its exclusive orientation toward the production of exchange value. The development from a general, anthropological idea toward a specific social-economic theory would present no problems were it not that the former continues to determine the latter despite its very different assumptions. It is not merely that the social-economic system only *partially* substantiates the ills which Marx denounces in his ever-present general critique. But the basic assumptions underlying the specific social-economic theory, the priority of economic production in the social process as a whole, is hard to reconcile with the more general critique. After the anticipated demise of capitalism, exchange value may be abolished; but material production remains the *base* of culture which continues to determine all human activity.[41] Marx assumes that with the abolition of exchange value fetishist relations and attitudes will disappear. But these phenomena of alienation result more from a *priority* of

40. Herbert Marcuse, *One-Dimensional Man* (Boston: Beacon Press, 1964), p. 11.
41. Cf. Rudolf Boehm, *Kritik der Grundlagen des Zeitalters* (The Hague: Martinus Nijhoff, 1974), p. 20. On this point my interpretation differs from that of Ernest Mandel, *Economic Thought of Karl Marx*, pp. 207 ff.

economic production than from the nature of the system in which this priority is expressed.[42]

As the next chapters will show, Marx unquestionably intended to liberate bourgeois society from the tyranny of the purely economic. Had his own principal concern not been to *reintegrate* the economic with the social? Nevertheless, in accordance with the theory and practice of late eighteenth- and early nineteenth-century economics which he attacked, he continued to grant material production a predominant place in the total scheme of human activity. In doing so he opened himself to the critique of objectivism which had inspired his early writings and which still underlies his attack on fetishism.

Surely, the economic "basis" of society *affects* all other aspects. But rarely, mostly in primitive conditions and periods of exceptional scarcity, has it ever determined the entire culture. It did so only after the more general trend toward objectivism that had developed in Western culture since the late Middle Ages culminated in the economization of all aspects of life. Marx deserves lasting credit for having detected the link that ties the dominance of the economic in recent times to this cultural objectivism. But he did so in a specific rather than a general way. He identified the capitalist system as the one that had made it possible for the economic thus to determine all aspects of culture. Historically he was unquestionably right. In denouncing *capitalist* economism, Marx attacked the particular form in which the economic factor had taken possession of all other aspects of modern life. But in attributing this "alienating" economization

42. Some of the most negative aspects of social life, which Marx attributes to a particular mode of production, are due to the more elementary fact of economic scarcity. Not until scarcity itself is proven to result from a particular system of production and distribution can the overcoming of that system be reasonably expected to eliminate those negative conditions. In a world of limited resources and alarmingly increasing populations, the possibility of such a proof would seem remote. Sartre, who in his later work fully accepted the social-economic origin of alienation, never succeeded in showing that the alienating conditions would permanently disappear in any system that must operate under the restrictions of material scarcity. Their *present form* would vanish with the capitalist mode of production. But it would be followed by unending cycles of alienation and reappropriation (*Critique de la raison dialectique* [Paris, 1960]).

exclusively to the capitalist system, he somehow deflected attention from the fact that it was not so much the *particular* nature of that system which was at stake as the more general dominance of the economic factor which that system had historically made possible. The distinction may appear overly subtle until one raises the question: Is there any reasonable hope that this *priority of economic production* will vanish with capitalism? I do not see how Marx's mature work could nurture such a hope. Occasionally Marx intimates the coming of a new era in which mankind would no longer be subject to the domination of economic production, but he did not substantiate this vision through his critique and usually expressed it in the economic terminology of work and leisure. Marx introduced historical development into economic theory beyond anything the classical economists had ever conceived. Yet the *priority* of the economic itself he assumed in the same permanent mode in which they had assumed it. With the hindsight provided by the all-pervasive problems resulting from unrestricted economic development as well as by the notorious failure of socialist societies to rid themselves of economism, we are more inclined to distinguish the priority of economic production from the particular form which it adopted in capitalism and to question this priority in its own right. Beyond the fetishism of commodities we also question the fetishism of economics. The cultural priority of material production poses a wider problem with which we can deal only at the end of this study. To understand it we must first evaluate the function of the negativity of praxis, in alienation, in the total dialectic of society, and indeed of all history.

2
Culture as Historical Process

THE NEW MEANING OF PROGRESS

In discussing the concept of culture we often forget that it is the outcome of a particular, historical process. Until we become aware of this process we fail to understand both the dynamic nature of the cultural reality and the inevitable relativity of our approach to it. Marx was among the first to have perceived the full impact of this historical perspective. In the preceding chapter we saw how he refused to separate culture from its natural basis, as had been customary in the modern age. Yet his refusal did not imply that culture can return to the simplicity of a natural harmony with nature, as some Romantics had believed. More and more he had objected to Feuerbach's theory of alienation because of its total neglect of the dialectical tension between nature and culture. Feuerbach's later evolution toward a straightforward materialism confirmed the correctness of Marx's insight. As early as 1844 Marx had felt the need to resume Hegel's dynamic conception of culture as a progressive attempt to humanize an ever-yielding yet every-resistant nature. Yet in contrast to Hegel's position, for him the real struggle between culture and nature took place not in the theoretical consciousness but in practice. Theory itself forms an integral part, but still only a part, of the more comprehensive practical transformation of nature. What Marx in the Paris Manuscripts hails as Hegel's discovery is mainly his own.

The outstanding achievement of Hegel's *Phenomenology* and of its final outcome, the dialectic of negativity as the moving and generating principle—is first that Hegel conceives the self-creation of man as a process, conceives objectification as loss of the object, as alienation and as transcendence of this alienation; that he thus

58

grasps the essence of *labor,* and comprehends objective man . . . as the outcome of man's own *labor.* [*MEGA* 1³: 156; *Coll. Works* 3: 332–33]

These lines set the stage for a historical theory of culture which Marx never wrote but constantly assumed. Ever since the Greek Sophists, the relation between culture and nature has been a topic of dispute. While the ancients generally assumed the basic identity of the two, modern thinkers mostly stressed their opposition. Yet, with the romantic reaction against the artificial culture of the eighteenth century and the upsurge of the natural sciences, the pendulum swung back to "nature." Marx's own "naturalism" may be regarded as part of this movement. But Marx firmly rejected the romantic as well as the materialist view of nature. For him, culture definitively transforms the nature both of man's environment and of his own being. Marx feels no sympathy for Feuerbach's romantic return to nature. In *The German Ideology* he writes:

> He does not see how the sensuous world around him is not a thing given direct from all eternity, ever the same, but the product of industry and of the state of society; and, indeed, in the sense that it is an historical product, the result of the activity of a whole succession of generations, each standing on the shoulders of the preceding one, developing its industry and its intercourse, modifying its social organization according to the changed needs. [*MEGA* 1⁵: 32; *Coll. Works* 5: 39]

For Marx, on the contrary, nature is what man leaves forever, the home to which he can never return. In fact, that home has ceased to exist, for the whole process of culture consists in transforming it. Henceforth the term *nature* in Marx carries a pejorative connotation. In discussing the division of labor in *German Ideology,* Marx refers to the "natural" society and the "natural" division of labor as essentially negative concepts that must be dialectically overcome.

> The division of labor offers us the first example of the fact that, as long as man remains in *naturally* evolved society, that is, as long as a cleavage exists between the particular and the common interest, as long therefore as activity is not voluntarily, but *naturally* divided,

man's own deed becomes an alien power opposed to him. . . .
[*MEGA* 1⁵: 22; *Coll. Works* 5: 47; emphasis mine]

The two terms "natural division of labor" and "natural society" are intrinsically connected, because a natural society is based upon a division of labor according to the predisposition of nature rather than upon the human needs of the laborer. Such a society is product-oriented rather than man-oriented: from the product's point of view it is profitable to exploit the worker's "natural" dispositions, even though such an exploitation runs counter to his human needs.

The same aversion for a fixed, given "nature" renders Marx very suspicious of any kind of human "essence." According to the "Theses on Feuerbach" (of uncertain date, but probably after 1844), human essence can be understood only "as 'species,' as an inner mute general character which unites the many individuals in a *natural way*" (*MEGA* 1⁵: 534; *Coll. Works* 5: 4). The true essence of man has nothing to do with "nature"—it is "the ensemble of the social relations" (*MEGA* 1⁵: 534; Thesis 6 in *Coll. Works* 5: 4). The "Theses" spell out explicitly what the Paris Manuscripts only imply. In them, and in the first part of *The German Ideology*, Marx formulated the general principles for a theory of history. He first conceived and later developed them, with an eye on the concrete case of capitalist society. Their scope undoubtedly reaches further. But even though they provide a general rule for evaluating the impact of the various factors that determine social development, they do not allow themselves to be applied indiscriminately to each and every society. Marx and Engels became increasingly aware of the difficulty of applying them universally. How did a theory of history come to be part of what started as a straightforward social critique?

In a letter written to Arnold Ruge the twenty-five-year-old Marx expressed his unqualified belief in an inevitable, historical progress toward a rational society.

Reason has always existed, but not always in reasonable form. The critic can therefore start out from any form of theoretical and practical consciousness and from the forms *peculiar* to existing reality develop the true reality as its obligation and its final goal. As far as real life is concerned, it is precisely the *political state*—in all its *modern* forms—which even where it is not yet consciously imbued with socialist demands, contains the demands of reason. [*MEGA* 1¹: 574; *Coll. Works* 3: 143][1]

As far as I know, this was the last time Marx mentioned "the demands of reason." But the fundamental trust in progress never left him. He never doubted that history, despite occasional cycles of regressive irrationality, on the whole develops toward ever greater rationality. This trust must, however, not be equated with the eighteenth-century faith in the *idea of reason* which, as from a superior plane, directs and determines all historical processes. Closer to Marx's view of progressing rationality stands Vico's theory of historical truth. Only what man himself *does*, does he know to be indubitably true—*verum facere*. Since man alone is the cause of history, even as God is the cause of nature, historical truth is, for Vico, the most reliable one. Similarly, for Marx history becomes rational to the extent that man succeeds in becoming its sole maker and emancipates himself from any submission to nature. In contrast to Vico, however, Marx conceives of the truth of history not as already made but as yet to be made. It is not a contemplative truth that reveals itself to the backward glance of the spectator of history, but the active truth-in-process that gradually develops under the impact of the forward-marching praxis. Not only do I know what I *have* done, but I anticipate what I *shall* do. The concept of praxis, then, uniting the past with the future guarantees progress toward ever greater rationality. We will not exaggerate its importance if we consider it the culmination as well as the transformation of the idea of progress.

Ever since the Enlightenment the idea of progress had been linked to radical political reform. Schemes for the improvement of society differed widely according to the degree of confidence the would-be reformers placed in human nature. Rousseau and Diderot deemed that nature was originally good: reform consisted primarily in liberating it from the accretions of an enslaving culture. Of course, neither Diderot nor Rousseau ever

1. Letter to Arnold Ruge, published in *Deutsch-Französische Jahrbücher* (1844).

favored a return to native simplicity. But their romantic idealization of Arcadian life-styles served as a convenient foil for criticizing established social structures. Not everyone agreed. Edmund Burke, though open to the idea of development, harbored no confidence in drastic political schemes. To the naturalist optimism of the Enlightenment he opposed civilization as reason's only weapon against a nature all too inclined to follow its primitive passions to their destructive ends. It was, in fact, to those passions that the revolutionaries catered in the name of abstract reason. But for Burke, society, which alone dresses man's "naked, shivering nature," develops not by the rigid rule of abstract reason but by the gentle impulse of organic growth. To disturb the fragile harmony of the social organism is to remand the human race to its original chaos.

Such were the political controversies around the idea of progress that eventually led to the French Revolution as well as to the Restoration. They had not subsided when Marx entered the university. The young Marx immediately fell in with the radical-political wing of the German Romantic movement that continued to promote a belated but more radical German revolution. It advocated an overthrow of the established religious and social as well as political order.

Yet the social theories of the Enlightenment and their radical development in German Romanticism do not hold the principal key to Marx's concept of history. For a more complete understanding we must turn to the early economists. Moved by the same hope and optimism as their enlightened contemporaries, the eighteenth-century pioneers of the new science regarded it as their special task to endow the ideals of progress with earthy practicality. Was wealth not the essential means toward the attainment of that terrestrial happiness which constituted the very goal of society? At last it had become possible concretely to define society's role in the pursuit of that goal. Unfortunately, different schools conceived of it in different ways. According to the Physiocrats, wealth had been with us all along: nations merely had to reap the bounty of nature instead of wasting their natural resources on mercantilist abstractions such as gold, silver, or a favorable international balance of trade. For Adam

Smith and his followers, wealth was even more universally available, since its one and only source was human labor. Material happiness was clearly within reach, provided man allowed "nature" (in this case, economic nature!) to follow its course and removed the obstacles placed in its way by misguided interventions. The capitalist system of production, more than any other factor, held the highest hopes for future happiness.

Yet their generous disposition did not prevent the economists from introducing a cautionary note into the harmony of progress. The French Physiocrats had long learned to distrust interventionist schemes that had wrought so much havoc in the national economy during the reigns of Louis XIV and Louis XV. The egalitarian essays that appeared in the *Encyclopédie* aroused their suspicion even more. Men may be equal in human dignity, but if all men should consider themselves evenly entitled to the wealth of this world, society would soon return to a pastoral state—and all progress would come to an end. The leveling tendencies that had intermittently surfaced during the revolution and had created such long-lasting economic problems fully justified the economists' distrust. Eventually even such an ardent advocate of social reform as Condorcet was forced to qualify the encyclopedic creed with a distinction between political and economic equality. While the former continued to be a worthy ideal, the latter had shown itself to be a dangerous utopia. British economists, traditionally more skeptical toward ideologies, spoke an even more sobering language. The study of economy compelled Adam Smith to question his own earlier belief in a universal harmony of nature. The production and distribution of economic wealth proved to be a most complex business that could hardly encourage egalitarian expectations. Only "industrious" workers, willing to labor for subsistence wages and eager to cooperate in the grand design of capitalist progress by saving even from their low wages, would keep the movement toward proprietary happiness alive.

There were other, even more ominous, portents. If happiness depended on material goods, then its sources were not unlimited. Malthus's dark warnings about the disproportion between the geometrical rate of population increase and the arithmetic development of wealth had little effect upon his contemporaries. Only his colleagues, though mostly unconvinced, considered them worthy of serious discussion. Clearly their idea of progress differed from the fashionable faith in an infinite improvement of the human condition. Economists dealt with tangible and therefore limited realities. Even social utopians such as Saint-Simon and Owen had to admit that the road to economic equality, however long, must come to an end somewhere. Once that end had been reached, no more genuine "progress" was possible. The difference between the encyclopedic and the economic point of view led to two distinct types of social progress: the former allows infinite development and has inspired political revolutions; the latter remains subject to the conditions of a finite closed system and has regulated economic planning.[2]

Marx consistently borrowed from both traditions. No single belief dominated his thought more than that man can and will improve his lot, and that he will do so by changing his political institutions. But when it comes to material development, we find him at the opposite end from the "philosophes," surpassing even the economists in realism. Indeed, Marx withdraws the concept of economic development from human interference altogether. The question of how much man could change economic trends had remained largely dormant under the liberal recipe "Laissez faire, laissez passer." Faith in the invisible hand had discouraged Physiocrats as much as Classicists from tampering with economic developments. But the underlying supposition has always been that it *could* be done. Early in life Marx had acquired the conviction that we cannot interfere with economic developments as long as we allow a particular system to continue existing. Man has no choice but to let it run its course or, if possible, to overthrow it altogether.

At this point a basic difference appears between Marx's concept of progress and that of the economists who preceded him. For while they were essentially optimistic about the outcome of the current development, Marx held it responsible for all social

2. On this distinction, see J. B. Bury, *The Idea of Progress* (1932) (New York: Dover Books, 1955), chap. 8.

evil and predicted that it would continue to generate misery at an ever-increasing rate. His expectation of a more equitable society was based not on the chances of improving the present system but on its inevitable breakdown. What supported Marx in predicting such a favorable outcome at the end of the capitalist collapse? It was, I believe, not empirical historical or economic evidence, even though such evidence was used to the full extent of its availability and beyond, but a philosophical conviction about the nature of the historical process. In his student years Marx had found ample philosophical support for a view so consonant with the optimistic climate of his age. The philosophical argument had lost its force, but the conviction remained: viewed in its entirety, history follows a rational course. That all reality ultimately must make sense is the principle which Marx had most severely denounced in Hegel's philosophy yet which he ended up most consistently assuming. It underlies, in fact, his lasting trust in the dialectical method.

THE RATIONALITY OF PRAXIS

Marx's critique of the past warranted no predictions about the future. "Whether or not the revolution will actually take place is the question to be answered by a 'scientific' study of the concrete social situation. It cannot be certified by a supposed insight into the logic of the historical process."[3] As we shall see in a later chapter, even an empirically proven dialectical pattern of movement fails to secure a favorable outcome to history. Nevertheless, Marx did predict not only the revolution but also the subsequent social condition, and at least for the latter he could claim no scientific evidence. Only the acceptance of a guiding rationality could have induced the necessity of the overall meaningfulness of history and excluded the possibility of its ultimate failure. Since Marx consistently rejected any transcendent rule of history, I find no other support for his historical optimism but that of an unshakable faith in man's ability and determination to

3. George Lichtheim, *From Marx to Hegel* (New York: Herder, 1969), p. 20.

remake the world in the image of reason.[4] Socialism does not result from certain social-economic conditions but from man's deliberate resistance to permanent irrationality. In the end the Marxist vision of history rests upon the inner logic of the rational will.

How much this logic dominates his interpretation of history appears most clearly in the famous statement of the preface to *The Critique of Political Economy:* "No social order ever perishes before all the productive forces for which there is room in it have developed; and new, higher relations of production never appear before the material conditions of their existence have matured in the womb of the old society itself (*Werke* 13: 9; *Sel. Works* 1: 363)."[5] This social-economic reflection has no ground in experience but in a particular concept of history. Marx's rational a priori comes even more to light in the next sentence: "Therefore mankind always sets itself only such tasks as it can solve; since, looking at the matter more closely, it will always be found that the task itself arises only when the material conditions for its solution already exist or are at least in the process of formation." It would be hard to find a sociological text inspired by greater confidence in the fundamental reasonableness of human nature and the rationality of historical developments. Indeed, here the faith in reason surpasses rational evidence altogether.

Of course, neither Hegel nor Marx ever understood rationality as Spinoza and Leibniz had understood it. For Hegel nature and history are filled with irrationality, while for Marx the social-economic condition of modern society is the least rational. However, rationality does not reside in isolated events or appearances. It is exclusively the quality of the *whole*. For Hegel, as

4. Ortega y Gasset describes the revolutionary temperament as the rationalist one in "The Sunset of Revolution," *The Modern Theme* (New York: Harper, 1961), p. 116.

5. G. A. Cohen, in his careful analysis of this preface, shows that the quoted statement permits regression (an economic structure being replaced by an inferior one) and stagnation (remaining locked in its economic form). Nevertheless, it forms part of a passage phrased in terms of "stages of development" of productive forces that shows a clear commitment to the progress thesis. Cohen, *Karl Marx's Theory of History* (Princeton: Princeton University Press, 1978), pp. 136–40.

Marx read him, this whole is essentially completed and the rationality of the world process vindicated. For Marx it cannot be completed unless a fundamental change occurs. Such a change is necessary *mainly because reason demands it.* Admittedly, Marx uses other, intrinsically economic arguments to support his claim. But the outcome cannot be justified by predictable social-economic development alone: it requires a *theory* of the rational and a *belief* that history will obey this theory.

In Marx's concept of praxis, the eighteenth-century idea of reason directing the course of history attained its final form. Two philosophers, Hegel and Cieszkowski, directly influenced its conception. Reacting against the abstract, ahistorical explanations of the seventeenth and eighteenth centuries and adopting Herder's theory of a national spirit, Hegel had introduced reason into the very development of social institutions. Yet he had soon found himself surrounded by conservative romantics who, denying all intrinsic rationality to social institutions, attributed their "organic" development exclusively to custom and habit. This battle had not been decided when Marx registered at the Berlin faculty of law. One of his teachers, de Savigny, in accordance with the principles of the historical school, attributed the development of law to customs directly springing from the inner impulse of the national spirit, while his professor of jurisprudence Edward Gans upheld the orthodox Hegelian thesis: "Whatever is produced by a people at a determinate epoch is produced by its force *and by its reason.*"[6] Marx himself soon joined the opposition against the historical school. In an early article he argued astutely that the historical school merely presented a variation of the old natural law theory that replaced the idea of an unchangeable nature by the even more static concepts of God or nation. Marx took a clear position with the Hegelian faction.

However, Marx equally objected to the speculative character of Hegel's rationality. Hence the crucial impact of the Polish Hegelian August von Cieszkowski, however slight Marx's direct acquaintance with his work may have been. In his ambitious

6. *Das Erbrecht in Weltgeschichtlichen Entwicklung* (Berlin, 1826), 1:xii.

Historiosophie, Cieszkowski rejected Hegel's past-oriented theory of history, but he did so in the name of Hegel's own *Logic.* Any understanding of history must include the future as well as the past, otherwise the totality which alone in Hegelian philosophy permits genuine understanding would be missing. But how can we know the future? Through the teleology of freedom. In the deed, the future presents itself before being realized. For the first time in history man has become sufficiently master of his activity to be able to determine the course of the future. Cieszkowski, a nobleman of mystical inclinations, insisted on couching this Promethean vision in Christian language: "The human race has now attained such a state of maturity that its own decisions come to coincide with the divine plane of Providence."[7] Henceforth knowledge of man must include knowledge of his destiny. Mere consciousness is only an intermediate stage between preconscious fact and transconscious deed.[8] The circle of pure cognition, opened when Aristotle raised thought above all other modes of being, closed when Hegel concluded to the ultimate identity of thought and being. The idealist consciousness can go no further: in achieving an identity of reality and thought it has completed its one-sided course. Philosophy must now claim its rights over the new territory of praxis. In realizing this outward movement, consciousness regains the *immediate* union with the real which thought had abandoned for the mediacy of reflection. Cieszkowski adds a moment of praxis to Hegel's theory of the Absolute Spirit. After having reached *Selbstdenken* in philosophy, consciousness must become *Selbsttun;* the *An-und-für-sich* must turn into the *Aus-sich.* Cieszkowski's presentation of this outward movement as a movement into the material, a "rehabilitation of matter," accelerated the Young Hegelian drift toward materialism. However, the primary factor here remains the conversion of theory into praxis. Marx's eleventh thesis on Feuerbach echoes the conclusion of the *Historiosophie:*

> Also philosophy must allow itself to become mainly applied and, even as the poetry of art turned into the prose of thinking, so must

7. *Prolegomena zur Historiosophie* (Berlin, 1838), p. 20.
8. Ibid., p. 97.

philosophy descend from the height of theory into the depth of praxis. Practical philosophy, or, more correctly, the *philosophy of praxis*—its most concrete impact upon life and social relations, the development of truth in concrete fact—this is the future task of philosophy.[9]

Philosophy can achieve its ultimate goal only by becoming "popularized" or, in Cieszkowski's oxymoronic expression, "Sie muss sich in die Tiefe verflachen."[10] By anchoring his expectations of the future in a philosophy of present and past, Cieszkowski hopes to steer clear of utopianism. The utopian, he writes, lacks an adequate awareness of the chasm between consciousness (of past and present) and reality. He ignores what is, in order to posit what *ought* to be. But in doing so he misunderstands the nature of *real* development and loses at the same time the *ideal* power of thought. The future can be understood only through a genuine dialectic of the present. Wherever the past has developed one-sidedly, a tendency in the opposite direction will develop in the future, and wherever two opposites have already emerged, their synthesis will be forthcoming.

According to this vision, history progresses toward an ever greater perfection. The content of Cieszkowski's "knowledge" of the future hardly exceeds what Hegel himself could have developed from his own premises. Yet underneath the Hegelian scheme we sense the presence of an idea that has little to do with "knowledge." The *Historiosophie* attempts, in fact, to provide a speculative charter not so much for *knowing* the future as for *making* it.[11] Nevertheless, Cieszkowski's projection remains rooted in the real present rather than in a purely ideal *ought*, and

9. Ibid., p. 129.

10. Ibid., p. 131.

11. Lukacs sees in it a return of Fichte's romantic *ought* to the philosophy of what *is*. His interpretation is confirmed by Hess, who admitted having taken the idea of praxis from Cieszkowski and who, precisely in his philosophy of action, explicitly refers to Fichte: "The time has come for the philosophy of spirit to become a philosophy of the deed. Not only thinking but all human activity must be lifted to a plane where all oppositions vanish. . . . Fichte in this respect has already surpassed the most recent philosophers" ("Philosophie der Tat," in *Sozialistische Aufsätze*, p. 50).

he even regards the philosophy of praxis as the only possible
way of overcoming the *ought* inherent in all thinking: "By its very
nature can the ought only be overcome through the deed."[12]
Cieszkowski opened the gate leading from Hegelian speculation
to action. The entire Hegelian Left was to pass through it. The
conversion of thinking into practice became the rallying cry of
the movement.

However, the method of converting thought into action—
a point on which Cieszkowski had remained uncomfortably
vague—would divide them again. According to the Berlin
Young Hegelians led by Bruno Bauer, historical progress consists essentially in a progressing consciousness. By relentlessly
criticizing its own creations, the mind enters upon ever higher
stages of consciousness. Originally Bauer had envisioned this
dialectic mainly as a critique of religion by philosophy. But gradually the Young Hegelian critique had turned more and more
against the conservative political regime of Prussia. The method
remained basically the same: the overthrow of established governments was to result primarily from new states of awareness
first achieved by philosophers and then conveyed to the masses.
This idealist concept of social progress prevailed even among
the more practically oriented Hegelians, who, under Arnold
Ruge's editorship, published the revolutionary *Hallesche Jahrbücher*. For them also political action consisted in the application of
philosophical ideas. On this point Marx's view essentially differs.

In *The Holy Family* and *The German Ideology* he settles his accounts with the Young Hegelian concept of history. Marx continues to agree with his former mentors that reason must be
embodied into concrete social structures and, since these structures do not exist at present, into revolutionary movements. But
he rejects the self-complacent elitism of the philosophical "critics" who consider themselves as the primary agents of history
and the masses as the "passive, spiritless, a-historical, material
element of history." To their view Marx opposes the primacy of a

12. Ibid., p. 143. This point is duly emphasized by Shlomo Avineri, *The Social
and Political Thought of K. Marx* (Cambridge: Cambridge University Press, 1968),
pp. 125–27, one of the few to have perceived Cieszkowski's significance for
Marx's theory of praxis.

proletarian class which embodies in its very existence the necessity for historical change. The struggle for survival will leave the proletariat no choice but to overthrow the system which has produced it. "The proletariat is compelled as proletariat to abolish itself and thereby its opposite, private property, which determines its existence and which makes it proletariat. It is the negative side of the antithesis, its restlessness within its very self, dissolved and self-dissolving private property" (*MEGA* 1³: 206; *Coll. Works* 4: 36). The inevitability of the proletarian revolution provided Marx with the Hegelian *necessity* of the future which, since Cieszkowski's work, the Young Hegelians had sought in vain. That revolution is not a matter of philosophical speculation but of social necessity.

As Marx phrased it later in the *Communist Manifesto,* the Communist predictions "merely express, in general terms, actual relations springing from an existing class struggle, from a historical movement going on under our eyes" (*Werke* 4: 475; *Sel. Works* 1: 46). The Young Hegelians, to the extent that they agreed to practical action at all, failed to take adequate account of the prevailing social conditions. Thus they introduced a Fichtean *ought* into Hegel's dialectic and actually regressed to a more idealist position. To Marx the dialectic of history is the dialectic of a *reality striving toward rationality,* not the dialectic of an *idea opposed to a reality.* Social change can be expected only from existing conditions that leave no alternative but revolutionary action. Only the class that incarnates those conditions is able to convert the idea into action. "As philosophy finds its *material* weapons in the proletariat, so the proletariat finds its *spiritual* weapons in philosophy" (*MEGA* 1¹: 504; "Contribution to the Critique of Hegel's Philosophy of Law," in *Coll. Works* 3: 187). But Marx had never attributed philosophical significance to the *ideas* actually existing among proletarians. The proletariat, he had written, represents the *negation* of philosophy qua philosophy. The proletarian class lacks all insight into its own universality, including the one that will be required for accomplishing its future task. It demonstrates the priority of practice over theory in the development of history.

However, the existence of the proletariat does not dispense

with theory: a dialectical consciousness is as essential a prerequisite for the socialist revolution as the material conditions of the proletarian class. But that class can become dialectically conscious only when its entire *existence* stands in dialectical opposition to the society which gave rise to it. To some Marxists this means that a revolutionary consciousness must first exist in the proletariat (Lukacs, Korsch); to others, that the theory must be implemented, by force if necessary, once the minimum social conditions exist (Lenin). But in either case the dialectical character of the proletarian class remains the main agent of history.

HISTORICAL REASON

In the first part of *The German Ideology* Marx outlines his concept of historical development. It bears the title "Feuerbach." Although he occupies a minor place in the actual discussion, Marx's reference to his former mentor is at least polemically appropriate. For while Feuerbach had based his anthropology upon the idea of a permanent, universal human nature, for Marx only man's historical character discloses his essence: the universal provides no information about man's specific nature. What concerned Marx was not the question why men think and act, or why they let themselves be guided by ideas and ideals, but why they think differently and nurture different ideas and ideals at different times. Prior to historical specification, the *universally* human would, from a Marxist perspective, be merely the prehuman.[13] For Marx man became historical as soon as he became human, long before he reached literacy. The science of man, then, consists essentially in the *history* of the human species.[14] Such a radically historical view of human culture did not

13. Karl Kautsky, *Die materialistische Geschichtsauffassung* 1:6–7, 392.

14. Habermas remains entirely within the compass of Marx's own thought in claiming that the natural sciences must be subsumed under the science of man, since the latter alone contains the principles from which a methodology of the former must be derived (*Knowledge and Human Interests*, trans. Jeremy Shapiro [Boston: Beacon Press, 1971], p. 50). Marx's refusal to distinguish the prehistorical from the historical stages of development reflected his aversion to the tendency of the Germans to "invent the prehistoric era" when they run out of positive material (*MEGA* 1⁵: 18; *Coll. Works* 5:42).

permit an abstract, general theory of history; for such a theory, as much as a general theory of man, would fail to take serious account of the historical specificity of each period. Marx therefore refused to expand what he considered to be no more than "a historical sketch of the genesis of capitalism in Western Europe" into "a historico-philosophical theory of the general path every people is fated to tread whatever the historical circumstances in which it finds itself" (*Werke* 19: 112).[15] It is important to keep this in mind when reading statements such as the following: "Our conception of history relies on expounding the real processes of production, starting out from the material production of life, and to comprehend the form of intercourse connected with this and created by this . . . as the basis of all history" (*MEGA* 1⁵: 28; *Coll. Works* 5: 53). Marx here undeniably states a universal principle, but one with limited practical applicability. For the term *material production* means different things in different societies. In a capitalist system, for instance, it is determined by specific forms of exchange, distribution, and consumption. Even more restricted is the application of the historical law according to which social relations determine property relations, since those relations themselves depend on a particular mode of production. Until property becomes a dominant factor in the production process (which only happens in its precapitalist and capitalist stages), it plays an insignificant part in the structuring of society. Even to refer to early forms of production as "Communist" is to compel into a later structure societies in which possession, private or common, had little significance. On the other hand, once property has acquired a primary role, it tends to translate itself immediately into social structures and to perpetuate them by means of property legislation. Thus it comes to dominate all social structures and to create constant conflicts between ever-changing modes of production[16] and those static structures.

On this point Marx's interpretation differs substantially from that of his immediate predecessors, the French historians of the

15. "Reply to Mikhailovsky" (1877), translated in *Marx-Engels, Basic Writings on Politics and Philosophy*, ed. Lewis Feuer (New York: Doubleday, 1959), p. 440.
16. Production is constantly changing *only* in the kind of society where property plays a primary role.

Restoration. Partly under the impact of the French Revolution, those historians had come to accept the position that political relations are determined by economic conditions. Systems of government are solidly rooted in what Guizot calls *"l'état des personnes"*—their property relations.[17] Political changes, Mignet argues, are effected by the "needs" *(les besoins)* of the various social classes. Yet none of them investigates the origins of those property relations. Their static, eighteenth-century concept of an immutable human nature does not require such an investigation.[18] Marx's apparently universal law then turns out to be a specific historical one.

Only in the *Grundrisse* does Marx provide the full historical perspective from which the relative significance of property developments may be understood. In an important passage which deals with so-called precapitalist modes of production (but which in fact are mostly noncapitalist) Marx defines property in such abstract terms that any attempt to discuss the history of the entire human race in property relations as we understand them now becomes patently meaningless.

> Property originally means no more than a human being's relation to his natural conditions of production as belonging to him, as his, as *presupposed* along *with his own being;* relations to them as natural *presuppositions* of his self, which only form, so to speak, his extended body. He actually does not relate to his conditions of production, but rather has a double existence, both subjectively as he himself, and objectively in these natural non-organic conditions of his existence. The forms of these *natural conditions of production* are double: 1) his existence as a member of a community. Hence the existence of this community . . . ; 2) the relation to land and soil mediated by the community, as its own, as communal landed property, at the same time *individual possession* for the individual, or in such a way that only the fruits are divided, but the land itself and the labor remain common. [*GR* 391; NIC 491–92]

Slightly further on Marx summarizes this description of property as meaning man's "conscious relation . . . to the conditions

17. *Essais sur l'histoire de la France* (1860), p. 74.

18. Plekhanov, *The Development of the Monist View of History,* trans. Andrew Rothstein (New York: International Publishers, 1972), chap. 2.

of production as *his own,* so that the producer's being appears as in the objective conditions *belonging to him"* (*GR* 393; NIC 493). Such a broad definition extends far beyond the narrow relations of ownership described in *The German Ideology.* Marx himself explicitly states that the so-called precapitalist formations have little in common with what we understand by either private or common property relations.[19]

In none of the earlier forms does appropriation result from labor, as it does in capitalism: labor *presupposes* a particular possessive relationship to the conditions of production. "The chief objective condition of labor does not itself appear as a *product* of labor, but is already there as nature; . . . [man] thus appears from the outset not merely as a laboring individual but . . . has an *objective mode of existence* in his ownership of the land, an existence *presupposed* to his activity and not merely as a result of it" (*GR* 384–85; NIC 485). Hence those economic conditions which determine the development of history are not, as the succinct description of *The German Ideology* may suggest, a matter of private or communal ownership. They are wholly different forms of production.

Marx's survey of precapitalist formations in *The German Ideology* is restricted to those forms which played a role in the development of capitalism: the tribal society, the slave society of classical antiquity (described almost exclusively on the Roman model), the feudalism of the barbaric age, and the bourgeois society of the West. In the more detailed description of the *Grundrisse,* Marx has moved somewhat beyond this pattern by adding the "Oriental" system. Yet for general historical purposes, this would still present an unjustifiably limited basis. However, Marx intended neither to write a sketch of world history nor even to develop a theory of world history. The latter point becomes

19. Nor are private and communal possession mutually exclusive. The predominant pattern of land possession in Asia is that of a comprehensive unity standing above the little communities which belong to it in hereditary possessions (*GR* 376–77; NIC 472–74). In other forms where the private is more clearly separate from the communal, membership in the commune still remains the condition for appropriation (Rome) (*GR* 378–79; NIC 475–76). The two forms may also appear together as in the Germanic type.

increasingly clear as Marx over the years weakens the link connecting one system of production to the next one. Even in *The German Ideology* the systems leading to capitalism were not linked entirely by intrinsic connections. They rather consisted of a succession of *types* which emerged as much because of fortuitous circumstances as inner necessity.[20] The feudal society replaced the ancient one, not merely because the ancient had disintegrated, but because tribes of an entirely different social system had moved in and *destroyed* the old forces of production. The ancient and the feudal systems presented social *alternatives* linked only by the fact that the latter destroyed the former.[21]

What Marx understands under the Asiatic mode of producing fits even less in a developmental pattern. Not only does it not "lead" to a capitalist mode of production but, being essentially stagnant, it cannot be said to prepare any other system. Change here must come strictly from without. The beginning of capitalist society lends itself more willingly to a purely economic interpretation. But even here contingent factors appear. First, it should be noted that whatever "necessity" there is in the emergence of capitalism was due, as Marx has always emphasized, not so much to rectilinear development of the feudal economy as to opposition *against it*. The towns were able to develop because serfs fled the country, and commerce grew partly out of an active desire on the part of the towns to unite against the feudal lords.[22] Historical development follows a dialectical course (in contrast to the materialist interpretation of history): it moves by

20. This, of course, is not to deny that some law of causality applies, but only that the theory of historical materialism alone is insufficient to explain the entire course of history.

21. Eric J. Hobsbawm in Karl Marx, *Precapitalist Economic Formations*, ed. and intro. E. J. Hobsbawm (New York: International Publishers, 1964), p. 32.

22. "In the Middle Ages the citizens in each town were compelled to unite against the landed nobility to defend themselves. The extension of trade, the establishment of communications, led the separate towns to establish contacts with other towns, which had asserted the same interests in the struggle with the same antagonist. . . . The conditions of life of the individual citizens became—on account of their contradiction to the existing relations and of the mode of labor determined by this—conditions which were common to them all and independent of each individual. The citizens created these conditions insofar as they had torn themselves free from feudal ties, and were in their turn created by them

opposition rather than by continuous progress. On the other hand, the rise of the manufactures results *directly* from the growth of the city population and the adopted principle of division of labor. No universal scheme applies. Internal as well as external factors determine the course of history, and it may well have been one of Marx's principal merits to have shown how intimately they are interwoven.

In the *Grundrisse* Marx describes the conditions needed for the transition from feudalism to capitalism as a series of dissolutions.

1. The dissolution of the relation which directly connects the laborer to the inorganic conditions of production and which allows appropriation of one with the other.

2. The dissolution of the relation in which the laborer appears as the proprietor of the instrument of his labor (*GR* 197; NIC 497–98).[23]

3. The dissolution of the relations of production in which use value predominates. This occurs mostly through the accumulation of wealth (gathered by trade and usury) in the form of money (*GR* 397, 402; NIC 497–98, 502).

According to this presentation, the transition from one stage to another occurs clearly through dialectical, that is, self-generated, oppositions. Yet a closer look reveals that those oppositions themselves are contingent upon particular, historical circumstances. Marx and Engels provide only scattered information on the nature of those circumstances. Apart from the passage in the *Grundrisse,* the principal texts appear in *Capital* 1, (pt. 8 and chaps. 14, 15) and *Capital* 3 (chaps. 20, 36, 47).

---

insofar as they were determined by their antagonism to the feudal system which they found in existence" (*MEGA* 1⁵: 42–43; *Coll. Works* 5:76).

23. Marx shows how the two "dissolutions" are connected: "The same process which divorced a mass of individuals from their previous relations to the *objective conditions of labor,* relations which were, in one way or another, affirmative, negated these relations, and thereby transformed these individuals into *free workers,* this same process freed—δυνάμει—these *objective conditions of labor*—land and soil, raw material, necessaries of life, instruments of labor, money or all of these—from their *previous state of attachment* to the individuals now separated from them" (*GR* 402; NIC 503).

The Marxist economist Maurice Dobb[24] has attempted to give a historically more sustained account of the complex, dialectical transitions from late feudalism to industrial capitalism. He attributes the disintegration of the feudal economy principally to its inability to satisfy the needs of the ruling class for more revenue. Yet those needs resulted not from the feudal mode of producing as such, but from particular, historical circumstances such as the effects of war and brigandage and the necessity of strengthening military resources. Increasing feudal exactions to meet this ever-rising demand caused massive desertions from the land, emancipation of the serfs, and availability of more labor power in the towns. The dissolution of the monasteries and the enclosures of land for sheep farming accelerated the drift from the country to the city. Historically "overdetermined" also was the process by which the emerging merchant class came to dominate the entire production. The enormous accumulation of wealth without which the capitalist mode of production would never have become possible derived not from the intrinsic usefulness of commerce, but from the systematic exploitation of less developed regions and monopolistic protection.[25] Even so, accumulation would have been insufficient had the distintegrating feudal order not made available a class of dispossessed. The formation of a proletariat completed the conditions for making mercantile investment in manufacturing profitable. "The new society had to be nourished from the crisis and decay of the old order."[26] The historical-materialist interpretation assumes the existence of those conditions; it does not "deduce" them from the previous period.

24. *Studies in the Development of Capitalism* (New York: International Publishers [1947], 1963).
25. "The law that the independent development of merchant's capital is inversely proportional to the degree of development of capitalist production is particularly evident in the history of the carrying trade, as among the Venetians, Genoese, Dutch, etc., where the principal gains were not thus made by exporting domestic products but by promoting the exchange of products of commercially and otherwise economically underdeveloped societies and by exploiting both producing countries. . . . But this monopoly of the carrying trade disintegrates, proportionally to the development of the peoples whom it exploits" (*Werke* 25: 341; *Cap.* 3:328).
26. Dobb, *Development of Capitalism*, p. 18.

Intrinsic and extrinsic elements had to cooperate even more intimately in bringing about the industrial revolution. However much capitalism invites technical progress, its internal development alone neither explains nor produces it. Scientific inventions (the steam engine, the cotton gin, etc.) do not follow by internal determination from the preindustrialist mode of production. On the other hand, practical inventions are not made until they are needed. Even when the scientific principles are available, the application must wait until the economy demands it. When Papin first invented the steam engine he found little use for it in his semifeudal principality of Hessen. So the tradition now honors James Watt, an English technician who merely repaired and slightly improved an existing model for the invention of which he never claimed credit. Watt's reputation rests on the fact that he adapted the new engine to meet an actual, economic need. Still, need alone could not have generated the required technology had there not existed a scientific theory independent of the immediate economic realities.

From the very beginning Marx opposed substituting historical-materialist theory for the empirical study of history. The *ultimately determining factors* are never the only ones and, hence, they must be understood in their total context. "Empirical observation must in each separate instance bring out empirically, and without any mystification and speculation, the connection of the social and political structures with production" (*MEGA* 1[5]: 14; *Coll Works* 5: 35).[27] Nevertheless, the assumption of rational progress guides Marx's factual analyses of history as well as his interpretation of historical succession. The idea of a *directed development* explicitly appears in the *Contribution to the Critique of Political Economy*. "In broad outlines Asiatic, ancient, feudal, and modern bourgeois modes of production can be designated as *progressive epochs* in the economic formation of society" (*Werke*

---

27. Engels also was aware of this problem: "Political economy is therefore essentially a *historical* science. It deals with material which is historical, that is, constantly changing; it must first investigate the special laws of each separate stage in the evolution of production and exchange, and only when it has completed this investigation will it be able to establish the few quite general laws which hold good for production and exchange as a whole" (*Werke* 20: 136; *Anti-Dühring* 163).

13: 9; *A Contribution to the Critique of Political Economy,* in *Sel. Works* 1: 363). Even orthodox Marxists find it hard to take this statement at face value. Thus Eric J. Hobsbawm comments:

> In the literal sense this is plainly untrue, for not only did the Asiatic mode of production coexist with all the rest, but there is no suggestion in the argument of the *Formen,* or anywhere else, that the ancient mode evolved out of it. We ought therefore to understand Marx *not* as referring to chronological succession, or even to the evolution of one system out of its predecessor (though this is obviously the case with capitalism and feudalism), but to evolution in a more general sense. . . . The statement that the Asiatic, ancient, feudal and bourgeois formations are 'progressive' does not therefore imply any simple unilinear view of history, not a simple view that all history is progress. It merely states that each of these systems is in crucial respects further removed from the primitive state of man.[28]

Indeed, *with respect to capitalism* feudalism marks an unquestionable progress over the so-called Asiatic formations. It immediately precedes capitalism because it creates the factual conditions for it. However, this proximate position does not imply that feudalism opens the only possible road to capitalism, even less that the Germanic tribes which overran the Roman Empire were the only ones to found a feudal society. Earlier we noted that Marx never attempted to write an outline of world history. We may add: neither did he attempt to write a history of economic systems. He only discussed previous economic systems according to their proximity, actual or possible, to capitalism. Indeed, in an economic history the usage of such broad concepts as "the Asiatic forms of ownership" or "feudalism" would be almost meaningless. Marx's reading of history is consciously hermeneutical. He interprets the past on the basis of a comparison with the present.[29]

28. *Precapitalist Economic Formations,* pp. 36, 38.

29. "He opens a general perspective on history precisely to the extent that he develops his analysis of the present: *i.e.,* precisely to the extent that he seizes the extreme or essential differences by which the present defines or illuminates, even if indirectly, the past." Lucio Colletti, *From Rousseau to Lenin* (New York: Monthly Review Press, 1974), p. 23.

Still the question remains in what even the relative progress of one social system with respect to another consists. Early in his career Marx had claimed that it was a matter of increasing rationality, and all indications are that he never abandoned this view. As a society progresses it becomes more rational. But what precisely distinguishes a more rational social structure from a less rational one? Nowhere does Marx answer that question. We may assume, I suppose, that any form of social integration that makes a society more flexible in its responses to outside and inside challenges also renders it more rational. For Marx such a development happens under the impact of the two principal agents of social change, namely, the forces of production and the social relations through which a society appropriates them. We shall have more to say about these factors in the next section. But even without trying to define them we may wonder whether they provide an adequate basis for social development. In simple terms: does all social development originate in the mode of production? Habermas, after having given the question considerable attention in a study on the reconstruction of historical materialism, concluded that social progress depends more on a society's ability to learn than on its mode of production. The latter depends on the former. Only when new learning, theoretical and practical, has found its way into the entire culture of a society and has affected even its general world-view is the decisive factor available for transforming the established form of social integration in accordance with its new needs. "Only this new form of social integration makes possible a further increase in system complexity—*e.g.,* the social utilization of productive forces, the shaping of new organizational forms, new media, etc."[30] History then becomes a directional process of learning,

---

30. "Geschichte und Evolution," in *Zur Rekonstruktion des Historischen Materialismus* (Frankfurt, 1976), p. 235. Cf. also the excellent analysis of Thomas McCarthy, *The Critical Theory of Jürgen Habermas* (Cambridge, Mass.: MIT Press, 1978), pp. 234–71. Hans Blumenberg's pioneering study on the emergence of the modern world-view, *Die Genesis der Kopernikanischen Welt* (Frankfurt: Suhrkamp, 1975), defines the condition for the ability to learn new things as an opening up of theoretical freedom: "What spurs inventiveness is the liberation from obstructing positions around the critical area, which previously allowed no

and progress directly depends on the amount of new learning a society has been able to assimilate.

The question arises, however, whether such an interpretation may still be called Marxist. It is, of course, not what Marx intended. But is it at least compatible with his principles? Habermas has, I believe, successfully defended himself against the charge of "idealism" in his interpretation. Learning creates only the possibility, the "logical space" within which new structures *may* be erected. Whether they actually will be depends on contingent circumstances. In any event, he has, as Marx had, restricted the increase of rationality to actual praxis, not to any speculative a priori. Such a model never allows us to interpret any period of history, the past no more than the future, by any single factor—such as, for instance, the class rule in capitalist society. For the practical will must constantly assert itself against forces that are by no means rational—that is, intelligible by inner necessity. When the barbaric tribes invaded the Roman Empire and destroyed its social-economic structure, no rational necessity in that structure "caused" this destruction. From the Roman point of view the invasions were highly irrational intrusions upon their society. Nor did any overreaching reason secure a more rational state of affairs afterwards. The practical reason that motivates a society consists in its elementary drive toward survival.

Marx assumes that over a sufficient period of time (allowing for setbacks and even total destruction by external forces) a society as a whole will respond rationally to its historical challenges and thereby increase its potential to survive. However, such an assumption guarantees no improvement of the human condition as a whole until the time when all societies have become economically interdependent (a situation initiated by modern capitalism), and then only after a long development. Solely his conviction that the current economic system is by its very nature bound to overtake all others and then to destroy itself emboldened Marx to predict a better future for the entire hu-

---

room for light thought-experiments and play with possibilities" (p. 158). He correctly emphasizes that the more a field of scientific investigation develops, the more it answers its own questions and the less it depends on extrinsic factors.

man race. Even if such an economic unification takes place, the question remains whether it provides a sufficient basis for a *total* interpretation of history. Any historical periodization reflects the concerns of the interpreter's age. Marx's attempt is no exception, even though it was oriented toward the future. Nor should the inevitable relativity of its historical perspective be held against his theory. But he who criticized past interpretations of history never raised the critical questions about our way of asking questions. He failed to confront the fact that his attempt at periodization was also done from within a particular, time-conditioned perspective.

BASE AND SUPERSTRUCTURE

Marx's conception of history would not have been remembered if it had merely been a variation on the idea of progress. Even his notion of praxis alone would hardly be memorable: Cieszkowski and Hess, who developed it, remain known today only to historians of ideas. What uniquely distinguishes Marx's contribution is the synthesis of those ideas with a concept of society that directly relates *all* cultural achievements to man's life-sustaining activity. At one point Marx formulated that connection in the ambiguous principle of the primacy of the social-economic. We actually possess two versions of this principle: a longer and, on the whole, more radical one, in *The German Ideology;* and a shorter, more ambiguous one in the *Contribution to the Critique of Political Economy.* The former is stated in both a positive and a negative form. The mode of production is the principal agent of history. "Men are the producers of their conceptions, ideas, etc.—real, active men, as they are conditioned by a definite development of their productive forces and of the intercourse corresponding to these, up to its furthest forms. Consciousness can never be anything else than conscious being, and the being of men is their actual life-process" (*MEGA* 1^5: 15; *Coll. Works* 5: 36). Negatively, pure consciousness is denied the role of primary agent of history. Consciousness is determined by language, and language derives from social relations, which themselves are determined by the mode of production. "Consciousness is ... from the very beginning a social product, and remains so as long as men exist at all" (*MEGA* 1⁵: 20; *Coll. Works* 5: 44). It is conditioned by the productive forces and the social intercourse to which they give rise. We must keep in mind that *The German Ideology* is a polemical work, written against theories that attributed an absolute primacy to states of consciousness. The reaction drove Marx to such extreme expressions as the following, never repeated evaluation:

> We set out from real, active men, and on the basis of their real life-process we demonstrate the development of the ideological reflexes and echoes of this life-process. The phantoms formed in the human brain are also, necessarily, sublimates of their material life-process, which is empirically verifiable and bound to material premises. Morality, religion, metaphysics, all the rest of ideology, and their corresponding forms of consciousness, thus no longer retain the semblance of independence. [*MEGA* 1⁵: 15–16; *Coll. Works* 5: 36]

The unquestionably materialist tenor of this text—"reflexes and echoes," "phantoms formed in the human brain"—did not prevent Marx from attributing an irreducible role to consciousness within the production process. Reflection and foresight are most essential in the process of production.[31] Consciousness may have a natural origin, but once it has emerged, it places itself in opposition to its "natural" context, including the particular social-economic context in which it originated. Dependence here means anything but identity. The specific mode of dependence of consciousness is precisely that it stands in opposition to that on which it depends. Hence it is as true to claim that social relations depend on consciousness as that consciousness de-

31. The connection of culture with elementary biological needs is, of course, neither controversial nor exclusively Marxist. Already Schiller had written in a school essay: "Hunger and nakedness made man first into a hunter, a fisherman, a cattleman, a farmer and an architect. Lust founded families and the vulnerability of the individuals drew shepherds together" ("Ueber den Zusammenhang der tierischen Natur des Menschen mit seiner Geistigen," in *Werke* 5:259). The controversy begins with the mode in which this connection is conceived. In *The German Ideology*, Marx separated language and consciousness from material production. Such a separation appears neither in Schiller nor, as far as I know, in any other writer before Marx.

pends on social relations. Against German idealist philosophers ("ideologists") Marx emphasized the latter aspects, but against Feuerbach he stressed the former. In the face of Feuerbach's increasingly materialist leanings, Marx strongly asserted the active relation of consciousness to nature. "Feuerbach does not see how the sensuous world around him is not a thing given direct from all eternity . . . but the product of industry and of the state of society" (*MEGA* 1^5: 32; *Coll. Works* 5: 39). The "Theses on Feuerbach," written around the same time, suggest that man is more a producer of nature than a product of nature: "The chief defect of all materialism up to now (including Feuerbach's) is that the object, reality, what we apprehend through our senses is understood only in the form of the object of contemplation; but not as sensuous human activity, as practice" (*MEGA* 1^5: 533; *Coll. Works* 5: 3). Insofar as materialism abstracts consciousness from its oppositional *relation to nature*, it basically coincides with idealism. In either case the two elements cease to be *actively* related to one another.

The relation between consciousness and reality did not receive its definitive expression until the preface to the *Contribution to the Critique of Political Economy*.

> In the social production of their existence men inevitably enter into definite relations which are independent of their will, namely, relations of production appropriate to a given stage in the development of their material powers of production. The totality of these relations of production constitutes the economic structure of society, the real foundation on which arises a legal and political superstructure and to which correspond definite forms of social consciousness. The mode of production of material life conditions the general process of social, political, and intellectual life. It is not the consciousness of men that determines their existence, but their social existence that determines their consciousness. [*Werke* 13: 8– 9; *A Contribution to the Critique of Political Economy* (Dobbs-Ryazanskaya) 11]

This text deserves a closer analysis than it usually receives. What are those material powers of production which determine the relations of production? They include the technical "means of production." But neither raw material nor instruments constitute economic powers until they are integrated within a social system. As Marx wrote in *The Poverty of Philosophy:* "Machinery is no more an economic category than the bullock that drags the plough. Machinery is merely a production force. The modern workshop, which depends on the application of machinery, is a social production relation, an economic category" (*Werke* 4: 149; *Coll. Works* 6: 183; Also *Werke* 27: 456; *Sel. Works 2:* 445). Even labor, though it naturally results in the production of use value, remains "only the manifestation of a force of human labor power," and hence is not properly economic until it becomes part of a social production system (*Werke* 19:15; *Critique of the Gotha Program,* in *Sel. Works 2:* 18).

But then the question returns all the more urgently: What are the so-called powers of production which determine social relations?[32] Obviously, in singling out the *material* powers of production Marx wished to emphasize that those factors to which his contemporaries had given the priority, such as the social environment (*l'opinion* of French historians) or the developing consciousness (the *Geist* of German idealists), originated in the more basic dialectic between man and nature. But that does not explain the *primacy* of the material powers. If the relation to nature is social and cultural from the start, why should the material powers be given any kind of priority? Marx's writings provide little help in clarifying this thesis. Yet the distinction between "material" and "social" relations which appears clearly in *Capital* 3 and in the letter to Annenkov of December 28, 1846, shows that he did not reduce social relations to the "material" relations directly involved in the economic production process.[33] They enjoy a far more independent status than the material relations—a fact which orthodox Marxism often overlooks. Still the question remains whether even this broader definition of the mode of production, in which social relations possess a far greater initiative, forms an adequate basis for explaining cul-

32. The Preface is by no means the only place where the primacy of the productive forces is asserted. It appears explicitly in *The Poverty of Philosophy* and *The Communist Manifesto* and is anticipated in *The German Ideology.* Cf. Cohen, *Marx's Theory of History,* pp. 142–47.

33. Cf. Cohen, p. 162.

tural development in every conceivable society. Aware of the narrowness of such an economic basis, Habermas has proposed a more limited interpretation of Marx's principle. According to him, the dependence on the mode of production applies only to those phases during which a society is passing to a new stage of development. Thus the economic base would "determine" the superstructure only in periods of social evolution.[34] But even in this qualified reading one may wonder (with Habermas himself) how useful the principle is for understanding the innovation of *all* societies. Economic production and the social relations it requires may well play such a determining role in a capitalist society. But other societies appear to be less prone to economic development, and, indeed, occasionally their social structures inhibit such a development. Marx himself concedes this in the case of the "Indian" society. To universalize the primacy of the mode of production, then, is to generalize the primacy of an economic development typical only of a particular society. At this point we do not want to criticize this universalization of the priority of the economic, but merely to take note of the limited validity of the economic principle.

The expression "independent of their will" by no means implies that production relations are imposed upon man from without, as the "environment" is given in the materialist concept of history. Those relations are forged in a society's active response to its environment. Certainly, the individual is not free to choose his original social environment, but he constantly changes it. Unlike the early determinists, Marx conceives of the group as a field of dynamic forces. As all human activity takes place within the relation to nature, so all individual activity takes place within the relation to society. Even the solitary genius expresses the nature of the society in which he lives. The originality of Marx's theory consists in having brought out the primary character of the social and productive qualities of all human activity. The question of individual freedom which looms so

---

34. "Reconstruction of Historical Materialism," in *Zur Rekonstruktion des Historischen Materialismum* (1975). English translation in *Communication and the Evolution of Society,* p. 143.

large in the discussion of his theory of history does not even arise.

The term *superstructure (Ueberbau)* remains, of course, controversial, with its implied assertion of the more fundamental nature of the mode of production. The architectural connotations of the term, as if a planned structure were projected by a master builder, are particularly misleading.[35] Yet this questionable schema has been made worse by the equation of the base with the material forces of production. This leads Marx's social theory back to that of his main adversaries. Indeed, as Hobsbawm has claimed, Marx's principal impact upon historiography has come from his resistance to the positivist tendency to reduce social science to the science of nature. Societies, for Marx, are systems of relations which gradually acquire enough autonomy to maintain themselves throughout internal changes and external pressures. Each system has its own internal dynamics, its own ability to innovate or lack of flexibility to respond to new challenges. According to its power to assimilate, a society will also stimulate new forces of production and appropriate them in new modes of production. According to Marx, no single factor is more influential in causing social change.

As I hope to show in my concluding chapter, in their actual analysis of cultural and political events Marx and Engels pay little attention to the base-superstructure model. Instead, they view social life in its totality as a complex web of relations in which all factors remain interconnected. In our time structuralist historians appear to have developed those long-range connections between the various factors operative in a given society more carefully than traditional Marxist theoreticians who, by and large, have too exclusively concentrated on the structure-superstructure distinction. Unfortunately, the concept of social structure now generally accepted is all too often articulated against the earlier positivist model of biological evolution in a way that excludes historical development. At this point Marx's distinction between structure and superstructure assumes a new importance. For the dynamic tension between different social

35. Karl Kautsky, *Die materialistische Geschichtsauffassung*, 1:812.

layers allows it to account for the development of societies in a way that structuralist theories generally fail to do. "The immense strength of Marx has always lain in his insistence on both the existence of social structure and its historicity, or in other words its internal dynamic of change."[36] Yet this dynamic relation presupposes the relative independence of the superstructure as well as its causal effectiveness. Unless the superstructure has an impact of its own, there can be no dialectical conflict and, consequently, no genuine historical development. This in itself excludes the possibility that one may be reduced to the other.

Rational, aesthetic, and even erotic activity enter as much into economic production as into cultural creations. The more "basic" character of the economic sphere may refer to the primary character of man's active involvement with nature in the material production process. Yet to represent this process as cause and all cultural creativity as effect is to miss the organic quality of the relationship entirely. The "superstructure" also affects the structure. Man conceives of his economic activity as he conceives of himself, and this all the more so as he progresses culturally. His practical activity increasingly reflects his cultural image. That religious world-views have influenced economic attitudes in the past has been proven.[37] Today their influence has been weakened under the impact of the very secularism they helped to create. Along with them the normative systems that produce moral habits suitable for work are rapidly losing their authority. The bourgeois society can no longer count on the support of an ideological system, which it needs as much as it does raw materials and exchange channels.[38] The interaction between structure and superstructure is also noticeable on the level of everyday living. The value we attach to leisure and aesthetics plays a lead-

36. Eric J. Hobsbawm: "Karl Marx's Contribution to Historiography," in *Ideology in Social Science*, ed. Robin Blackburn (New York: Pantheon Books, 1972), p. 276.

37. Tawney and Weber have shown this for the relation between Protestantism and the rise of capitalism. But Islam presents an even more striking instance, as its economic impact is felt in culturally heterogeneous societies.

38. Cf. Jürgen Habermas, *Legitimation Crisis* (Boston: Beacon Press, 1975), chap. 7.

ing role in our contemporary economy. To explain this value as a *result* of the material production process strains credibility. A purely "economic" view of history would be as absurd as one in which history is no more than a succession of battles fought to satisfy princely ambitions. There is no plausible way of reducing the erotic qualities of Cleopatra's nose to the mode of production of the Hellenistic-Egyptian society. Yet Pascal was right: that nose did change history.

Even political factors cannot simply be reduced to economic ones. Their subordination to class divisions created by the production process must not be *assumed* as a general, a priori principle. The so-called Marxian theory of history consists, above all, in a critical reading of history. The structure and development of a society reflect the production relations of *that particular* society, and they are intelligible only in the light of that society's own origins and aspirations.[39] Never did Marx or Engels pretend to provide a master key that would unlock indiscriminately the secrets of all historical developments. In his review of Marx's *Critique of Political Economy,* Engels explicitly cautioned against such uncritical applications of Marx's principle: "History often proceeds by jumps and zigzags, and if it were followed in this way, not only would much material of minor importance have to be included but there would be much interruption of the chain of thought" (*Werke* 13: 475; *Coll. Works* 16: 475). Marx provided the method for a critique of history, but both he and Engels felt that this method should be learned from their actual historical writings rather than from their theoretical remarks. When questioned about the historical-materialist method, Engels invariably referred to Marx's *The Eighteenth Brumaire of Louis Napoleon* (1852), a monograph that even today earns the respect of historians of the period.[40] In this work and in *The Class Struggles in*

39. "In order to examine the connection between spiritual production and material production it is above all necessary to grasp the latter itself not as a general category but in definite historical form" (*Werke* 261, 267; *TSV* 285).

40. Cf. Engels's letters to J. Bloch (Sept. 22, 1890), C. Schmidt (Oct. 27, 1890), H. Starkenburg (Jan. 25, 1894), in *Werke* 37: 464, 493; 39: 207; *Sel. Works* 2: 489, 496, 506. A contemporary historian who used Marx's works extensively is George Duveau, in *1848: The Making of a Revolution* (1965), trans. Anne Carter

France 1848–50 (1850) Marx shows, in a detailed analysis of the events in France during the critical period 1848–51, how political alliances were made and broken on the basis of class interests. Thus the allegiance of the Legitimists to the Bourbon dynasty and of the Orleanists to the Count of Paris had no more to do with royalty than the Republicans' commitment to the Republic. Landed property (Bourbon), high finance (Orleans), commerce and industry (Republican)—those, not dynasties and constitutions, were the real interests which divided the political parties. The moment those interests merged, the political goals that identified the parties were happily sacrificed to their real objectives (*Werke* 8: 139; *The XVIII Brumaire,* in *Sel. Works* 1: 272).

In Marx's view the principal effect of the revolution was the total defeat of the workers, the class which had made most of the sacrifices. Yet in the long run this defeat polarized the bourgeoisie and the proletariat, providing the latter with the unity and determination needed for the decisive struggle.

> What succumbed in these defeats was not the revolution. It was the pre-revolutionary traditional appendages, results of social relationships which had not yet come to the point of sharp class antagonisms—persons, illusions, conceptions, projects from which the revolutionary party before the February Revolution was not free, from which it could be freed not by the *victory of February,* but only by a series of *defeats.* In a word: the revolution made progress, forged ahead, not by its immediate tragi-comic achievements, but on the contrary by the creation of a powerful, united counter-revolution, by the creation of an opponent in combat with whom, only, the party of overthrow ripened into a really revolutionary party. [*Werke* 7: 11; *The Class Struggles,* in *Sel. Works* 1: 139]

The workers' defeat was necessary for the development of an industrial bourgeoisie without which the proletariat would never come to power. Until 1848 the industrial faction of the bourgeoi-

---

(New York: Random House, 1967). It is noteworthy that Marx's contemporary, Alexis de Tocqueville, whose political sympathies were diametrically opposed to his own, likewise interpreted the revolution and the subsequent events as having been determined by class struggles. Cf. *The Recollections of Alexis de Tocqueville* (New York: Meridian Books, 1959).

sie had remained under the rule of the financial aristocracy. To attain full development the industrial bourgeoisie first had to "shape all property relations to suit itself" for the purpose of conquering a share in the world market. Together with the peasants and the petty bourgeoisie, the proletariat had heavily contributed to this bourgeois emancipation. However, when the workers pressed the new regime for their share of the spoils, they found themselves confronted by the same army and national guard which had helped them to win the victory of 1848. They were beaten back into prerevolutionary obscurity. The peasants and petty bourgeoisie had also been cheated out of the victory of 1848. But they staged a spectacular comeback with Louis Napoleon, who skillfully exploited the frustration and financial hardship of the lower-middle class in postrevolutionary France by means of a dynastic name that was a symbol of domestic peace and national glory.

It is in the very complexity of those subpolitical social dynamics that the real qualities of Marx's method appear. For class interest which determines political attitudes is by no means the same as economic class egoism. It consists of the entire outlook on culture, morality, and politics by which a class universalizes its own position into that of the common good. This was particularly the case for the petty bourgeoisie which, in view of the privileged condition of the industrial bourgeoisie and the lowly status of the proletariat, regarded itself as the class of the "people." In rising to power and imposing its own moral and cultural standards, it expected to emancipate all of society (*Werke* 8: 141–44; *The XVIII Brumaire*, in *Sel. Works* 1: 275). Unlike the industrial bourgeoisie and the proletariat, the petty bourgeoisie was possessed of national pride and inspired by patriotic symbols.

The complex character of class *consciousness* renders a narrow interpretation of history in terms of class *interests* impossible; for the two are separated by a world of prejudice, vanity, misunderstanding, and narrowmindedness. Political strategies are shaped by a consciousness that includes—besides a more or less adequate perception of genuine class interests—miscalculations, short-sightedness, individual and social ambitions, and the generally human capacity of being deceived—all of which make political life into an unpredictable hustle-bustle. Engels, in his 1895 preface to *The Class Struggles in France,* observes that it takes hindsight to interpret events accurately and that current history never reveals the *ultimate* economic causes (*Werke* 7: 511; *Sel. Works* 1: 119).

Social-economic movements start long before the crises which they provoke and continue long after them. The year 1848 was a time of relative economic stability. Only the study of these larger waves allows us to reconstruct the relations between structure and superstructure. But also, only those larger movements can inform us about what properly belongs to the structure. Gramsci has rightly observed that in the structure itself some movements are organic while others are purely incidental.[41] An economic crisis may be produced by the instability of a government or by a particular piece of legislation. To ascribe it to the social-economic structure as such is far too simplistic. Not all economic developments belong to the "basis."

Of course, the notion of class consciousness would not amount to a fruitful principle of historical interpretation if it were not accompanied by more specific rules. Why, for instance, did the petty bourgeoisie, despite all its political naiveté, become the ruling class shortly after it had been defeated by the industrial bourgeoisie? And why did nothing of the sort happen to the proletariat? In answering those questions Marx fully reveals the dialectical character of his theory. The political life of the ruling class in a capitalist society follows the self-contradictory movement of the capitalist system itself: every new victory brings it a step closer to its final defeat. The bourgeoisie brought itself to power by promoting the cause of freedom and democracy. Yet after its victory, freedom and democracy became the principal instruments of its downfall. They threaten its rule by transferring power to the subjugated majority. Marx credits the bourgeois parties with having perceived this more clearly than the socialists, who continue to wallow in utopian dreams: "The bourgeoisie had a true insight into the fact that all the weapons which it had forged against feudalism turned their points against itself,

41. *The Modern Prince and Other Writings,* p. 168.

that all the means of education which it had produced rebelled against its own civilization, that all the gods which it had created had fallen away from it" (*Werke* 8: 153; *The XVIII Brumaire* in *Sel. Works* 1: 287). Thus the capitalist class digs its own grave precisely by its attempt to perpetuate its life. The "secret" of socialism is none other than this inevitable decline of the ruling class, which will drag all other classes along in its fall and, in the end, spark a general rebellion in the class that has collected all the cast-offs of the others. The success or failure of proletarian revolutions are entirely conditioned by the degree of decline. This explains why the workers were beaten in June 1848, while in 1851 the petty bourgeoisie managed to overthrow the rule of the industrial bourgeoisie.

Until the other classes have completed their rule, the proletariat is the powerless class par excellence. Fully understanding their weakness, the bourgeoisie intended to rid itself from its restless former partners by forcing them into the June insurrection. This, the ruling class hoped, would clear the road to bourgeois progress of its last obstacle. Yet it failed to take into account the effect of the confrontation and of the defeats themselves. For the confrontation exposed the fact that freedom and democracy were not its concern (the bourgeois parties even abolished the universal suffrage), but "the state whose admitted object is to perpetuate the rule of capital, the slavery of labor" (*Werke* 7: 33; *The Class Struggles,* in *Sel. Works* 1: 162). The defeat taught the proletariat its real position and gave it a group consciousness. A succession of such defeats are needed for the workers to realize that they are not a particular section of the democratic system—indeed, that they do not belong to that system at all. They cannot succeed within the parameters of a capitalist society. The sooner they learn this lesson, the sooner they may turn their defeats into victories. But until such a genuine proletarian consciousness emerges, victory means defeat and defeat, victory.

Here, then, appears the main difference between proletarian and bourgeois revolutions. While the latter are clearly conceived and methodically executed, the former stumble along from one defeat to another until a situation occurs where no other choice remains but a desperate fight. Only at that point can the proletariat hope to win a revolution.

> Bourgeois revolutions, like those of the eighteenth century, storm swiftly from success to success; their dramatic effects outdo each other; men and things seem set in sparkling brilliants; ecstasy is in the everyday spirit; but they are short-lived. . . . On the other hand, proletarian revolutions, like those of the nineteenth century, criticise themselves constantly, interrupt themselves continually in their own course, come back to the apparently accomplished in order to begin it afresh, deride with unmerciful thoroughness the inadequacies, weaknesses and paltrinesses of their first attempts, seem to throw down their adversary only in order that he may draw new strength from the earth and rise again, more gigantic, before them, recoil ever and anon from the indefinite prodigiousness of their own aims, until a situation has been created which makes all turning back impossible, and the conditions themselves cry out: *Hid Rhodus, hic salta!* [*Werke* 8: 118; *The XVIII Brumaire*, in *Sel. Works* 1: 250–51]

In the final statement of this passage Marx expresses what is often overlooked—namely, that only at a few decisive moments in history does the structure simply break the superstructure which it has gradually built up over the years, sometimes over the centuries. Only in the final stage of the capitalist epoch, the proletarian revolution, can we consider the social-economic factor the sole effective agent of history.

However, Marx had not always defended this notion of a discontinuous revolution. In fact, hardly more than a year before he wrote the preceding lines he had held the exactly opposite view. In his 1895 preface, Engels points out how the first three parts of *The Class Struggle in France* were still written under the impression that the revolution of 1848 marked the beginning of the decisive combat between the proletariat and the bourgeoisie. It would be a long struggle. But it would be a continuous one until the final victory, with the proletariat gaining more power at each new uprising. The proletarian revolution would follow the basic pattern of all previous European revolutions. After the victory of a particular party, the more radical wing of that party would turn against the more moderate one and, while pretending to safeguard the original victory, would in fact initiate a new stage of revolution.

Marx's disappointment with the outcome of the 1848 revolution did not deter him from yet again and again supporting insurrectional activity before any evidence of the imminent social-economic collapse of capitalism disappeared. But he never expected those "premature" revolts to lead *automatically* to the definitive proletarian uprising. They could only prepare for it; and to do so they had to be *manipulated*. Thus, in his 1850 "Address to the Communist League," Marx exhorted the German proletariat to exploit the "imminent" bourgeois revolution for its own purposes and, rather than wait for a future proletarian revolution, to fashion the coming events into the beginning of an uninterrupted revolution that would result in a complete proletarian takeover. Marx never doubted the need for a lengthy preparation for the final struggle, but he came to regard control over the next revolution "the first act of this approaching drama" (*Werke* 7: 254; *Sel. Works* 1: 116). Even in a bourgeois revolution proletarians make most of the sacrifices. They should keep the revolutionary spirit alive after the aims of the petty bourgeoisie have been attained, and transform it into a *continuing* revolution.

> While the democratic petty bourgeois wish to bring the revolution to a conclusion as quickly as possible . . . it is our interest and our task to make the revolution permanent, until all the more or less possessing classes have been forced out of their position of dominance, until the proletariat has conquered state power and the association of proletarians, not only in our country but in all the dominant countries of the world, has advanced so far that competition among the proletarians of these countries has ceased and that at least the decisive productive forces are concentrated in the hands of the proletarians. [*Werke* 7: 247–48; *Sel. Works* 1: 118]

The continuity or discontinuity of the proletariat's victorious rebellion with earlier revolutions in which it plays a subordinate part is an issue with far-reaching theoretical and practical consequences. It has divided the Marxist camp into two incompatible factions. One emphasizes the need for the actual presence of all the social-economic conditions and discourages premature revo-

lutionary action. The other assumes that the conditions necessary for the final confrontation will emerge earlier if the proletariat deliberately supports *any* revolutionary movement. Lenin
referred to Marx's address to support his claim that Russia's
unpreparedness for a proletarian uprising posed no obstacle to
the immediate instigation of revolutionary activity. In *Two Tactics*
(1905) he first advocated the strategy of turning the beginning
bourgeois revolution into the first stage of a "permanent," proletarian one. Yet Marx had posited an advanced capitalist industry
as a first condition for such a revolution to succeed. This would
never be attained if capitalist development was disrupted from
the start by egalitarian rebellions. Lenin was fully aware of the
lack of a proletarian class consciousness in Russia. Yet he defended the possibility of a proletarian revolt because he viewed
the entire capitalist economy as a single unit. Industrial capitalism *as a whole* had become ripe for the revolution, and this revolution was more likely to erupt in "the weakest link" of the capitalist chain, as Russia was in 1905, than in the areas of its greatest
strength. The revolution which Marx had expected in Germany
never took place, while in imperial Russia the suppression of the
bourgeois revolution and the impoverished state of the peas-
antry had created an "objectively revolutionary" situation. Not
only the proletariat, Lenin felt, but all classes must be possessed
by a spirit of rebellion for a social revolution to succeed. This
condition was fulfilled in Russia when the national crisis of the
war with Germany and the persistent suppression of the liberal
bourgeoisie incited all strata of the population to revolt. "It is
only when the *'lower classes' do not want* to live in the old way, and
the *'upper classes' cannot carry on in the old way* that the revolution
can triumph."[42]

Lenin's greater emphasis on revolutionary action than on social-economic conditions calls for a strong revolutionary theory.
The socialist revolution is not a spontaneous explosion of social-
economic conflicts. It directly results from the propagation of a
doctrine developed by thinkers of the possessing class: "By their
social status, the founders of modern scientific socialism, Marx

42. *Left-Wing Communism, an Infantile Disorder,* in *Collected Works,* 31:85.

and Engels, themselves belonged to the bourgeois intelligent-
sia."[43] A socialist consciousness does not automatically spring
from the proletarian class struggle, but from a scientific knowledge of that struggle which the proletariat itself is unable to
produce.[44] Yet such a knowledge must not be conceived as a
descriptive theory of social facts. Facts alone, certainly social
"facts," would never have allowed Marx to predict the specific
developments leading to the final revolution. Action is needed,
and the function of theory is to *guide* it, not merely to describe it.
The existence of a proletariat creates only the *possibility* of radical
change: its actualization depends on the presence of proletarian
consciousness.

In the end, the controversy between determinists and voluntar-
ists presents a struggle between two different aspects of the
fundamental rationality that underlies Marx's concept of history: the rational law of social-economic development, and the
rationality deliberately imposed upon that development by the
rational will. The former without the latter leads to economic
determinism; the latter without the former, to utopianism.
There is no dilemma between necessity and conscious action in
Marx because, as Kolakowski has pointed out, the class consciousness of the proletariat *is* the historical process itself in its
ultimate state.[45] The rational law of social-economic development culminates in the proletariat's will and necessity to replace
an irrational system by a rational one.

PREHISTORY AND THE END OF HISTORY

Marx never held the economic deterministic theories that have
discredited so much "Marxist" historiography. Yet a more basic
question persists. In singling out material production as the *ultimately* determining factor of history, does Marx not adopt precisely the kind of transhistorical, universal principle which his

43. *What Is to Be Done?*, in *Collected Works* 5:375.
44. Ibid., p. 383.
45. Kolakowski, *Main Currents of Marxism* 1:148.

own concept of history excludes? Marx was not unaware of the problem, for by all accounts he appears not to have considered the principle of production directly applicable to primitive, so-called prehistorical societies. According to Engels, he estimated Lewis Morgan's *Ancient Society* (1877) so important for his own theory that he planned to write an essay on its conclusions. Nothing came of the project, but Engels claims that he mainly developed Marx's own ideas in *The Origin of the Family*. It is, of course, impossible to verify this claim, yet Marx's recently published ethnological notebooks appear to support it. Hence there is every reason to take Engels's work as, at least in substance, concordant with Marx's latest development. Now that work clearly relativizes the primacy of the economic factor in history.[46] According to *The Origin of the Family*, the family system plays a more important role than production relations in the early development of social institutions. Only when labor reaches a certain level of productivity and complexity do social structures begin to be determined by production relations. This will eventually lead to a society "in which the family system is entirely dominated by the property system, and in which the class antagonisms and class struggles . . . now freely develop" (*Werke* 21: 28; *Sel. Works* 2: 171). Engels's study introduces a new element, yet not one that conflicts with Marx's basic principle of historical interpretation. Far from invalidating that principle, Engels in fact gave it much needed support; for he showed how the determining factor of history is itself historical, not only in its particular appearance, but in its very existence. Economic production remains the basic agent of history, but that agent itself has emerged from a prehistory. Engels radicalized the Marxist principle of historicity by showing how even the determinant factor in history had a historical origin. In addition, he pointed out the

---

46. Cf. Lawrence Krader, "Karl Marx as Ethnologist," in *Transactions of the New York Academy of Sciences*, ser. 2, vol. 35, no. 4 (April 1973), pp. 304–13. Ever since the German social democrat Heinrich Cunow first drew attention to the apparent discrepancy between Engels's work and Marx's published views, Leninists have generally rejected Engels's work to the extent that it contradicts the absolute primacy of the economic factor.

connections between the final transformations of the prehistorical family and subsequent property relations.

In Morgan's report of a conflict between the more conservative consanguinity systems and the more rapidly developing family relations, Marx and Engels saw their own view of the dialectical relation between the dynamic mode of production and the more static social structures confirmed. The overthrow of the matriarchal system was, in Morgan's theory, a direct result of the division of labor. The male who provided the food and procured the implements necessary thereto, had gradually acquired ownership over them. Yet the matriarchal system precluded his children from inheriting his possessions, since the children belonged not to his, but to their mother's *gens*. A quiet revolution transferred the rights of the *gens* to the father and the monogamous marriage emerged, "the first form of the family based not on natural but on economic conditions, namely on the victory of private property over original, naturally developed common ownership" (*Werke* 21: 68; *Sel. Works* 2: 224). To serve his own proprietary interests, the male drove the female into monogamy, while he himself remained basically committed to the greater sexual freedom of an earlier day. Yet even as the current family system originated when property relations began to dominate the process of production, so it will disappear with the abolition of its economic foundation. Once inherited wealth becomes social property and wage labor disappears, prostitution, the necessary concomitant of strict monogamy, will lose all support. The proletariat already anticipates this future equality of the sexes. Due to the absence of property and to economic equality in the industrial labor market, woman has regained her real right to separate from and the means to overcome male domination. Engels moved beyond Morgan's analysis in his explanation of the origin of the state. The moment property came to dominate social relations, it had to be safeguarded against the communal traditions of the past. The political sphere raised it into the very goal of society. The classical state represents the first social institution totally unrelated to the older family relations and entirely determined by the economy of property. Not consanguinity (in Athens the *gentes* and *phratries*), but the place of domicile *(demes)*, the center of economic activity, became dominant.[47] Marx's reluctance to draw any significant distinctions between history and prehistory had exposed him to a number of objections. Especially his failure to mention family relations as a determining factor in the structuring of society made his theory of social development appear overly simplistic. Yet once property relations themselves were shown to be derived from family structures, his theory gained a great deal of credibility. The invention and perfection of tools which in *The German Ideology* inaugurated the process of civilization, then, is no longer *the* determining factor of prehistorical development, no more than production itself is. Both must now be seen as elements which *at the historical stage* would play a primary role, *but not until the appropriate family relations had allowed it to play this role.*

It is interesting how recent research has confirmed the qualifications of the primacy of production relations with respect to primitive society. Habermas has shown that social labor alone is insufficient to distinguish humans from hominids, who also had a social organization of labor and even a primitive technology (weapons, tools). An adequate characterization of the specifically human requires that we add an organization along kinship lines.[48] Moreover, such a society does not always develop because of changes in its production system. A variety of problems (demographic, social, ecological) may emerge which a society based on the kinship organization is unable to solve. At that point it will try out new structures according to the learning capacity it has acquired.[49]

In this context we may wonder whether Marx sufficiently observed the limits imposed by his historical principle. Has he not

47. That the family continues to play a crucial role in the social structure of industrialized societies is a fact well known to Marx and by no means incompatible with the priority of the social-economic factor, for the family mediates the social-economic structure with the superstructure. It functions as the channel through which a class conveys its values, ideas, and prejudices to the next generation.

48. "Reconstruction of Historical Materialism," in *Communication and the Evolution of Society,* p. 138.

49. Ibid., pp. 161–63.

weakened his own principle of historicity in universalizing the priority to the social-economic factor? Has he not unduly generalized the particular situation of his own age by extending the primary importance of the economic factor for all other ages? To be sure, material production plays a substantial role in any kind of society, and the mode in which it satisfies human needs has substantially contributed to the cultural shape of every epoch in history. But economic activity does not determine the specific differences of most societies. At the time and in the countries where Marx wrote, it did; at no previous epoch was man more preoccupied with his material needs and the means of satisfying them. Property had assumed an unprecedented importance and had come to be regarded as the very bulwark of liberty. Since the end of the eighteenth century, economic expansion, private and corporate, had come to dominate all other concerns of public life in advanced countries. In that context the theory of a social-economic substructure as the ultimately determining factor of all cultural, moral, and political expression holds a great deal of plausibility. Yet the principle loses much of its plausibility for other periods of history. Not because material needs were not essential—they always were—but because economic production and commerce were so intermingled with other aspects of a culture as to exclude a meaningful distinction.

Already in Marx's day an article in a German-American newspaper raised the objection that the primacy of production over other aspects of social life holds true for our epoch "in which material interests preponderate, but not for the middle ages, in which Catholicism, nor for Athens and Rome, where politics reigned supreme" (*Werke* 23: 96; *Cap.* 1: 82). Marx's answer makes one wonder whether he grasped the full impact of the distinction: "This much is clear, that the middle ages could not live on Catholicism, nor the ancient world on politics. On the contrary, it is the mode in which they gained a livelihood that explains why here politics, and there Catholicism, played the chief part" (ibid.).

Social-economic factors may well be the most *fundamental* ones, in the sense that none are more elementary to any society. They also may have been the factors that specifically determined the culture of rising industrial capitalism. Yet by distinguishing them from the rest of the culture we project our own concerns and aspirations upon societies that were guided by others. The legitimacy of viewing all cultures as conditioned by the particular mode in which basic human needs are being satisfied, does not in itself justify the universal cultural primacy of the economic activity *as such*. To assume such a primacy conflicts with the more fundamental principle of the radical historicity of all social structures. Marx himself repeatedly criticized the classical economists for attributing the principles and structures of capitalist society to human nature itself. The primacy of the economic, if universalized, should fall under the same criticism.

Of course, however general his statements were, Marx always had one particular type of society in mind—the bourgeois. His observations in the ethnological notebooks, as well as his agreement with Morgan's work, suggest that he was far less prepared to extend the principle of the primacy of production relations than his more sweeping statements indicate. Engels felt it repeatedly necessary to qualify the principle, even in relation to developed societies. In the letter to Joseph Bloch in which he explicitly invoked Marx's authority for his position, Engels wrote:

> The Prussian State also arose and developed from historical, ultimately economic causes. But it could scarcely be maintained without pedantry that among the small States of North Germany, it was precisely Brandenburg that had to become the great power embodying the economic, linguistic and, after the Reformation, also the religious differences between North and South, because of economic necessity and not also because of other factors. . . . It is hardly possible without making oneself ridiculous, to explain in terms of economics the existence of every small State in Germany, past and present. . . . [*Werke* 37: 464; *Sel. Correspondence,* p. 395]

Marx himself qualified the principle of the primacy of the economic not only for the prehistorical age but also, and even more significantly, for the Communist society of the future. Here economic activity becomes fully integrated with self-expression. Such a vision need not be as naively utopian as in the description of *The German Ideology,* where man can "hunt in the

morning, fish in the afternoon, rear cattle in the evening, criticize after dinner . . . without ever becoming hunter, fisherman,
shepherd or critic." As Marx, older and wiser, suggested at the
end of *Capital* 3, with the advent of the Communist society all the
work toward the making of a new man is still to be done. Yet at
least the overcoming of the purely economic then becomes an
attainable reality.

Meanwhile a more fundamental question encumbers the final
scenario of the dialectic of history. Must the contradictions of
capitalist economy *inevitably* result in the advent of a socialist
society? Even Marx's followers have felt the need to consider
alternatives to the outcome Marx predicted at the collapse of
the current social-economic system. Thus Lenin, impressed by
the renewed strength of the capitalist economy at the turn of the
century, inserted an additional stage—imperialism—before the
predicted collapse. Kautsky and some of the Frankfurt Marxists
attempted other adjustments of Marx's projection to new economic realities.[50] Others more radically questioned the very assumption that the internal development and collapse of capitalism would ever suffice to create the conditions for a full social
emancipation. Doubts about this inspired Horkheimer and
Adorno to combine cultural critique on an even footing with the
social-economic one, while virtually abandoning Marx's structure-superstructure model in favor of a basically Hegelian critique of culture.

Even if we assume Marx's scenario of the future to be correct,
does it follow that in the final stage of socialism major social-
economic conflicts will be definitely precluded? Do not the very
factors that enable a society to overcome one conflict situation
create a new one? The question was most cogently formulated
by Sartre in his *Critique of Dialectical Reason*. A dialectic of praxis,
he argues, always carries within itself the opposites of self-realization and self-reification. It presents the endless possibilities of
a creative freedom. But any partial realization of these possibili-

---

50. See, for instance, Friedrich Pollock's discussions of state capitalism and
Henryk Grossmann's attempt to square Marx's law of accumulation with the
predicted collapse.

ties restricts the pursuit of others. Any attempt toward total realization merely results in fragmentary achievements. In history man realizes his infinite potentiality—*but only within the limits set by scarcity,* limits that are as much subjective as objective. This restriction excludes the possibility of a society without social-economic antagonisms. Even if material scarcity could ever be overcome in a world of abundance, the realization of certain possibilities would still prevent the realization of others. An individual bound to exist as a *particular* person is forced to neglect the development of his *entire* potential. The same applies to society. The achievement of a "partial totality" creates conflicts with the "total totality."[51] Each society lives by its own ideals, defines itself in particular concepts, sets itself specific goals—all of which determine it as one-sided, restrictive, and, however hospitable to foreign influences, inherently exclusive. The point is not merely that each society suffers from its own defects and tensions, but also that in adopting a particular form it imposes its own value system even upon those who would prefer not to share it—dependent societies and dissenting members. The violent hostility displayed by a number of traditional or semitraditional societies toward the United States has other and deeper roots than their obvious aversion to economic imperialism. Along with the economic factor the fear for the transformative impact of a secular, modern culture plays a considerable part. It is the fear of being absorbed by a different society powerful enough to draw others into its own ambit and thereby powerful enough to deny them the possibility of structuring their world according to their own needs. Nor is the totalization less oppressive *within* the controlling societies. For the growing complexity of high technological communities requires the kind of relentless discipline on the part of its members which Freud, in *Civilization and Its Discontents,* denounced as the major source of unhappiness in modern culture.

For that reason some neo-Marxists have abandoned the notion of a dialectic of history that would result in a definitive liberation. According to Sartre, such a state would conflict with

51. Jean-Paul Sartre, *Critique de la raison dialectique,* pp. 165-72.

the Marxist concept of praxis. There is a dialectic *in* history, the dynamic pattern of social change, leading from contradiction to resolution. But there is no dialectic of history leading to a final resolution of all conflicts. Wherever creative freedom operates, conflicts arise.[52] Even the social revolution cannot prevent new conflicts from emerging. Nor is the postrevolutionary society the ideal toward which history moves. It constitutes merely one stage of an ever-developing freedom: the present class conflicts will cease to exist but new forms of social alienation, already observable in existing socialist societies, will emerge. This reinterpretation limits Marx's dialectic to the single phase of capitalism, the one on which Marx in fact focused his exclusive attention.

Earlier we saw that Marx justifies his notion of progress only in reference to the capitalist society. The "Asiatic" mode of producing does not "progress" to another mode of production. Indeed, being essentially static, the Indian village system (Marx's usual model) might never have changed had it not been invaded by capitalist powers. Nor can one claim that the ancient societies of the Near East and of the Mediterranean basin perished to make room for more advanced systems of production. They broke down altogether in a general, cultural decline or they succumbed to foreign invasions and, as Marx repeatedly notes in the case of the Roman Empire, they *regressed* to a more primitive social-economic status. Even the incursions of capitalism into undeveloped countries did not mark "progress" from the invaded societies' point of view. Capitalism destroyed their entire social fabric in a manner "sickening to human feeling." Yet, Marx insists, the capitalist annexation meant progress *insofar as only capitalist society can, by its inevitable internal collapse, bring about full social liberation.* In a *New York Daily Tribune* article of June 25, 1853, he wrote: "The question is, can mankind fulfill its destiny without a fundamental revolution in the social state of Asia? If not, whatever may have been the crimes of England she was the

---

52. Cf. George Allen, "Sartre's Constriction of the Marxist Dialectic," in *The Review of Metaphysics* 33 (1979):106.

unconscious tool of history in bringing about that revolution"
(*Werke* 9: 133; *Political Writings,* ed. Daniel Fernbach [New York:
Vintage Books], 2: 307). This statement is important for two reasons. First, it assumes
that capitalism, and only capitalism, inevitably leads to a socialist
society which, in principle, is a liberated society. Second, the
creation of such a liberated society is assumed to be the immanent goal of history that will be reached even through actions
intentionally opposed to it and resulting in an immediate deterioration of the affected societies. The second point formulates
the much more comprehensive principle that history as a whole
follows a progressive course. With this Hegelian-sounding principle Marx moves from the particular (with respect to capitalism) to a general idea of progress (all of history *must* move toward the ultimate, postcapitalist state of perfection). Marx
himself repeatedly declared that his historical analyses applied
only to the capitalist era. Is the idea of historical progress, then,
not an undue generalization of a restricted situation? If progress
is taken as an *inherent* quality of history, as many Marxists appear
to think, Marx's general principle must, indeed, remain wholly
unsupported. But if we understand capitalism to be a de facto
existing economic power which happens to be stronger than all
other economic systems and therefore destined to overtake
them, the idea of universal progress through capitalism legitimately extends the limited analysis of the capitalist world. This, I
believe, is the correct reading of Marx's more general statements
about historical progress.[53]

Yet in this interpretation the general principle is based entirely upon the particular and must share its unproven assumptions. Specifically, it suffers from all the weakness derived from

53. Kolakowski confirms my interpretation: "It might be seen that . . . capitalism itself was an accident—a system that had happened to arise in a particular,
not very large part of the world and had subsequently proved strong and expan-
sive enough to impose itself on the whole planet. Marx did not himself draw this
inference [corrected from: influence], although significantly, he observed at a
later stage that the analysis in *Capital* applied only to Western Europe" (*Main
Currents of Marxism* 1: 350–51).

the failure to exclude alternatives to Marx's disaster scenario and inevitable sequence of socialist society at the end of the capitalist era.

Even when restricted to the historical past, the base-superstructure model, if consistently maintained, would create serious difficulties for the interpretation of history. We noted, however, that Marx did not strictly adhere to it and that he also used a more organic model of society in which each element codetermines all others. A new mode of production leads to a new social system with a different political structure, and, in the end, to a new stage of cultural development. But the new modes of thinking and the new fashions in artistic expression themselves result in new politics and new social relations which, in turn, spawn new modes of production. The question then occurs whether such an organic codetermination is compatible with a continued use of the base-superstructure model. How can society be both an organic whole of which the various parts influence one another and still allow one part to assume a definitive priority? The answer to this question will emerge in the concluding chapter. But even now it seems certain that only a conception that reduces the various parts of the totality to relative *moments* can prevent any single dominant factor from destroying the organic quality of the whole. Such a conception Marx finds in the dialectic. Marx's dialectic, then, holds, in the final analysis, the key to his interpretation of culture. It alone enables us to decide whether that interpretation follows a rectilinear, causal course or whether it preserves an organic conception in which the base still holds a priority, but no longer an absolute one. In the second case, the primacy of the base would consist in the primacy of the more elementary and the more immediate over the less elementary and the more reflective moments of society. A decision on this issue requires a far more thorough reflection on Marx's dialectic than this chapter has provided. Marx's historical analysis mostly *assumes* the existence of a dialectical method; it does not justify it. What are its principles and limitations? To find out we have to turn to the more consciously developed dialectic of the base.

3
The Structural Dialectic

DIALECTIC FROM HEGEL TO MARX

In the preceding chapter we investigated Marx's dialectic of history as he defined it in *The German Ideology* and in the preface to the *Critique of Political Economy,* and as he applied it in his historical writings. We learned there about the complex relation by which production relations determine the entire process of cultural development in its legal, philosophical, aesthetic, and religious aspects. In his economic writings, starting with *The Poverty of Philosophy,* Marx analyzes the structural dialectic that supports this historical pyramid: the interaction between economic forces and production relations as well as its reflection in economic concepts and theories. This structural dialectic differs considerably from the historical one. Nevertheless, one always presupposes the other. While the dialectic of history rests on an intricate web of synchronic oppositions, these oppositions themselves result from a historical process. To this synchronic (yet never ahistorical) dialectic we now turn.

In the dialectic of the base, Marx applied his method most self-consciously. This is understandable enough since he devoted most of his attention to a critique of capitalist economy where he found the root of the legal, aesthetic, and philosophical developments of culture. Without a discussion of the "basic" dialectic, then, Marx's concept of culture cannot be understood. Moreover, as I pointed out in the Introduction, economic activity itself forms an essential part of the real (as opposed to the merely apparent) cultural process. Unfortunately, Marx's followers have not sufficiently distinguished the relations between base and superstructure. Marx himself never adequately clarified the distinction and Engels admitted that this was a genuine lacuna in their theory. In their case, this was due to an all too understandable lack of time. But later interpreters, less excusably, felt thereby justified in transposing the dialectic of the basis to the entire realm of culture. Such, of course, is not my position. If we turn to the dialectic of economics, we do so not because we believe that it provides an adequate explanation of the entire cultural process (neither did Marx!), but because it forms an essential part of it and the part where Marx most reflectively applied his method. In this chapter we shall only investigate the method itself, while reserving its concrete application in the area of economics for the next one. Since we shall be dealing here with the formal aspect of Marx's dialectic (much of which applies to the historical as well as to the structural), we must first clarify how dialectical thought differs from other forms of reflection as well as how Marx's application of it differs from that of his sources.

Not until Plato can we claim with any degree of assurance that the dialectic has been formalized into a *method* of thinking. By modern standards, to be sure, it is an easy-going method with none of the forbidding formality of present treatises on logical argumentation. Plato's dialectic, particularly in his early dialogues, consists of the art of conversation, but a conversation which leads to reflection and disclosure; reflection on one's position and disclosure of reality. By exposing inherent prejudices, unfounded assumptions, unexamined options, Socrates shakes the initial convictions of his interlocutors and hints at their proper place in a rational totality. Clearly the method was devised for attaining insight into reality, but the *internal, moral* reality of the mind rather than the sensible one of the cosmos. Plato's dialogues open up a new, inner dimension in the real where truth in the end consists not so much in knowing how things are as in adopting the right attitude toward them. The real becomes intrinsically connected with moral righteousness. An essential characteristic of Plato's dialectic is that it is exclusively a method: there is no indication of the real itself being dialectical. Hegel describes Plato's dialectic as a "generation of the universal" from the particular, immediate experience. His own dialectic is a process of *reality* as well as of thought. In this respect it owes more to Aristotle than to Plato.

Aristotle is not generally thought of as a dialectical thinker, and his influence may well have counteracted the mode of thinking which Plato's dialogues initiated. Nevertheless, when he proclaimed thought itself to be the object of thinking, Aristotle paved the way for the central idealist thesis that the implicit identity of thought and being becomes explicit as the process of thought, gradually overcoming all oppositions, attains unity. But it could do so only because of a second Aristotelian principle, the principle of act and potency, which allowed motion to determine the object of thought as fully as the thinking process. The notion of potency introduced a dynamic quality into the relation between the determinations of the thought object, thus providing it with what Hegel has called "das Prinzip der lebendigen Subjektivität"—that is, the power of self-movement.[1] Dialectical negativity here is converted from an opposition between two related ideas into a principle of development: the idea opposes itself to itself, and willfully abandons its original unity for the sake of attaining a more comprehensive integration. Hegel found this dynamic quality more present in Aristotle than in Plato. "While in Plato the affirmative principle, the Idea as only abstractly self-identical, prevails, in Aristotle the moment of negativity, not as [mere] change nor as nothing, but as differentiation, as determination appears and is being emphasized."[2]

Still the term *dialectical* does not suit Aristotle's philosophy as a whole. His logical writings reveal no trace of an attempt to incorporate negative opposition as a constructive principle into the formal method of thought. It was Kant who, however unintentionally, provided this decisive element in his theory of unresolvable oppositions.

Hegel attempted to convert this expression of metaphysical agnosticism into the very method for uniting thought with its intended real object. To him the dynamic tension of their con-

---

1. G. W. F. Hegel, *Vorlesungen über die Geschichte der Philosophie. Gesamtausgabe* (1831), 14:285.
2. Ibid., p. 286.

flict serves as the power that moves them onto a higher level of unity. "By dialectic is meant the indwelling tendency outwards by which the one-sidedness and limitation of the predicates of understanding is seen in its true light, and shown to be the negation of them.—Thus understood the dialectical principle constitutes the life and soul of scientific progress."[3] Critical in this process is the movement of negation, resulting from the opposition of two limited concepts. But this negation does not leave pure destruction in its wake: it merely surpasses the finite and views it in a more comprehensive totality which reconciles the opposites. "It is in this dialectic as it is here understood, that is, in the grasping of opposites in their unity or of the positive in the negative, that speculative thought consists."[4]

All thinking confronts contradiction—its own internal opposition as well as its opposition to the real. Those oppositions, we rightly believe, reveal limits of thinking. But the limits themselves are not absolute. Thinking constantly overcomes them in the process of moving from ignorance to insight. As thought progresses, however, oppositions increase until we reach the limits of rational thinking itself. At that moment, Hegel proposes, one further step must be taken to found all the preceding ones: we must *think the opposition itself*. Through that final step Hegel establishes the fundamental unity of thought and reality which his dialectic had postulated from the start. Through the gradual *disclosure* of the rational nature of the real (which rationalism had totally failed to provide) thinking actively participates in the development of the real. Philosophy does not merely "describe" the dialectical movement of reality, as some Marxist interpreters of Hegel have claimed.[5]

Marx understood the practical power of this dialectical realism. But to release it philosophy had to do more than "understand" what is and thereby give it a semblance of rationality. It had to *change* the world in conformity to its own rational principles and thus convert speculation into practical energy. Marx

3. *The Logic of Hegel*, trans. W. Wallace, 3d ed. (New York: Oxford University Press, 1975), p. 147.
4. Ibid., p. 56.
5. Alexandre Kojève, *Introduction to the Reading of Hegel*, trans. H. Nichols (New York: Basic Books, 1969), p. 179.

objected to Hegel's conception of the real in *the form of pure thought*. His disagreement passed through successive stages. In his doctoral dissertation he simply and somewhat idealistically posits that philosophy must be *realized* in social action—a phrase well known through its last echo in the "Introduction to the Critique of Hegel's Philosophy of Right" (1844). According to this early, critical conception, ideas exist prior to social reality and determine it according to their own patterns of rationality. A philosophical system, however conservative, inevitably turns into a critical power as soon as a new generation compares it to the existing reality, because the political reality will inevitably be at variance with the philosophical model, if for no other reason than that the model *idealizes* the reality. Thus philosophy inevitably provokes a critical attitude toward the existing conditions. Hegel failed to grasp this practical function of philosophy. "It is a psychological law that the theoretical mind, having become free in itself, turns into practical energy and, leaving the shadowy empire of Amenthes as *will*, turns itself against the reality of the world existing without it" (*MEGA* 1[1]: 64; *Coll. Works* 1: 85).

In thus pitting itself against the existing world, philosophy ceases to be self-contained. It confronts a reality that is different and which philosophy can control only by converting its theory into practical energy: "The result is that as the world becomes philosophical, philosophy also becomes worldly, that its realization is also its loss, that what it struggles against on the outside is its inner deficiency" (*MEGA* 1[1]: 64; *Coll. Works* 1: 85). Hence the liberation of the world through philosophy is also the liberation from philosophy.[6] In such a "realization," dialectical philosophy radically transforms the Hegelian task of understanding "what is" and brings the real world to its ideal completion. Nevertheless, Marx's concept of philosophy remains within the idealist orbit and substantially differs from his later theory which emerges from, and develops with, praxis. It also differs, though to a lesser degree, from the position which he defended during the short period following the completion of his dissertation.

6. On the distinctness of this early, Young-Hegelian phase in Marx's thought, cf. Hans-Martin Sass, "The Concept of Revolution in Marx's Dissertation," in *The Philosophical Forum*, vol. 8, nos. 2–4, pp. 241–55.

This second phase is strongly marked by Ludwig Feuerbach's anthropological reinterpretation of Hegel's dialectic. In an article, "Toward a Critique of Hegel's Philosophy,"[7] Feuerbach had argued that philosophy, instead of being the science of the spirit, should reduce all spiritual ideas and ideals to their human origin. In *The Essence of Christianity* he applied this anthropological method to man's main projection, the idea of God. His anthropology, Feuerbach claimed, "places philosophy *in the negation of philosophy,* that is, it declares that alone to be the true philosophy which is converted *in succum et sanguinem,* which is incarnate in man."[8] Such a program required the abolition not only of religion, but also of all "speculative" philosophy. Yet the end of speculation did not spell the end of dialectical thought. In order to convert dialectical philosophy into anthropology, it sufficed to reverse it. Hegel's method remained fundamentally valid, insofar as it overcame the opposition between thought and reality. "But it abolishes the opposition *only within the opposition itself,* within one of the two elements—thought. Thinking for Hegel is being: thinking is the subject, being the predicate. The true relation between thinking and being is where being is the subject and thinking the predicate. Thinking proceeds from being, but being does not proceed from thinking."[9] To set things aright the predicate must become subject and the subject, predicate. Instead of starting from itself, philosophy must start from its antithesis.

In retrospect Feuerbach's "reversal" appears to have little more than the name in common with Hegel's dialectic. For what characterizes Hegelian dialectic is not so much the opposition between antithetic moments as their *intrinsic and necessary relatedness.* For Hegel the connection between the notion and its appearance is wholly determined by the inner development of an all-encompassing spiritual reality. To remove this ideal support in favor of what Feuerbach calls "the principle of sensualism" is

7. "Zur Kritik der Hegelschen Philosophie," in *Sämtliche Werke,* ed. W. Bolin and F. Jodl (Stuttgart, 1959), 2:158–204.

8. *Das Wesen des Christentums,* in *Sämtliche Werke,* 7:283; *The Essence of Christianity,* trans. George Eliot (New York: Harper, 1957), p. xxxv.

9. "Vorläufige Thesen zur Reform der Philosophie," in *Sämtliche Werke,* 2:238.

to forfeit the inner necessity of the dialectical development. All that is left, then, is the old antithesis between mind and nature, and a purely empirical relation between the two. Such a relation, based exclusively upon de facto observation, can never be more than contingent. Whatever necessity Feuerbach ascribes to his "dialectic" he derives from logical principles which he has ceased to accept. Thus he replaces the dynamic relation between internally connected moments by a purely extrinsic, dialectical frame of thinking, the moments of which lack all inner cogency.

It did not take Marx long to realize the inadequacy of such a method. Yet at the time when he had been trying unsuccessfully to find the right angle of approach for a fundamental critique of Hegel's *Philosophy of Right*, Feuerbach's "key" unlocked his own thought. The fragment of Marx's commentary which has reached us was written shortly after the publication of Feuerbach's *Theses* and shows their influence throughout. Hegel's philosophy is criticized for reducing the real to a mere appearance of the ideal. By "real" Marx understands, with Feuerbach, the empirically verifiable, and he accuses Hegel of substituting an ideal effect to a real cause. Family and civil society, the real basis of society, are presented as subordinate, "finite" moments of the "concrete" Idea, the state. The entire empirical realm becomes a mere "mediation" which the Idea performs upon itself. Marx unquestioningly accepts Feuerbach's interpretation that for Hegel thought is the subject and being the predicate.[10] By presenting the concretely real as emerging from the Idea, Hegel creates an effect of logical mysticism. Thus, concerning the organic structure of the state, Hegel writes: "This organism is the development of the Idea to its differences and their objective actuality."[11] The Idea appears incarnate in the concrete powers of the state and the constitutional monarch is born as a living individual out of the self-concretizing Idea.

> Had Hegel started with the real subjects as the bases of the State it would not have been necessary for him to let the State become

10. Ibid., p. 262.
11. *The Philosophy of Right*, trans. T. M. Knox (New York: Oxford University Press, 1967), p. 269.

subjectified in a mystical way. . . . Subjectivity is a characteristic of subjects and personality a characteristic of the person. Instead of considering them to be predicates of their subject Hegel makes the predicates independent and then lets them be subsequently and mysteriously converted into their subjects. [*MEGA* 1¹: 426; *Coll. Works* 3: 23][12]

For all his loyalty, Marx is extending Feuerbach's principle to the realm of politics in a manner which its author never intended and could hardly have agreed with.

Soon Marx would experience more substantial difficulties than the limitations of Feuerbach's principle. In Feuerbach's dialectic the negation, which is simplistically equated with "alienation," signifies merely an imperfect state of consciousness that must be "overcome." But he presents no compelling argument for its appearance nor, for that matter, for the necessity of its overcoming. To surpass a dialectical moment it is not sufficient to declare it a "mystification." *Without intrinsic connection* between the present and the future state the dialectical necessity vanishes altogether and the "negation" is reduced to a mere criticism of the present. Having by then become a full-fledged revolutionary, Marx needed a method which would allow him to predict the future with certainty. The *necessity* of change had to appear in the very structure of the present. This necessity Marx only found in Hegel's philosophy, to which he returned in 1844.

The Economic and Philosophical Manuscripts of the Paris period reveal a careful study of the nature of dialectical negation in Hegel.[13] Yet Marx avoids attacking Feuerbach by name. Instead he directs his sarcastic wit toward the Young Hegelians: "After all these entertaining antics of idealism which is expiring in the form of criticism, the Critical School has not even now intimated that it was necessary to discuss critically its own source, the dialectic of Hegel; nor has it given any indication of its relation with the dialectic of Feuerbach" (*MEGA* 1³: 151; *Coll. Works* 3: 328

12. *Critique of Hegel's Philosophy of Right*, trans. Joseph O'Malley (Cambridge University Press, 1970), p. 23.
13. See, above all, the "Critique of Hegel's Dialectic," which concludes the third manuscript.

slightly altered). He even praises Feuerbach as "the only person who has a serious and critical relation to Hegel's dialectic" and credits him with having replaced Hegel's negation of the negation "which claims to be the absolute positive," by a self-subsistent principle founded on itself (*MEGA* 1³: 152; *Coll. Works* 3: 328). While the Young Hegelian attempt to salvage the dialectical method from Hegel's political and religious conservatism still remained an intraphilosophical corrective, Feuerbach presented a more radical critique. "In Hegel the negation of the negation is not the confirmation of the true essence, effected precisely through negation of the pseudo-essence. With him the negation of the negation is the confirmation of the pseudo-essence. . . ." (*MEGA* 1³: 164; *Coll. Works* 3: 339–40). Instead of negating the illusion, Hegel has merely negated its *external* existence and internalized it. At the end of the reappropriation process the subject merely discovers itself in a "self-confirmation," which is "not yet sure of itself, which is therefore burdened with its opposite" (*MEGA* 1³: 152; *Coll. Works* 3: 329). In contrast to such a doubtful reappropriation, Feuerbach's sensuous being is perceptually indubitable and grounded upon itself.

Nevertheless, as we saw in the previous chapters, the Manuscripts owe more to Hegel than to Feuerbach. Specifically, the crucial concept of the dialectic as a self-creating process is Hegelian.

> Thus by grasping the *positive* meaning of self-referred negation (although again in estranged fashion) Hegel grasps man's self-estrangement, the alienation of man's essence, man's loss of objectivity and his loss of realness as self-discovery, manifestation of his nature, objectification and realization. (*MEGA* 1³: 167; *Coll. Works* 3: 342).

As the dynamic moment that launches the subject beyond its given condition, Hegel's negation presents a possibility of revolutionary development that is wholly absent in Feuerbach's concept of alienation.

In the dialectic of the Paris Manuscripts the economic factor appears as the negative moment of what remains essentially an anthropological process. The capitalist mode of production has become the main obstacle in man's social development. Yet the economy of capitalism not only prevents genuine social development: it also suffers from internal contradictions. Marx notes their existence at the beginning of the Manuscripts and summarizes them in the section on alienated labor (*MEGA* 1³: 81; *Coll. Works* 3: 270). It is on those contradictions that Marx's critique of society will henceforth concentrate.

THE DIALECTIC OF ECONOMIC CONCEPTS

Until 1845 Marx had used dialectic primarily as a method for an anthropological critique of capitalist society. The dialectical negation had consisted in the opposition between prevailing social-economic conditions and an ideal, humanist model. The writings of *The German Ideology* drastically changed the perspective. Henceforth the contrast was no longer between a transhistorical idea of man and a present historical reality, but between opposing historical stages. History itself moves by way of conflict, a conflict that originates in the opposition between production forces and production relations. Thus Marx at once laid a social-economic basis for the dialectic of history and converted the critique of history into a critique of economics. At the same time *The German Ideology* established that economic categories themselves result from a historical process. The so-called structural dialectic of economics is the outcome of a particular historical development.

In his 1847 critique of Proudhon's *The Philosophy of Poverty,* Marx adumbrated an entirely new approach to the study of economics. Major economic developments are touched off by internal conflicts in the prevailing system. Proudhon's total disregard for the historical origins of economic concepts in his "Hegelian" theory forced Marx to reflect on the proper method for a dialectic of economics. *The Poverty of Philosophy* did not take him very far along that road. Yet his sarcastic and not always fair critique of Proudhon's "Hegelianism" effectively cleared the way for a development of his own dialectic.

The dialectical movement of Proudhon's economic categories does not really result from internal oppositions, nor is it the outcome of the actual production relations from which they derive their origin. In Marx's view, it consists entirely in the purely logical formula of movement mechanically applied to intrinsically static economic concepts. Proudhon fails to see altogether the dynamic character of economic categories. He treats them as "immutable laws, eternal principles, ideal categories." Nevertheless, he feels the need to criticize them and to show their potential for social reform. To provide the necessary change in his immobile economic universe he turns to what he has learned from Hegel's *Logic*. Treating them as expressions of a self-developing Idea, he conveys to economic relations *ab extrinseco* the movement which their own nature lacks. Thus economic systems come and go, not according to the intrinsic necessity of their actual conflicts, but according to a supereconomic Idea. Hegel's triadic schema must substitute for insight into the nature of economic development. Accepting his categories ready-made from the classical economists, Proudhon is satisfied with placing them in a rational (but not historical!) order of succession. He converts political economy into logic, even as Hegel had reduced religion, morality, and right to developments of an Idea. But unlike Hegel, Proudhon is a poor dialectician: even his logical connections lack consistency.

> What then does M. Proudhon give us? Real history, which is, according to M. Proudhon's understanding, the sequence in which the categories have manifested themselves in order of time? No! History as it takes place in the idea itself? Still less! That is, neither the profane history of the categories, nor their sacred history. [*Werke* 4:134; *Coll. Works* 6: 169]

From this confrontation with a purely "logical" (in Proudhon's, not in Hegel's sense) dialectic of economic categories Marx learned the important lesson that no structural analysis can be adequate without having solid foundations in history. This may appear to be no more than a conclusion drawn from *The German Ideology*. Of course, in a sense it is. But *The German Ideology* had led the critique of history to a point where it had to become a critique of social-economic relations. A mere dialectic of history such as he had undertaken in his earlier work was no longer sufficient. If history was to be more than one more ideology, a variation on Hegel's self-propelling Spirit, then concrete, simultaneously existing social-economic conflicts had to be analyzed in their structural opposition. But in such an analysis the use of the dialectical method might easily degenerate into a mere exercise in Hegelian logic, as had happened with Proudhon. In heaping sarcasm on the unhappy Frenchman Marx was in fact settling accounts with his own past. Proudhon had done in his analysis of economic concepts what Marx—in a more expert way—might have done himself. Indeed, Proudhon's marginal remarks on Marx's critique show his bitterness at being criticized for doing what Marx himself had taught him to do. This interpretation may be partly attributed to the inability of a mind untrained in Hegel's philosophy to grasp subtle but crucial distinctions. I suspect, however, that what Marx had taught Proudhon about the use of Hegel's method in social theory may at least in part have been reflected in *The Philosophy of Poverty*.

At any rate, by the time he was finished with Proudhon, Marx had become convinced that an effective critique of economy should expose the internal conflicts within the existing economic structure, but *with constant reference to their historical origins*. Concretely, this meant a critique of economic conflicts and concepts through the production relations which gave rise to them, and of the producton relations in turn through the powers of production that had conditioned them. It was not a finite analysis such as Proudhon had attempted and as Marx himself at one point may have envisaged, but an ongoing process never to be completed. A delicate balance was to be struck between mere concept analysis and historical generalizations. But at least Marx had understood that the proper method for dealing with the economic basis of society was through economic facts rather than through anthropological ideals or general historical laws. What Marx learned from his critique of Proudhon was not so much the importance of studying the historical origins of present conditions—this he already knew—but the possibility of achieving an analysis of historical concepts with the full instrumentation of abstract logical tools, without having to abandon a critique of those concepts from a historical perspective.

In the light of those experiences we should be able to evaluate the difficult text which Marx wrote as an introduciton to his *Critique of Political Economy* but discarded before its publication.[14] At the beginning of the methodological part of this essay Marx advances that the proper method in economy is not from the concrete-particular (for instance, population) to the universal (capital), but from the abstract to the concrete (*GR* 21; NIC 100). To start a scientific investigation with a concrete, historical complexity is to begin with "a chaotic picture of the whole."

> The economists of the seventeenth century always begin with the living whole, with population, nation, state, several states, etc.; but they always conclude by discovering through analysis a small number of abstract, general relations such as division of labor, money value, etc. As soon as these individual moments had been more or less firmly established and abstracted, there began the economic systems, which ascended from the simple relations, such as labor, division of labor, need, exchange value, to the level of the state, exchange between nations and the world market. The latter is obviously the scientifically correct method. The concrete is concrete because it is the concentration of many determinations, hence unity of the diverse. It appears in the process of thinking, therefore, as a process of concentration, as a result, not as a point of departure, even though it is the point of departure in reality and hence also the point of departure for observation and conception. [*GR* 21–22; NIC 100–01]

We recognize Descartes's rule that the scientific investigation should move from the simple to the complex, a rule which itself echoes Galileo's *metodo resolutivo*. The concrete totality is the point of departure for observation and conception. In the expository analysis, however, it must be broken down into its abstract components lest it "evaporate" altogether. Only through general concepts can the economist hope to discover the "essence" of an economic development rather than its muddled "appearances" (*Werke* 23: 95; *Cap.* 1: 81) Such "essences" raise, of

---

14. The text, first published by Karl Kautsky in *Neue Zeit* and later reunited with the *Critique*, now usually appears as the first of the manuscripts published under the title *Grundrisse der Kritik der politischen Ökonomie* (1939), (1953).

course, verification problems of their own: they are not accessible to direct perception.[15] Nevertheless, they are justified by the unique function they serve in the understanding of historical processes.

Thus far Marx's position basically coincides with that of the classical economists. Yet in the final sentence Marx introduces a new element that has an unmistakably Hegelian ring. "The concrete is concrete because it is the concentration of many determinations, hence unity of the diverse." Here, clearly, a new element in the analysis is announced: Marx definitively takes leave of the empirical generalizations of the British economists that univocally fit every single "application," in favor of Hegel's universals that are transformed at each new stage of their realization. Yet, again, Marx's method eludes easy classification, for he immediately qualifies his allegiance to Hegel by restricting the dialectic to the mental order.

> In this way Hegel fell into the illusion of conceiving the real as the product of thought concentrating itself, probing its own depth, and unfolding itself out of itself, by itself, whereas the method of arising from the abstract to the concrete is only the way in which thought appropriates the concrete, reproduces it as the concrete in the mind. [*GR* 22; NIC 101]

Marx here reaffirms his early, Feuerbachian ("only in the mind") critique of Hegel's method. Nevertheless, on the cognitive level he accepts the notion of the self-concretizing universal. If he had satirized Proudhon's economic "Hegelianism," it was not because the French socialist had followed Hegel's method, but because he had reduced it to a mechanical application of the triadic schema. Proudhon had been too simplistic in his Hegelianism.

Meanwhile the relation between thought and reality, as Marx conceived it, creates some problems of its own. For the social-economic reality that Marx envisioned is to a great extent man-made and, consequently, "mental" as much as physical. Marx himself realized the full complexity of the problem even though he did not have a solution ready. (This may have contributed to his decision not to publish the introduction.) A few lines after his rejection of Hegel's "idealism" he raises the question: have not

---

15. Leszek Kolakowski, *The Main Currents of Marxism*, 1:317.

these simple categories also an independent historical or natural existence preceding that of the more concrete ones? The answer is far from the simple dismissal the reader might expect. Thus the "simple category" of ownership also *in reality* initiates the increasingly complex legal relations of society. But ownership itself presupposes the family, which is a more concrete legal category. Marx merely insists that the simple categories in that case reflect relations *dominating* in an immature concrete situation which become subordinate in a more advanced society. Further qualifications are needed to explain the origins of simple categories in early but highly "advanced"—that is, complex—societies.

> Thus in this respect it may be said that the simpler category can express the dominant relations of a less developed whole, or else those subordinate relations of a more developed whole which already had a historic existence before this whole developed in the direction expressed by a more concrete category. To that extent the path of abstract thought, rising from the simple to the combined, would correspond to the real historical process. [GR 23; NIC 102]

Despite all the qualifications, this conclusion considerably exceeds the epistemological limits Marx had set to his structural dialectic. He himself had ruled out a total separation of the order of reality from that of conceptual analysis. The dialectic of history which Marx had started to develop in his earlier works requires at least a parallelism between idea and reality. He restates this principle in the introduction:

> Just as in general when examining any *historical or social science,* so also in the case of the development of economic categories it is always necessary to remember that the subject, in this context contemporary bourgeois society, *is presupposed both in reality and in the mind,* and that therefore categories express forms of existence and conditions of existence of this particular society, the subject. [GR 26–27; NIC 106. My emphasis]

Categories do not merely picture but directly *reflect* historical development. The question is, however, whether the convergence of dialectical structure and social-economic reality should be expressed by a parallelism in the development from the simple to the complex. Even if actual social developments tend to move in the direction of increasing complexity (which they may well do), this does not justify an equation with the *logical* development from the simple to the complex. Marx here introduces principles of Hegel's historical dialectic into a procedure from which he had explicitly excluded their applicability. Rationalist philosophers who followed the same logical path and who presupposed the existence of a parallelism between the *ordo rerum* and the *ordo idearum* were nevertheless more cautious in distinguishing the *rules* of the method from the development of reality.

Nevertheless, Marx's basic intuition is right: to the extent that their historical development *intrinsically* determines the economic categories, the structural analysis cannot ignore its *direct* relation to concrete reality. (I write *direct,* because obviously the entire economic analysis deals with the real and its verification must come from empirical observation. The only question here is whether the *ordo inventionis* or *expositionis* is also the *ordo successionis.*) At the same time, Marx correctly perceived that a *critique* of political economy required more than a tracing of the historical origins of its institutions, techniques, and production relations. The dialectic of succession outlined in *The German Ideology* and applied in his historical works would not suffice for this purpose. Even though the categories reflect their historical origins, they do so through the prism of their present, original structure.

> It would be inexpedient and wrong therefore to present the economic categories successively in the order in which they have played the dominant role in history. On the contrary, their order of succession is determined by their mutual relation in modern bourgeois society, and this quite the reverse of what appears to be natural to them or in accordance with the sequence of historical development. The point at issue is not the role that various economic relations have played in the succession of various social formations appearing in the course of history; even less is it their sequence 'as concepts' *(Proudhon)* (a nebulous notion of the historical process), but their position within modern bourgeois society. [*GR* 28; NIC 107–08. S. W. Ryazanskaya-Dobb translation]

A critique requires an analysis of capitalist economy in its *present* structure. Marx now claims that such an analysis would have to be dialectical. But it is not the kind of dialectic for which he can make the same reality claims as for his dialectic of history. Being a constructive model for the interpretation of economic structures, it is in principle restricted to the order of *presentation*.[16]

The principal characteristic of this structural dialectic is that it organically connects the various phases of the economic process which classical economy had separated. For Marx, production already contains consumption and distribution itself is a form of producing (*GR* 11; McLellan 23–24).[17] This interrelatedness of all economic categories marks a clear innovation in economic thinking made under the direct impact of Hegel's philosophy. In his review of Marx's *Critique of Political Economy*, Engels describes the difference:

> Political economy begins with *commodities,* begins from the moment when products are exchanged for one another—whether by individuals or by primitive communities. In exchange a product becomes a commodity. It is, however, a commodity solely because a *relation* between two persons or commodities attaches to the *thing,* the product, the relation between producer and consumer who are here no longer united in the same person. [*Werke* 13: 475; *Sel. Works* 1: 374][18]

Marx uses no "simple" concepts, only conceptualized relations. Each term must ever anew be defined in accordance with the complex web of relations in which it appears.[19]

16. Cf. William L. McBride, *The Philosophy of Marx* (London: Hutchinson, 1977), pp. 58–67.

17. Nor should this interconnection of production, distribution, and exchange be interpreted in a formalistic "Hegelian" way, as if production *universally* appropriated the products of nature while distribution determined which *particular* group was to partake of those products, and consumption constituted the *individual* enjoyment of them (*GR* 11; NIC 89).

18. Review anonymously published in *Das Volk* on August 20, 1859. *Werke* 13:475.

19. Bertell Ollman has made this interrelatedness the central theme of his study, *Alienation: Marx's Concept of Man in Capitalist Society* (New York: Cambridge University Press, 1971).

THE HISTORICAL PRINCIPLE RADICALIZED: *CAPITAL*

Did Marx retain the methodological principles he formulated in the introduction to the *Critique of Political Economy?* With regard to the interrelatedness of economic concepts, undoubtedly yes! In other respects, however, some unexpected development seems to have occurred. In the "Afterword" to the second German edition of *Capital* (1873) he distinguishes the order of scientific inquiry from the order of presentation. Both follow a dialectical pattern, but that pattern is not immediately obvious to the investigator while he is still engaged in collecting data and examining possible connections. At first sight Marx's distinction merely suggests a growing awareness of the "mental" character of the dialectic and an attempt to hone its distinctness from the real movement to a finer edge. But the picture becomes considerably more complex when Marx, against Hegel's idealism, insists that "the ideal is nothing else than the material world reflected by the human mind, and translated into forms of thought." Marx thus restates the "reflection" theory enunciated in *The German Ideology* and never repeated since. The dialectic of presentation is now said to reflect the subject matter "ideally—as in a mirror" (*Werke* 23: 27; *Cap.* 1: 19). But for a dialectical presentation to reflect the real movement as a mirror, reality itself must be dialectical independently of the mind. By the same token the earlier distinction between the order of presentation and the movement of reality vanishes.

Capital no longer features the kind of methodological considerations that had marked Marx's earlier essay. Explicit references to Hegel have sharply decreased.[20] But the impact of Hegel's dialectic of history has increased. Much of *Capital* and most of the preparatory *Theories of Surplus Value* is spent in showing the intrinsically historical character of all economic concepts. This, more even than their internal relatedness, distinguishes

---

20. The few that remain point to Marx's continued loyalty to "Hegel's method." Thus he (unfairly) dismisses John Stuart Mill as being "as much at home in absurd contradictions as he feels at sea in the Hegelian contradiction, the source of all dialectic" (*Werke* 23: 623; *Cap.* 1:596).

Marx's categories from those of the classical economists.[21] To him the capitalist system is not the logical product of common sense and Western inventiveness, but the outcome of specific social and technical developments, subject to historical metamorphoses and constantly passing through distinct but interconnected cycles of production, circulation, sales, and reinvestment. It negates a previous system of production and will, in time, be supplanted by a new system that synthesizes the two preceding ones. Capital is "a definite social production relation, belonging to a definite historical formation of society" (*Werke* 25: 822; *Cap.* 3: 814), and capitalist production is "by no means an absolute form for the development of the productive forces and for the creation of wealth" (*Werke* 25: 274; *Cap.* 3: 263–64).

Nowhere is the historical relativity of economic concepts more evident than in Marx's discussion of *value*. Even this first and foremost concept intrinsically depends on a particular, historical mode of production. The utility of a product turns into *value* only after it has become part of a social exchange system. Though the obvious value of a product appears to consist in its use, in the current system exchange value alone possesses economic significance. Exchange has gradually detached itself from use and adopted a meaning of its own, independent of the specific nature of the product. "All that these things now tell us is that human labor power has been expended in their production, that human labor is embodied in them. When looked at as crystals of this social substance, common to them all, they are— values" (*Werke* 23: 52; *Cap.* 1: 38). Such a claim may hardly seem to go beyond the fundamental principles of the classical economists but, in truth, constitutes a revolutionary innovation. For Marx here presents value itself as resulting *from a particular*

21. That reality is essentially a dynamic process is a principle Marx had adopted from Hegel at an early age. In the Manuscripts of 1844 appears the well-known passage: "The outstanding thing in Hegel's *Phenomenology* and its final outcome—that is, the dialectic of negativity as the moving and generating principle—is thus first that Hegel conceives the self-genesis of man as a process . . ." (*MEGA* 1³: 156; *Coll. Works* 3:332). This text, of course, considers only *man* as a process being. But Marx, and ever more so, regarded man as the moving principle of all reality.

mode of production. Value is a universal economic category *only within the capitalist economic system.*

The same system which reduces all products to "mere congelations of undifferentiated human labor" (*Werke* 23: 81; *Cap.* 1: 67), renders the value-producing activity into an abstract, strictly capitalist mode of producing. The term *labor,* according to Marx, applies exclusively to that specific productive activity which supports a value-and-exchange system that is at least relatively independent of use. Indeed, it is precisely labor which allows the production of use value to be converted into one of exchange value. Hence its peculiar ambiguity: labor by its very nature produces use value, yet in the capitalist economy it is the substance and measure of what is not useful, of exchange value.[22]

Because of its abstract nature, value can be measured in quantities of an arbitrarily chosen and arbitrarily valued metal. Money is the concrete expression of abstract value. With it comes price, "the money name of the labor realized in a commodity" (*Werke* 23: 116; *Cap.* 1: 101), which allows any commodity to be exchanged for any other commodity. However, since this concrete expression of value as such is itself a commodity and possesses a value of its own, money in a capitalist economy is far more than a mere means of exchange: it becomes the real end which directs the purchase of commodities (the putative end). Money's principal function consists not in the acquisition of goods but in the expansion of capital: its ultimate purpose is not to buy but to sell. It allows the economic process to sever all direct connections with use: the abstract price represents abstract value produced through abstract labor. All that counts is the *process* of value. "In the circulation m(oney)—c(ommodity)—m(oney) both the money and the commodity represent only different modes of existence of value itself, the money its general mode, and the commodity its particular or, so to say, disguised mode. It is constantly changing from one form to the other without thereby becoming lost, and thus assumes an automati-

---

22. Klaus Hartmann, *Die Marxsche Theorie* (Berlin: Walter de Gruyter, 1970), p. 268.

cally active character" (*Werke* 23: 168; *Cap.* 1: 153). Value, the real agent, becomes value in process through the circulation of capital.

Capital depends on the presence of specific historical conditions. Though classical economists were well aware of that fact, Marx criticizes them for simply assuming that those conditions "naturally" emerge. Thus Ricardo, who possessed the concept of surplus value, never concerned himself with the conditions of its origin. "He treats it as a thing inherent in the capitalist mode of production, which mode, in his eyes, is the natural form of social production" (*Werke* 23: 539; *Cap.* 1: 515). According to Marx, the very existence of those conditons must be investigated. They may have been historically inevitable but were by no means "natural" or intrinsically necessary, since they resulted from a specific mode of producing, not from production as such. Capital is but the final outcome of a long line of historical developments. It cannot be understood without an examination of all its preceding conditions. Ignoring the history of economic categories results in inaccurate interpretations. Thus classical economists define the value of labor as the price it takes to produce and maintain labor power. But such an intrinsically capitalist equation, Marx claims, aside from confusing value and price, identifies labor with its producer.

> In the expression 'value of labor,' the idea of value is not only completely obliterated, but actually reversed. It is an expression as imaginary as the value of the earth. These imaginary expressions arise, however, from the relations of productions themselves. They are categories for the phenomenal forms of essential relations. That in their appearance things often represent themselves in inverted order is pretty well known in every science except political economy. [*Werke* 23: 559; *Cap.* 1: 537]

In classical economy, labor value is simply defined by the current capitalist practice of determining its price by the maintenance cost of the *laborer*. "What economists therefore call value of labor, is in fact the value of labor power, as it exists in the personality of the laborer, which is as different from its function, labor, as a machine is from the work it performs" (*Werke* 23: 561; *Cap.* 1: 538).

Nowhere does the historical-dialectical character of Marx's concepts appear more clearly than in his most original contribution—the theory of surplus value. Marx presents the labor process which yields surplus value from two different points of view. In *Capital* 1 he describes the process of productive work *in its essential nature,* which its historical appearances, to a greater or lesser extent, realize. Far from being the only possible realization, capitalist labor is almost its direct negation.

> Labor is, in the first place, a process in which both man and nature participate, and in which man of his own accord starts, regulates, and controls the material reaction between himself and Nature. He opposes himself to Nature as one of her own forces, setting in motion arms and legs, head and hands, the natural forces of his body, in order to appropriate Nature's productions in a form adapted to his own wants. By thus acting on the external world and changing it, he at the same time changes his own nature. He develops his slumbering powers and compels them to act in obedience to his sway (*Werke* 23: 192; *Cap.* 1: 177).[23]

This kind of productive work corresponds entirely to the anthropological view, articulated in the Paris Manuscripts, of an active, dialectical relation between man and nature. The emphasis rests on human initiative: man starts "of his own accord," "regulates," "controls."

The other description presents the labor process as it takes place *within the capitalist production.* Here a very different picture emerges. Although the ability to buy and sell labor presupposes a "personal" independence which neither the slave nor the serf possesses, a capitalist economy leaves the laborer no real freedom to sell or to withhold his labor power: "The second essential condition . . . of finding labor power in the market as a commodity is this—that the laborer instead of being in the position to sell commodities in which his labor is incorporated, must be obliged to offer for sale as a commodity that very labor power, which exists only in his living self" (*Werke* 23: 183; *Cap.* 1: 168–69). All

---

23. Marx here does not use the term *labor* in the restrictive sense of the productive activity exclusive to the capitalist system, but of productive activity in general.

concepts of capitalist economy—labor, value, price, capital—are determined by its principal goal: the creation of surplus value. Surplus value alone determines what makes the capitalist economy move—profit. Circulation as such does not increase the value of commodities. The only source of value is labor, and to yield profit the created value must exceed the amount returned in labor wages. To achieve such a surplus the worker must be separated from his product, a state of affairs possible only in an economic situation where the producer is no longer able to support himself independently or to contribute the material conditions for the production. By providing him with the necessary conditions for production (place, machinery, distribution), capital places itself between the two and succeeds in appropriating the entire labor value. The resulting mode of producing admits no other goal than the creation of surplus value.

> Our capitalist has two objects in view: in the first place, he wants to produce a use-value that has a value in exchange, that is to say, an article destined to be sold, a commodity; and secondly, he desires to produce a commodity whose value shall be greater than the sum of the values of the commodities used in its production, that is, of the means of production and the labor-power, that he purchased with his good money in the open market. His aim is to produce not only a use-value but a commodity also; not only use-value but value; not only value, but at the same time surplus value (*Werke* 23: 201; *Cap.* 1: 186).

In the process capital expands, and it expands through an increase of the sole producer of value—labor (*Werke* 23: 223–25; *Cap.* 1: 208–10).

I shall pass no judgment on Marx's controversial thesis that labor is the exclusive source of value increase and that means of production never yield more value than they lose through operating expenses and amortization (*Werke* 23: 218; *Cap.* 1: 204). Here I am concerned only with his relativization of established economic concepts. Value, price, labor, all have become constitutive factors of the productive process *at a particular stage* of its development. For Marx, the current stage stands in a negative relationship to earlier ones: it is opposed to what productive work "essentially" is and historically was, namely, the "necessary condition for effecting exchange of matter between man and Nature" (*Werke* 23: 198; *Cap.* 1: 183–84) through which man "develops his slumbering powers" (*Werke* 23: 190; *Cap.* 1: 177).

DIALECTICAL CONTRADICTION REDEFINED

Development and interconnectedness alone do not constitute dialectical necessity. In addition, a *contradictory opposition* between dynamically connected moments is required. Here the problems of Marx's structural dialectic and of its impact upon the historical development confront us at once. What counts as a dialectical contradiction? The question was difficult in Hegel; but it became far more so after Marx reshaped the nature of the dialectical opposition into one of factual conflict. In the preface to the second edition of *Capital*, Marx explains what he understands by an inquiry of a dialectical development.

> Such an inquiry will confine itself to the confrontation and the comparison of a fact, not with ideas, but with another fact. For this inquiry, the one thing of moment is, that both facts be investigated as accurately as possible, and that they actually form, each with respect to the other, different moments of an evolution, but most important of all is the rigid analysis of the series of successions, of the sequences and concatenations in which the different stages of such an evolution present themselves. [*Werke* 23: 26; *Cap.* 1: 18]

Yet under what conditions do facts become dialectical oppositions? That certain states conflict with others poses, of course, no problem. But a mere conflict of "facts" lacks the necessity characteristic of true dialectic. In contrast to bourgeois economists, Marx's analysis of the current economic conditions includes, he insists, "the recognition of the negation of that state, of its inevitable breaking up" (*Werke* 23: 28; *Cap.* 1: 20). In treating the economic process as a dialectical development, Marx does far more than empirically describe it: he brings out the necessary inception and *inevitable* demise of historical systems of production because of their *inherent* (not contingent) contradictory elements.

A contradiction, strictly speaking, occurs only between logical propositions. How does this apply to the simultaneous appearance of incompatible claims or drives? Clearly, the deeper structures of a society are not logical structures in the sense in which systems of rules are related to the truth of propositions. How can we justifiably apply the term *contradiction*, then, to repeated confrontations between groups with incompatible claims? Habermas has argued that a necessary condition for social oppositions counting as contradictions is that they occur within a communications system where incompatible claims are made about the validity of norms of action. This he asserts is the case in class conflicts.[24] Yet I question whether even that is a necessary and sufficient condition for attaining the kind of necessity Marx claims for his contradictions. Most of what Marx refers to as contradictions consist not of social conflicts but of *opposite tendencies* coexisting in the same economic system.[25] But, more importantly, class conflicts do not per se possess the inevitability both of the breakdown and of the subsequently emerging system which Marx expects from dialectical contradictions.

What, then, provides the additional element that converts conflicting states into dialectical oppositions with a predictable, positive outcome? Marx himself, as well as Engels and Lenin, all refer to Hegel's *Logic*.[26] But clearly the dialectic of *Capital* lacks the moving agent of Hegel's philosophy: a Spirit which *by intrinsic necessity* negates itself and, then, by the same necessity negates its negation in a new affirmation. What substitutes for the Spirit in securing the inner necessity which alone could grant total predictability, especially predictability of a noncontradictory fu-

24. Jürgen Habermas, *Legitimation Crisis*, p. 28.

25. An example typical both of the choice and of the looseness of Marx's use of the term is the "contradiction" between the quantitative limitation and the measureless quality of money in *Grundrisse:* "Money as a sum of money is measured by its quantity. This measuredness contradicts its character, which must be oriented towards the measureless" (*GR* 182; NIC 271).

26. While he was working on the *Grundrisse* manuscripts, Marx wrote Engels (Jan. 16, 1858) that Hegel's *Logic* had been "of great service" to him "as regards the *method* of dealing with the material," and expressed the desire to make accessible "what is *rational*" in that method. *Werke* 29: 260; *Sel. Correspondence*, ed. S. W. Ryazanskaya, trans. I. Lasker (Moscow: Progress Publishers, 1955), p. 93.

ture? Various answers have been given to this question.[27] One recent critic of Marx's method claims to detect underneath the actual, economic contradictions the continued impact of an anthropological assumption from which alone the dialectical movement obtains its direction. Klaus Hartmann regards the so-called contradictions of capitalist society truly "contradictory" (i.e., dialectically negating) only with respect to an ever assumed but never admitted anthropological "thesis." Political economy thus is negatively and "contradictorily" related to a *positive vision of man*. Without this vision there would indeed be no true negativity at all and, consequently, no genuine dialectic. But since Marx does not grant any active function to the anthropological factor in his dialectic, Hartmann wonders where the movement finds its direction and, more specifically, what unifies the variety of tensions and oppositions ("contradictions") into a meaningful, predictable development. Marx continues to invoke Hegel's name, but, his critics charge, he invokes it in vain.

> Marx intends to present an intuitively concrete explanation of the social process, supporting his argument by a mirror type relation to Hegel's philosophy. But what he achieves is a concept of reality, a description, a representation. Such an approach does not enable him to explain the process, especially in its negative development, since all reality, all practice is positive. To be sure, in a particular instance one may compare a form of society to the anthropological model of species life and criticize it by that norm. But one has thereby not succeeded in explaining the negative.[28]

Marx's analysis of capitalist economy is negatively related to an assumed positive idea of man. Yet a social critique in itself does not constitute a dialectical negation, not even if this critique is presented in the form of inner tensions ("contradictions"). To *oppose* a historical-economic analysis to an assumed anthropological model is to pit against each other two different orders of

27. Long ago Rudolf Stammler located the presence of a teleological element in the conscious decisions which entering into social relations inevitably requires (*Wirtschaft und Recht*, 2d ed. [Leipzig, 1896], p. 421). Marxists consider the separation of conscious aspirations and economic necessity a "Kantian" error and prefer to concentrate on the second.

28. Klaus Hartmann, *Die Marxsche Theorie*, p. 226.

reality. Such an opposition does not constitute a dialectical negation. In the description of labor of *Capital* 1: 177 (quoted earlier), the assumed anthropological model surfaces when Marx defines work as man's self-realization through the control of nature. But is such an anthropological "thesis" truly *antithetical* to the present mode of production? What precisely does "human work" as opposed to capitalist "labor" mean on the economic level on which the dialectic is alleged to take place? It is easy to see how the emancipation of exchange value from use could constitute a threat to human development and even how it is opposed to the original goals of production. But it is difficult to conceive of such an emancipation as an *economic contradiction*. In fact, it is hard to imagine how it could have been avoided altogether and even harder to project a developed economic system that would exclude it *in principle*.

The question whether Marx's intrinsically economic "contradictions" manifest a fundamental discrepancy between the current social-economic situation and an anthropological model has resulted in two different interpretations of his dialectic. One radicalizes the anthropological element. Those who have adopted it realize, of course, that anthropology never *appears* in Marx's critique of economic theories. Nevertheless, what determines this critique, they insist, is an idea of man clearly formulated in Marx's early writings and never retracted. They ascribe the more "naturalist" interpretation of Marx's theory to Engels and his heavy-handed successors. Marx's own view would have remained humanistic to the end. The anthropological interpreters attempt to establish an original Marxian dialectic of freedom rather than having to borrow secretly from non-Marxian sources such as Hegel's philosophy of Spirit. The most important study inspired by this attitude is Sartre's *Critique de la raison dialectique*. The other interpretation simply denies that dialectical necessity and development require an overall "thesis"—least of all an anthropological one. Economic contradictions alone suffice to bring the process of history to the predicted overcoming of the capitalist system. Other factors play a role in this process, but they ultimately depend on the economic ones. Those who have chosen this approach concede that anthropological considerations are present in Marx's mature work, but they deny that they play a role *in the dialectic* as such. Among them we find all "official" theorists of communist parties, as well as a number of Marx's critics.

Though a few Marxists, most notably Lukacs and Gramsci, had emphasized the presence of anthropological elements in Marx's theory, the radically anthropological interpretation originated in French existentialist circles. It was prepared by Alexandre Kojève's seminar on Hegel's *Phenomenology*. By highlighting certain passages in the *Phenomenology* and detaching this work from the totality of Hegel's *System,* Kojève in fact laid the foundation for a wholly new dialectical philosophy, one that would dispense with such idealist notions as Absolute Spirit and Idea, and concentrate exclusively on the development of human freedom. This position, Kojève and his followers claimed, basically coincided with Marx's original one. Their selective reading was mainly responsible for the enormous postwar success of Marx's early writings and the relative neglect of his mature ones. The entire interpretation rests on a concept of freedom culled from the master-and-slave passage. The master is the individual who realizes that freedom can be achieved only through self-negation and who is willing to stake his life on the attainment of self-assertion and recognition. Yet his self-denial is limited to one heroic act. After his victory he is satisfied to depend on a slave for fulfilling his desires. The real dialectic of freedom begins with this slave's activity. For him also the road to freedom leads through self-denial. While cowardice deprived him of an instant access to full self-consciousness, his consequent daily self-negating labor proved in the end to be a safer path toward the achievement of genuine freedom. For by persistently overcoming the resistance of a material world, the slave gradually subjugates the entire cosmos and thus gains the kind of objective and lasting recognition which the master never received. The process from denial to freedom continues through the negative self-sufficiency of Stoic freedom, the unworldliness of the unhappy consciousness, the denial of monastic life, the detachment of the creative mind from its achievements and, most importantly, the alienation of the objective mind from its self-created culture.

Marx may not have agreed with most of this analysis: in the Paris Manuscripts he repudiates Hegel's alleged identification of alienation and objectification. But, his existentialist interpreters claim, he never questioned the main thesis that man creates himself in a process of self-negation. Searching for a dialectical necessity which they do not find in Marx's own writings, they developed his brief allusion to the master-and-slave passage at the end of the Paris Manuscripts into a full-fledged dialectical theory. Kojève's interpretation sheds some light on the dialectic of freedom in Marx's early writings, but it fails to provide the development of the capitalist system with the dialectical necessity which *Capital* requires. For the conflicts resulting from the capitalist system are precisely not the ones of freedom. As Marx presents them, they are created not by decisions and attitudes, but by objective modes of production and social structures. It may still be true that the "contradictions" of *Capital* derive their dialectical quality from an unstated anthropological "thesis," but there can be no doubt that Marx studiously avoided basing his argument on anthropological concepts. Consequently, any anthropological interpretation of his dialectic deviates from Marx's clearly stated intentions. Certainly he regarded the capitalist mode of production as incongruous with demands of human nature. But he did not want his *dialectic* to depend on this opposition. No anthropological or philosophical *thesis* initiates the social-economic process, because any general concept such as "human nature," "human work," is itself already the result of a preceding social-economic development and must therefore be regarded as "ideological," that is, secondary with respect to the process of production. It is a basic principle of hermeneutics not to neglect an author's own interpretation of his work until one has tried it and found it wanting. Now, according to Marx, *contradictions which already exist* within the economic process itself, not some preconceived idea of human nature, constitute the inner dialectic of the system and will cause its collapse. Economics as a science turns into a critique of economy, since an analysis of the present mode of production cannot fail to expose its multiple contradictions. Dialectical contradictions, then, are self-contradictions of the social-economic system.

Whether Marx succeeded in keeping his dialectic *within* the economic system is a question we may be able to answer at the end. That it was his intention to keep it within those limits is beyond doubt. We must, then, first study the contradiction on his own terms. *Capital* 3 defines the contradiction of the capitalist system as a whole. "The contradiction of the capitalist mode of production . . . lies precisely in its tendency towards an absolute development of the productive forces which continually come into conflict with the specific *conditions* of production in which capital moves and alone can move" (*Werke* 25: 268; *Cap.* 3: 257). These specific conditions, he has told us a few pages earlier, are the ones that foster and expand the surplus value of the existing capital. Yet as production increases, profit rates decline. The entire development of capitalist economy is determined by the attempt to overcome this built-in handicap of its system.

The general "contradiction" of the capitalist system manifests itself in a number of specific conflicts, starting with the first and most fundamental category of value. No economic value can be realized without use value. Yet economic value tends more and more to suppress the use value on which it depends. Because of the partial identity of the two "values," their opposition becomes a dialectical contradiction: "the two sides which tend to isolate themselves from each other, are nevertheless intrinsically linked and cannot exist independently. If the opposites were not related or indifferent to each other, no struggle would take place. Thus if a producer could produce even one single unit of value without use, all the difficulties and contradictions of production and exchange would vanish."[29] The same contradiction reappears in the opposition between concrete labor (resulting in use value) and abstract labor (producing value). In the process of exchanging one usable object for another, abstract labor tends to suppress concrete labor, on which it nevertheless depends.

Together value and labor lead to the contradiction of money.

29. M. Rosenthal, *Les Problèmes de la dialectique dans Le Capital de Marx* (Moscow: Langues étrangères, 1959), p. 174. This claim is based upon Marx's own exposition in *Theories of Surplus Value*, trans. Jack Cohen and S. W. Ryazanskaya (Moscow: Progress Publishers, 1971), esp. 1: 152–304 and 3: 453–540.

Value asserts its independent existence in money. Originally a mere means of circulation, money gradually turns into the real end of the circulating commodities. It brings to a close the simple form of exchange (commodity-money-commodity) and initiates the complex one (money-commodity-money) in which exchange value becomes the only goal of production. Money enables the producer to retain surplus value and to add it to his original capital. Thus what began as a means of circulation has turned into the main instrument for accumulating value. This accumulation allows capital to concentrate, mechanize, and thereby to expand the process of production. Yet in the end expansion will become capital's undoing. As production increases, capital must compensate for the declining profit rate. By lowering wages and lengthening working time, it extracts an ever greater amount of surplus value from the worker. This creates a conflict between an increased production and a decreased buying power that eventually results in a succession of economic crises. In them all the contradictions between use and value, between abstract and concrete labor, between commodity and money come to more and more explosive confrontations. Marx describes this development in *Capital* 3.[30]

Has this initial survey taught us what Marx understands precisely by "contradiction"? Hardly. In his critical study *On the Dialectical Method* (1868), Eduard von Hartmann attacked Hegel for presenting as contradictions what was in fact not at all contradictory in the commonly accepted sense of *mutually exclusive at the same time in the same respect*. Nor are Hegel's contradictions "contraries," for they do exist in the same subject. Marx's usage of the term suffers from the same ambiguities and some additional ones. It varies from logical inconsistency to practical incompatibility to social conflict.[31] The contradiction between use

30. Marx mentions a number of other "contradictions," such as the machine designed to shorten working time and to free the worker, which led in fact to an unprecedentedly long working day and the chaining of the worker to one restricted task at one machine.

31. The ambiguity has grown worse among Marx's contemporary followers. One student of Soviet logic concludes, in exasperation: "There are so many different notions of contradiction that one does not know where to begin. For

and exchange value refers to the capitalist tendency to make exchange into *the* economic value, while nevertheless use must remain the very basis of exchange. But is this tendency to transform a production process originally designed for the creation of use value a contradiction? Is a shift from concrete to abstract labor contradictory? Does money become contradictory when from a means of circulation it turns into the determining factor of the exchange process?

The inverted relation between profit rate and surplus labor value intrigued Ricardo, but he never thought of it as a contradiction. Other contradictions are economic tensions which may lead to social crises, such as the increasing productivity of industrial capitalism and an inevitable (in Marx's theory!) decline in buying power.[32]

The only reason for placing such a variety of meanings under the same nomer is that Marx regarded them all as creating conflicts which would eventually lead to the final crisis of capitalism. *Any tension that is expected to accelerate the final conflict is termed contradictory.* To understand the full implications one must read the story backward, so to speak, from the anticipated final crisis to the tensions whose cumulative effect will bring it about. Only the perspective of history as the preparation for an apocalyptic class war makes it possible to perceive those tensions and conflicts as "contradictory" (i.e., explosive). Such a perspective may not be unreasonable, but neither is it scientifically "necessary," as Marx and Engels thought. Even if the social-economic tensions were proven to destroy the system in which they appear, they would still provide no information about its successor except

---

some, contradiction is little more than the antagonism of vectors the effect of which are mutually exclusive. For others, contradiction is almost the same as the constitutive relation in the Hegelian sense. Between these two extremes there is place for almost anything." Guy Planty-Bonjour, *The Categories of Dialectical Materialism*, trans. J. J. Blakeley (New York: Frederick A. Praeger, 1967), p. 105.

32. Marx himself largely dispels the "contradiction" of a longer workday as a result of the introduction of machinery devised to shorten the manufacturing process, by the distinction he draws between constant and variable capital. If only the addition of labor (variable capital) allows capital to increase profits, then any investment in machinery (constant capital) for *whatever purpose* must be compensated for by an increase in labor.

that it would not contain the same contradictions to the same degree. Without accepting an overall, ideal structure of reality which *with logical necessity* directs the oppositions toward an ideal *telos*, one has no compelling reason for regarding them as dialectical, that is, as moments of an intrinsically meaningful and necessary development. Hegel provides such a teleological structure in his theory of reality as a self-developing Spirit. But Marx recognizes no all-comprehensive spiritual reality. Dialectical movement, according to him, results exclusively from the simultaneous existence of conflicting states of being. The oppositional relations between the moments must be determined strictly by the structure of the contradictory elements, not by the anticipatory effect of any final cause. Yet teleological assumptions abound and are occasionally expressed. In *Capital* 3 we read: "The capitalist mode of production is, for this reason, *a historical means* of developing the material forces of production and creating an appropriate world-market and is, at the same time, a continual conflict between this its historical task and its own corresponding relations of social production" (*Werke* 25: 260; *Cap.* 3: 250).[33]

Moreover, without a teleological assumption nothing warrants a positive outcome to Marx's dialectic. Unceasing conflict accounts for movement; it does not determine the direction of the movement. In giving his dialectic a progressive interpretation, Marx reveals his unwavering allegiance to an unavowed teleology. These "unstated millennial assumptions" cannot be dismissed as mere remarks of a Hegelian past.[34] How can contradictions lead to an ascending development without assuming an

33. This was no mere slip of the pen. In the *Grundrisse*, where we find his thought in process, Marx states: "*The historical vocation* of capital is fulfilled as soon as, on the one hand, demand has developed to the point where there is a general need for surplus labor beyond what is necessary, and surplus labor itself arises from individual needs; and on the other, general industriousness has developed . . . and has been passed on to succeeding generations, until it has become the property of the new generation; and finally when the productive forces of labor . . . have developed to the point where the possession and maintenance of general wealth requires, on the one hand shorter working hours for the whole society . . ." (*GR* 231; McLellan 85; NIC 325).

34. Robert Heilbroner, *Marxism: For and Against* (New York: Norton, 1980), p. 87.

overall logical construction which unifies the separate agents into a single consistent movement?

Even the term *contradiction*, if it is to mean more than the simultaneous existence of *different* realities, implies the presence of a mental factor. Admitting this presence, some commentators have granted the mind an ordering role in establishing the dialectic of opposing economic tendencies. (Soviet Marxists have traditionally rejected interpretations of this sort as Hegelian, yet their own purely "objective" reading ends up attributing to Nature all the ideal qualities of Hegel's Spirit.) The French Marxist Henri Lefebvre, for instance, considers all dialectical categories mental, yet rooted in objective, social structures.[35] An empirical study of economic data reveals their connectedness and opposition. The dialectical construction in which the mind subsequently orders those data allows one to understand them beyond their empirical givenness and to predict their future development.

> The basic economic category—exchange-value—is developed and, by an internal movement, gives rise to fresh determinations: abstract labor, money, capital. Each complex determination emerges dialectically from the preceding ones. Each category has a logical and methodological role, it has its place in the explicative whole which leads to the reconstitution of the given concrete totality, the modern world. It also corresponds to an epoch and the general historical characteristics of the epoch in question—the framework for events and actions—can be deduced by starting from the category essential to it. This theoretical deduction must thus agree with the empirical and specifically historical research into documents, eye-witness accounts and events.[36]

Even this most Hegelian of all interpretations falls short of yielding the certainty which Hegel's dialectic derives from the all-encompassing active Notion. A repeated observation which, by virtue of induction, receives a certain *a priori* character cannot

35. Cf. *Dialectical Materialism*, trans. John Sturrock (London: Jonathan Cape, 1968), pp. 88–89.
36. Ibid., p. 95.

accomplish what Marx's dialectic purports to do.[37] How much empirical evidence is required to make the dialectic more than a heuristic device or a working hypothesis? Does the available evidence support at least a moral certitude?

Those difficulties increase if we turn to other, less "idealist" interpretations, the only ones, it should be noted, officially recognized by communist regimes and parties. All of them are solidly rooted in Engels's "realist" account of the dialectic. Marxists of existentialist leanings tend to dismiss this account as a betrayal of Marx's theory. Yet they conveniently overlook the fact that Marx himself left the task of justifying his method entirely to his collaborator. Nor did he remain in the dark about the nature of Engels's interpretation. For Engels personally read the *Anti-Dühring*, the only finished exposition of the method, to Marx. His work may not exactly express Marx's own *thought* but, having no information on this thought, we must give serious attention to the sole interpretation of his method which he himself approved.

Engels initiated the "realist" interpretation of historical materialism in a review of Marx's *Contribution to the Critique of Political Economy*. Commending Marx for divesting Hegel's logic "of its idealist trappings," he describes the dialectic as a "real process" of interacting and conflicting economic relations.[38] The mind merely retraces this extramental dialectic but plays no active role in connecting its moments: they are intrinsically related by themselves.[39] Nor is the dialectic restricted to social-economic

37. Official Marxism is understandably reluctant to admit this point. *Fundamentals of Marxism-Leninism* dogmatically asserts: "Owing to their universal character, the laws of dialectics are of a methodological importance and serve as pointers for research" (Moscow: Foreign Languages Publishing House, 1963; p. 87). But nowhere is this universal character justified.

38. Marx-Engels, *Selected Works*, 1:374.

39. This "reality" of the contradictions distinguishes what Marxists call "dialectical" from "metaphysical" thought. Thus Maurice Cornforth writes: "According to the common, metaphysical conception, contradictions occur in our ideas about things, but not in things. . . . This point of view regards contradiction simply and solely as a logical relation between propositions, but does not consider it as a real relation between things." *Materialism and the Dialectical Method* (New York: International Publishers, 1971), p. 92.

relations or to human affairs. Dialectic constitutes an essential feature of reality as such. Indeed, it is reality itself insofar as reality is in constant development. Dialectic, we read in *Anti-Dühring*, is "an extremely general . . . law of the development of nature, history and thought" (*Werke* 20: 131; *Anti-Dühring*, p.154).[40] Engels equates motion with contradiction and matter with motion.[41] Even simple mechanical change can occur only because of a body's being at the same time in one place and in another.[42]

Of course, in Hegel also motion is dialectical. In the *Logic*, becoming results from the opposition in identity of pure Being and pure Nothing,[43] and in the *History of Philosophy* we read: "The reason why dialectic first seizes upon motion as its object lies in the fact that dialectic is itself this motion; or put another way, motion is the dialectic of all that is."[44] But Hegel's moving reality is essentially spiritual. Now, without Spirit a dialectical theory of *human praxis* is still possible (as Lukacs and Korsch have shown), but a dialectical theory of nature is excluded unless one endows "Nature" or "matter" with the same kind of teleological qualities Hegel attributes to his Spirit. We shall see later that this is what happens in orthodox Marxism, though neither methodically nor consistently. In his *Philosophical Notebooks* Lenin

40. *Herr Eugen Dühring's Revolution in Science*, trans. Emile Burns (New York: International Publishers, s.d. [1966]).

41. "Motion is the mode of existence of matter. Never anywhere has there been matter without motion. . . . Matter without motion is just as unthinkable as motion without matter." *Anti-Dühring*, p. 68. Together the two assertions provide the entire "justification" for a dialectic of nature.

42. Ibid., p. 132. To support this assertion, Engels refers to Hegel's "rejection" of Aristotle's principle of noncontradiction—a dubious support, since Hegel explicitly claims Aristotle's authority for his own theory of motion. Cf. Hegel, *Wissenschaft der Logik* (Hamburg: Felix Meiner, 1934 [1967]), 1:192–93; *Science of Logic*, trans. A. V. Miller (New York: Humanities Press, 1969), p. 198. Such an affirmation and negation at the same time in the same respect, an outright rejection of the fundamental principle of traditional logic, even Soviet scholars find hard to swallow (Planty-Bonjour, *Categories of Dialectical Materialism*, p. 118).

43. *Wissenschaft der Logik* 1:67; *Science of Logic*, p. 83.

44. *Gesamtausgabe* (Berlin, 1832), 13:313.

qualified Engels's equation of development and dialectic by specifying that the development must be a *unity of contraries*.[45] But by and large textbooks returned to the simpler version and simply assumed that all development is contradictory.[46]

THE AMBIGUOUS LEGACY: THE THREE LAWS OF DIALECTIC

Engels converted contradiction into progressive movement by means of three fundamental laws: the unity of contraries, the negation of negation, and the transformation of quantity into quality.[47] Since the entire nature of Marxist dialectic as it has been traditionally interpreted depends on these laws, we must consider them in some detail. The dynamic quality of the dialectic originates in the so-called unity of contraries, that is, the *simultaneous* existence of opposite qualities in the same subject. Our earlier discussion of the contradiction should make us realize the difficulty of attaching a precise meaning to this most general law. What are contraries/contradictories? (The terms are used inconsistently.) What is the same subject? This much is clear enough: the contradiction is a conflict between *internally*

---

45. V. I. Lenin, *Collected Works*, trans. Clemens Dutt (Moscow: Progress Publishers, 1961 [1972]), 38:258. It is worth noting that in an early polemical work on the dialectical method Lenin restricts it to *social* development: "What Marx and Engels called the dialectical method is nothing more nor less than the scientific method in sociology, which consists in regarding society as a living organism in a constant state of development, the study of which requires an objective analysis of the relations of production which constitute the given social formation and investigation of its laws of functioning and development" (*What the "Friends of the People" Are and How They Fight the Social Democrats, Collected Works*, 1:165).

46. For instance, *Fundamentals of Marxism-Leninism* (Moscow, 1964) states: "All development, whether the evolution of stars, the growth of a plant, the life of a man or the history of society is contradictory in its essence" (p. 79).

47. In the *Dialectics of Nature* they appear as follows: "The law of the transformation of quantity into quality and vice versa; the law of the interpenetration of opposites; the law of the negation of the negation" (*Werke* 20:348). Trans. C. Dutt (New York: International Publishers, 1940), p. 26. Lenin reversed the order of the first two.

connected aspects of the objective world.[48] But the internal contradiction requires the existence of internal relations. That Marx assumed their existence is, I believe, beyond doubt. Without it his entire critique of political economy becomes unintelligible. In *Theories of Surplus Value* (*Werke* 26³: 394; *TSV* 3: 503) he criticizes "vulgar" economists for not perceiving the *internal connections* among the oppositions which they encounter in their science and thus failing to bring out their antagonistic character. Yet Marx rarely ventured beyond the *man-made* contradictions of economic systems. Engels did, and his treatment became decisive for the further development of the problem. For him, *all* reality is in process and all its aspects are, therefore, internally related. The great merit of Hegel's system, he claims, is that "the whole natural, historical and spiritual world was presented as a process, that is, as in constant motion, change, transformation and development; and the attempt was made to show the internal interconnections in this motion and development" (*Werke* 20: 22; *Anti-Dühring*, p.30). Both nature and history present an endless maze of relations and interactions. Not to see the inner connections between individual things is to overlook their coming into being and their passing away (*Werke* 20: 2; *Anti-Dühring*, pp.26–28).[49] The universal existence of internal relations is a primary condition for a reality conceived as creative process. Only because they "mutually penetrate each other" (*Werke* 20: 21; *Anti-Dühring*, p.29) do the oppositions of reality result in constant novelty. For Engels the inner relations constitute the moving power of the dialectic: oppositions become dynamic only when they exist *within* one and the same reality, when a thing is *internally* divided against itself and its own constituents are in conflict with each other.[50]

48. Cf., for instance, Ts. A. Stepanyan: "Contradictions in the Development of Socialist Society," *Voprosy Filosofii* 2 (1955): 69–86, and comments in Gustav Wetter, *Dialectical Materialism*, trans. Peter Heath (New York: Frederick Praeger, 1958), pp. 343–45.

49. Also: "The first thing that strikes us in considering matter in motion is the interconnection of the individual motions of separate bodies, their being determined by one another" (*Dialectics of Nature*, p. 304).

50. Cf. Gustav A. Wetter, *Dialectical Materialism*, p. 337.

Lenin and Stalin faithfully followed Engels's doctrine. "Dialectics in the proper sense," Lenin writes in his *Notebooks*, "is the study of contradiction *in the very essence of objects*."[51] Stalin explicates: "Contrary to metaphysics, dialectics holds that internal contradictions are inherent in all things and phenomena of nature, for they all have their negative and positive sides, a past and a future, something dying and something developing."[52] It is the existence of internal relations which makes Soviet philosophers so confident that nature is *self-moving* and no longer needs an extramundane mover.

Yet how can internal relations exist without some logical and teleological structure which unites all elements in an organic totality? Bertell Ollman responds that the internal nature of the "parts" rather than the function of the whole qua whole provides the connection.[53] He supports his claim by what he considers to be independence of internal relations in Leibniz's monads of the totality. But the very term *parts* ("whatever parts") implies an idea of a *totum*. The reference to Leibniz seems particularly inappropriate—both logically and ontologically—since each monad is directly related to the principle of totality and harmony (God) and *only through it* to all other monads which it internally "reflects." By themselves monads constitute separate ("windowless") worlds incapable of direct interaction. Ollman finds the philosophical underpinnings of this theory in Marx's contemporary, the self-made German philosopher Joseph Dietzgen.[54] But Dietzgen starts from the idea of a totality and then attempts to show how universally recognized parts can be established, while the problem in Marxist theory is precisely the existence of such a totality. Dietzgen *presupposes* it on the basis of cognitive processes which cannot conceive of the real except as relational. But that argument falls short of showing that the

51. *Philosophical Notebooks,* in *Collected Works,* 38: 253.

52. *Dialectical and Historical Materialism* (New York: International Publishers, 1940 [1972]), p. 11. See also Maurice Cornforth, *Materialism and the Dialectical Method,* p. 90.

53. Bertell Ollman, *Alienation,* p. 35.

54. Ibid., p. 38.

relations must be *internal* in the real "parts," unless one assumes idealistically that the relations of the mind *are* the relations of things. Engels and possibly even Marx made precisely such an assumption. How would the dialectic apply to nature as well as to history, except on the supposition that nature obeys the same laws as the human mind? The "materialist" reversal of the relation between nature and mind in no way eliminates the idealist identity of the two. On the contrary! That the mind follows dialectical laws in its relation to nature is in itself no idealist thesis: the notion of logical law is implied in that of mind (whether derived or original). But by conceiving those laws as existing in reality—*independently of the mind*—one moves not away from the monist identity, but closer to it.

If nature and mind are aspects of the same totality, the dialectic of history must inevitably entail a dialectic of nature and *vice versa*. Marx may not have been quite ready for this conclusion. But I see no consistent way of escaping it on Engels's principles. As Ollman has pointed out, the universal existence of internal relations leaves no other choice but to integrate the dialectic of history with a dialectic of nature. "If nature and society are internally related (Marx explicitly denies nature and history are 'two separate things'), an examination of any aspect of either involves one immediately with aspects of the other."[55] This interpretation correctly reflects Engels's thoughts, yet the assumption of a single homogeneous reality comprehending both mind and nature differs only in name from idealist monism. Materialist monism has the same roots as the idealist variety. To eliminate it, it is not sufficient to reverse the order and to replace a priori methods by empirical ones. Idealists often present their own method as fundamentally empirical.[56]

---

55. Ibid., p. 58. Also: "The same kind of response can be given to the question whether the dialectic is in the world or in people's minds thinking about the world. When the logical distinction between the two is rejected, a question which assumes it cannot be asked" (p. 269).

56. Thus Kojève characterizes Hegel's method in the *Phenomenology* as empirical and descriptive insofar as Hegel "looks at the real and describes what he sees,

Few thinkers have genuinely escaped the idealist interpretation of Marx's theory.[57] Among Western Marxists Louis Althusser spearheaded the drive against idealism. According to Althusser, Marx's presentation of his own dialectic as a mirror image ("right side up") of Hegel's fails to account for the novelty of his enterprise. For Marx's dialectic proceeds not by "cumulative internalization," as Hegel's Spirit does, but by "the accumulation of effective determinations (deriving from the superstructures and from special national and international circumstances) on the determination in the last instance by the economic."[58] Rather than being *internal* contradictions created by a single self-developing reality, Marx's contradictions are caused by the *external* collisions of the economic structure with determinations of the superstructure. They originate through *overdetermination.*[59] Althusser has correctly identified the theory of internal contradictions as idealist. The question arises, however, whether a "dialectic" of external contradictions can still claim to follow a

---

everything that he sees, and nothing but what he sees." *Introduction to the Reading of Hegel*, p. 176.

57. One of them is the Soviet philosopher T. S. Bakradze. In his study on *System and Method in Hegel's Philosophy*, he openly rejects the possibility of internal contradictions and, in general, of internal relations: "Only an idealist, specifically a Hegel, can speak of internal contradictions of concepts, of internal and immanent connections, about transitions from one into the other, because the immanent connections—the transition of one concept into another—are equivalent to the self-movement of the concepts." If ideas are secondary to reality, internal relations cannot be assumed to exist in reality, since such connections presuppose an *ideal* structure of the real. *Sistema i metod filosofii Gegelja* (Tbilisi, 1958), p. 438. Cf. the discussion of Bakradze's thought in Planty-Bonjour, *Categories of Dialectical Materialism*, pp. 53–70.

58. Louis Althusser, *For Marx*, trans. Ben Brewster (New York: Pantheon Books, 1969), p. 113.

59. Althusser's theory is not entirely new. Already Plekhanov had cautioned against a simplistic understanding of the economic determination, claiming rightly that Marx's theory of *interaction* between productive forces and social relations excludes the simple economic determinism of which he is so often accused (*Fundamental Problems of Marxism* [Moscow: Progress Publishers (1908), 1976], pp. 52–56). Karl Kautsky, in his classical study on the materialist concept of history, is even more explicit. "Let us not forget: only in the *final analysis* is the whole juridical, political, ideological complex to be regarded as a superstructure

predictable, logical pattern. On what basis can the innumerable external determinations acting on one another be said to establish a homogeneous, relatively simple structure of development with a clearly foreseeable outcome? A dialectical contradiction cannot simply be equated with social conflict: it consists of a historically *necessary* conflict that will result in an equally *necessary* "resolution."

If Althusser fails to answer the question, another structuralist, writing under his influence, has attempted to show the validity of a dialectic of external contradictions. Maurice Godelier, in an essay on "Structure and Contradiction in *Capital*,"[60] distinguishes the internal contradictions of an economic structure, such as the relation between capital and labor, from the contradiction between two different structures, such as the oppostion between the social conditions of production and the forces of production. The latter oppositon is external because the forces of production constitute "a reality completely distinct from the relations of production and irreducible to them." It is precisely because one does *not* imply the other that the opposition between the two becomes revolutionary. The second contradiction "does not contain within itself the set of conditions for its solution" and *therefore* results in violent conflict.[61]

Unfortunately, the text of *Capital* supports no such distinction between internal and external contradictions. For Marx, simple production and circulation lead directly to capitalist production and circulation and, eventually, to revolutionary conflict. The original opposition between use and exchange value *contains* all subsequent ones. It is true enough that the contradiction immanent in the commodity from the beginning only creates the *possi-*

---

upon an economic infrastructure. It does not necessarily apply to any individual phenomenon in history. Whether it be economic, ideological or other, in some relations it may function as infrastructure, in others as superstructure." *Die Materialistische Geschichtsauffassung* (Berlin, 1927), 1:837.

60. First published in *Les Temps Modernes* 246 (November 1966) and later translated in a collection, *Ideology in Social Science,* ed. Robin Blackburn (New York: Pantheon Books, 1972), pp. 334–68.

61. "Structure and Contradiction in Capital," *Ideology in Social Science,* p. 356.

bility of social conflicts, and that for this possibility to become actualized a number of conditions must be fulfilled which are not *given* with the existence of the commodity as such.[62] Yet those conditions, those circumstances, are not simply *extrinsic* to the internal contradiction. They follow from it *directly* and *necessarily*, though *not immediately. In and through its own development* capitalist production creates the conditions which convert the possible into the actual conflict.[63] The contradictions in Marx's theory cannot achieve what they are supposed to achieve without being internal. The structuralists can win the battle against idealism only by sacrificing the dialectic itself.

The problems created by the idealist heritage in Marx's dialectic increase with the law of the negation of negation. Simply stated, the second negation prevents the dialectical movement from coming to an end after the first conflict. It is responsible for the progressive nature, what Lenin termed "the spiral form," of the dialectic. In Hegel the second negation includes a positive aspect as well as a negative one, since it resolves the original conflict in a new synthesis. The first negation, the contradiction, is not fully understood until it is understood also as a *unity* of contraries. Hegel himself insisted on the twofold function of this

62. "The antithesis, use-value and value; the contradictions that private labor is bound to manifest itself as direct social labor, that a particularized concrete kind of labor has to pass for abstract human labor; the contradiction between the personification of objects and the representation of persons by things; all these antitheses and contradictions, which are immanent in commodities, assert themselves, and develop their modes of motion, in the antithetical phases of the metamorphosis of a commodity. These modes therefore imply the possibility, and no more than the possibility, of crises. The conversion of this mere possibility into a reality is the result of a long series of relations . . ." (*Werke* 23:128; *Cap.* 1:114). See also, *GR* 310, NIC 406.

63. Marx also distinguishes an external from an internal opposition. But one directly entails the other. "Commodities, first of all, enter into the process of exchange just as they are. The process then differentiates them into commodities and money, and thus produces *an external opposition corresponding to the internal opposition* inherent in them, as being at once use-values and values. Commodities as use-values now stand opposed to money as exchange-value. On the other hand, both opposing sides are commodities, unities of use-value and value" (*Werke* 23: 119; *Cap.* 1:104).

second negation when he envisioned the possibility of distinguishing four moments rather than three in the dialectical process.[64]

Yet Marx's dialectic differs from Hegel's on a crucial issue. While for Hegel the second negation completes the cycle and brings the dialectical movement to a temporary conclusion, Marx admits in principle no concluding synthesis, not even a temporary one. Conflicts are not resolved: they *intensify* until their combined effect explodes in a revolution. Nor is this a later interpretation of Marx's theory. Marx's reaction against Hegel's triadic cycles dates back to his student years in Berlin. From his fellow Young Hegelians he had learned to distrust the dialectical "synthesis" through which the German philosopher had brought the revolutionary power of his method to rest in a religious and political conservatism. Hegel's syntheses, according to his emancipated disciples, merely serve as stepping stones toward the final synthesis of the Prussian, Protestant state. They betray the dialectical principle which by its very nature must criticize and change the established reality. Marx soon repudiated the purely theoretical critique of the Young Hegelians: the real dialectic of history occurs not through speculation but through practice, and a practice negates not universally but selectively. Yet he never questioned the unending character of the dialectical negation. This creates serious problems with respect to the "spiral form" of the development resulting from the law of negation of negation. To the best of my knowledge, Marx applies the negation of negation only to social developments. In *Capital* 1 he uses it to explain the evolution of property. Capitalist production, which expropriates both the workers' products and their instru-

---

64. G. W. F. Hegel, *Wissenschaft der Logik* (Hamburg: Meiner), 2: 497. Comments in Eric Weil, "The Hegelian Dialectic," in *The Legacy of Hegel*, ed. J. O'Malley, K. W. Algozin, H. P. Kainz, and L. C. Rice, p. 58. Lenin understood this dual nature of the second negation. Quoting Hegel's statement about the dialectical negation negating only the immediate he comments: "Not empty negation, not futile negation, *not skeptical* negation, vacillation and doubt is characteristic and essential in dialectics . . . no, but negation as a moment of connection, as a moment of development, retaining the positive . . ." (*Philosophical Notebooks*, in *Collected Works* 38:226).

ments of production, will itself be expropriated in the inevitable socialization of the means of production.

> The capitalist mode of appropriation, the result of the capitalist mode of production, produces capitalist private property. This is the first negation of individual private property, as founded on the labor of the proprietor. But capitalist production begets, with the inexorability of a law of nature, its own negation. It is the negation of negation. This does not reestablish private property for the producer, but gives him individual property based on the acquistions of the capitalist era: i.e., on cooperation and the possession in common of the land and of the means of production. [*Werke* 23: 791; *Cap.* 1: 763]

We find other instances of the dialectical negation of negation, but always in social-economic developments.

Engels extended the law to all natural processes. In *Anti-Dühring* he applies it, with dubious success, to botany, geology, and mathematics as well as to history and anthropology. What does it mean that a grain of barley germinates, ceases to exist as a grain (negation) and becomes a plant which, in turn, produces new grain and dies (negation of negation) (*Werke* 20: 126; *Anti-Dühring*, p. 169)? Does Engels say anything more than that natural developments follow a cyclic pattern? Not only is this noninformative, but it is nondialectical, for in such a presentation the *distinctness* of the third moment from the first is lost.[65] Yet this distinctness is essential to a dialectic of social revolution. Not surprisingly, then, most contemporary Marxists have quietly abandoned Engels's scientific simplifications. Maurice Cornforth, for instance, denies that the law of negation of negation applies to all forms of development, even though he upholds the dialectical character of all development.

> The importance of this concept of negation of negation does not lie in its supposedly expressing the necessary pattern of all development. All development takes place through the working out of contradictions—that is a necessary universal law; but specific con-

---

65. Kautsky has pointed out other inadequacies in Engels's presentation, especially the obvious fact that the new life is not caused by the death of the old. Karl Kautsky, *Die materialistische Geschichtsauffassung* (Berlin: Dietz, 1927), 1:132.

tradictions do not necessarily work out in such a way that an earlier stage of development is repeated at a later stage—sometimes
that may happen and sometimes not, depending on the specific
character to the processes of development. Yet the repetition of an
earlier stage *is* a notable feature of some processes of development
and, moreover, to bring it about is often an important aim of
practice.[66]

Yet the real difficulty concerns the nature of the synthesis. A
mere negation resulting from a "contradictory" state of affairs
presents nothing really new *unless one assumes that the development
follows an upward direction.* But this "spiral" movement does not
follow from the negation of negation: it is *presupposed* by it. In
Hegel a self-realizing Spirit justifies this upward trend. But for
Marx progress must emerge from the contradictions themselves.
Thus the difficult question arises: how does Marx's second negation differ from the first or, for that matter, from any other? It is
hard to conceive of the negation of negation as resulting in a
positive state without introducing teleological considerations. A
dialectic consisting exclusively of a collision of different aspects
of a moving reality ("objective contradictions") provides no clue
whatever about the outcome of its contradictions. Even Lenin's
"apparent return to the old"[67] must remain wholly unsupported.

Ever since Engels, a number of Marx's interpreters have attempted to derive from Darwin's theory of evolution the kind of
directed movement with which the Absolute Spirit had provided
Hegel's dialectic. Dialectical philosophy, Engels writes, "reveals
the transitory character of everything and in everything; nothing can endure before it except the uninterrupted process of
becoming and of passing away, of endless ascending from the
lower to the higher. And dialectical philosophy itself is nothing
more than the mere reflection of this process in the thinking
brain" (*Werke* 21:261; *Sel. Works* 2: 363). Engels concedes that the
"natural science" on which this theory of dialectical progress

66. *Materialism and the Dialectical Method,* p. 117. Plekhanov also expresses
reservations about its universal application.

67. *Philosophical Notebooks,* in *Collected Works* 38:222. My critique is confirmed
by Wetter: "It is clear that a twofold negation by no means necessarily lands one
back at the starting point (even at a higher level)" (*Dialectical Materialism,* p. 364).

purports to be based also predicts a descending movement for this planet as a whole, leading to the eventual extinction of all life. But this long-range prediction of doom in no way dampens his optimism about the near future. "We still find ourselves a considerable distance from the turning point at which the historical course of society becomes one of descent." To us, rather, it would seem that from the start serious problems accompany the equation of historical progress with biological evolution. The Darwinian priority of "the fittest" holds no promise of constant progress or even of temporary improvement, for "fit" is any condition that is able to cope with present favorable and unfavorable forces. What survives will be more compatible with the prevailing conditions than what perishes, but nothing guarantees that it will possess a higher degree of *intrinsic* perfection. The "fittest" does not mean the best possible or even the "better," except in the one respect of being adequately equipped to deal with its environment. Nevertheless, Marxist philosophers usually regard a developing reality to be an upward-moving reality. Cornforth, whom earlier we found distinguishing processes that are truly progressive (negation of negation) from others that are not, denies that the distinction depends on any difference between "nature" and "spirit." In his view, a movement can have direction without any consciousness to direct it (the hypothesis of God being explicitly excluded). But then *what* determines some movements as progressive in contrast to others? Cornforth's answer blatantly begs the question: "If some processes have direction and others have not, this depends solely on the particular character of the processes themselves and of the conditions under which they happen."[68] We cannot speak of the direction of everything, he claims, "but only of the direction of the particular things in which we are interested such as the 'forward' movement from feudalism to capitalism to communism."[69] Clearly this is too arbitrary to merit discussion.

More to the point, Kautsky observes that each organism possesses its own structure for self-preservation and procreation,

68. Cornforth, *Materialism and the Dialectical Method*, p. 109.
69. Ibid., p. 110.

and may be considered more perfect as it is better equipped to cope with both. "It is impossible to say that this teleology and perfection increase in the course of development of a series of organisms, that the more highly developed ones, which are farthest removed from the forms of their ancestors, are better organized, more vital and more affirmative than the simple ones."[70] Precisely because of its anthropomorphic teleology, in which he detects the influence of Kant, Kautsky rejects any equation of Marxist dialectic with a Darwinian theory of evolution.

The Marxist attempt to retain Hegel's ascending movement has not succeeded in retaining a teleological direction without a spiritual mover. Some Marxists implicitly admit this and consider the law to be nothing more than the dialectical negation (understood in the Marxist sense of pure contradiction) brought to its ultimate conclusion. Others attempt to give it a separate status by distinguishing it as a particular species of the generic law of negation.[71] Most consistent was Stalin, who rejected the law of negation of negation altogether (replacing it by two others of his own making) for being either redundant or idealist. Once the negation is reduced to a simultaneous presence of "contrary" elements in reality, no resources remain from which "positive" meanings can be extracted. The dialectical movement then is reduced to a natural process of evolution extended to include social developments.[72]

70. Karl Kautsky, *Die materialistische Geschichtsauffassung,* p. 139.

71. Plekhanov thus describes the negation of negation: "Every phenomenon, developing to its conclusion, becomes transformed into its opposite; but as the new phenomenon, being opposite to the first, also is transformed in its turn into its own opposite, the third phase of the development bears a *formal resemblance to the first*" (*The Development of the Monist View of History,* trans. Andrew Rothstein [New York: International Publishers, 1972], p. 81). Of course, resemblance is not identity, yet Plekhanov's reservations about the triadic character of the dialectic indicates that he is in the dark as to how the second negation could essentially differ from the first. Lenin also places it at the end of the list in his "Elements of Dialectics" (*Notebooks, Collected Works,* 38:221), as if it were implied by the doctrine of the unity of opposites (cf. p. 223). On the questions which Soviet philosophers have begun to raise about the same point, see Guy Planty-Bonjour, *The Categories of Dialectical Materialism,* pp. 136–38.

72. Godelier also concludes that the negation of negation has lost its validity in

But if the third movement brings nothing new, has the dialectic not changed from triadic to dyadic? Most Marxists continue to pay lip service to the triadic form, but they often do so with little conviction. Plekhanov, while upholding the triadic schema against Mikhailovski, estimates that "it does not at all play in Hegel's work the part which is attributed to it by those who have no idea of his philosophy."[73] His judgment may be erroneous for Hegel, but it certainly applies to Marx. Lenin, in his early polemic with the same Mikhailovski, claims that attempts to prove the correctness of the triad are but a relic of Hegelianism: Engels does not even mention the triads in his method.[74]

If the second negation introduces no positive element into the dialectic, is the Marxist still justified in expecting a final synthesis, a positive and permanent state of society? Here the critique of orthodox Marxism by the Frankfurt School becomes particularly pertinent. How could all contradictions be resolved in a socialist society without bringing the dialectic to the same arbitrary closure which Marx and the Young Hegelians had denounced in Hegel?[75] Orthodox Marxists have not remained un-

---

a dialectic that is no longer propelled by a self-moving Spirit. Marx's dialectic must dispense with all internal teleology. It consists entirely in a conflict of incompatible but relatively independent structures. Unlike Stalin, Godelier does not appeal to some self-evident law of evolution according to which conflict must result in greater perfection. Yet he nevertheless assumes a progressive movement.

73. *Monist View of History,* p. 79.

74. *What the Friends of the People Are and How They Fight the Social Democrats,* in *Collected Works,* 1: 164. Some contemporary Soviet philosophers express similar reservations. T.A. Kazakevich and A.G. Abolentseva conclude their article on "Some Problems concerning the Law of the Negation of Negation": "Marxism by no means rejects the triad, but nor is it regarded as a universal master key which can be used to prove everything. As understood in dialectical materialism, the triad is above all expression of the path of double negation pursued by all natural and social phenomena as well as our knowledge, in the course of their development" (*Vestnik Leningradskogo Universiteta* 23 (1956): 76.

75. As Adorno wrote, "To negate a negation does not bring about its reversal; it proves rather that the negation is not negative enough. . . . This is the decisive break with Hegel. To use identity as a palliative for dialectical contradiction . . . is to ignore what the contradiction means." *Negative Dialectics,* trans. E. B. Ashton (New York: Seabury Press, 1973), p. 159.

aware of the problem and have conceded the continued existence of contradictions while at the same time rendering them harmless. Thus Lenin distinguished "antagonism" from "contradiction": the former would disappear, while the latter would remain and become the moving power in the development of the Communist society.[76] Stalin admitted the actual presence of genuine contradictions, such as the conflict between the peasant class and the proletariat, in the socialist society of the Soviet Union. Even permanent contradictions between relations of production and the productive forces of society he considered inevitable, since the development of production always lags behind the development of productive forces.[77] Yet Stalin did not regard those contradictions as "antagonistic," since economic planning prevents them from breaking out into open conflicts. Mao alone among the political leaders of communism fully accepted the consequences of a negative dialectic. He declared the existence of genuine contradictions between individuals and society to be "nothing strange" in a Communist society, and in 1957 he criticized Stalin for having treated internal contradictions, such as the oppositions between mass and leaders, as external antagonisms.[78]

The proliferation of scholastic distinctions between Communist and other oppositions suggests that Marxists have not been able to account satisfactorily for a "positive" synthesis in a dialectic of internal conflict. Nor is this surprising. The orthodox version of the negation of negation introduces an evolutionary pattern in what is in fact a dialectic of revolution. Since continuing revolution is the last thing an established society desires, orthodox Communists tend to halt the negation of negation as soon as the state has taken possession of the means of production. Such

76. V. I. Lenin, "Remarks on N. I. Bukharin's *Economics of the Transitional Period*" (May 1920), *Collected Works*.

77. "Economic Problems of Socialism in the U.S.S.R. (1952)," in *Current Soviet Policies*, ed. Leo Gruliow (New York: Praeger, 1953), p. 14.

78. Arthur A. Cohen, *The Communism of Mao Tse-Tung* (Chicago: University of Chicago Press, 1964), pp. 160–63. Already in his early work, *On Contradiction* (1937), in *Selected Readings* (Peking, 1971), Mao advances a theory of permanent contradiction.

an arbitrary suspension of the negative movement merely results in state capitalism.[79]

As the status of the negation of negation became more and more dubious, the law of transformation from quantity to quality gained in importance. Stalin and his followers who had dropped the former strongly emphasized the latter. The reason is not difficult to grasp. If the negation of negation was considered to be too idealist, some other principle had to be found to provide the dialectic with an ascending direction. More and more Marxists started looking for a theory that by purely empirical methods would educe intelligible patterns of development out of conflict and thus in some way justify the expectation of continuing progress. Neo-Darwinism particularly appealed to Marxist dialecticians because of having dislodged teleology from its last stronghold. The survival of the fittest alone sufficed, or so it was thought, to account for the emergence of ever more developed forms. At the same time, the theory of evolution so intimately combined conflict with movement that it might be regarded as the scientific counterpart of Hegelian dialectic. Already Marx and Engels had taken a lively interest in Darwin's theory. But they had rejected, as Hegel himself did, the concept of a *gradual* change from one species to another: dialectic progressed by sudden reversals. De Vries's discovery of genetic mutations dispelled the dialecticians' reservations.[80] Where once the negation of negation had been needed to secure the "upward turn" of the dialectic, henceforth the law of quantity and quality, interpreted in a Neo-Darwinian fashion, would suffice to give the dialectical movement a "progressive" direction. Hegel's principle asserted that purely quantitative increases eventually result

79. Raya Dunayevskaya, *Philosophy and Revolution* (New York: Delacorte, 1973), p. 54.

80. This is not to say, of course, that Marxism simply threw in its lot with Neo-Darwinianism. Lysenko's now discredited attempts to revive Lamarck's theory of the inheritance of acquired habits, officially accepted through most of the Stalin era, reminds us of the contrary. In Engels's unpublished papers, one passage criticizes Darwinism as a simplistic transposition of Hobbes's *Bellum omnium contra omnes* and bourgeois economic struggles to the development of nature, *Archiv K. Marxa i Engelsa* (Moscow), 2: 62.

in qualitative changes "and," Engels adds, *"vice versa."*[81] Marx applies the principle to the transition from precapitalist to capitalist possession of money and commodities.[82] Other instances are the transformation of value from use value to money and the transitions between the successive modes of cooperation that lead to capitalist production. Engels points out similar transitions in the fourth part of *Capital* 1 and universalizes the law so as to include the entire present flora and fauna.

Characteristically, Plekhanov and Lenin removed the law from the first place which it had held with Engels. The two Russians were anxious enough to provide social theory with a "scientific" foundation, but they considered change essentially subordinate to *conflict.* Both were primarily concerned with social conflict: one as a philosopher of revolution, the other as a practical revolutionary. In Hegel's dialectic they found, above all, a method for the understanding of social dynamics. Their interest in the positive sciences was entirely secondary. Yet, they felt, the dialectic would remain idealist unless it was integrated with the determinist laws of the material universe. As Z. A. Jordan has suggested, Plekhanov's reasons for adopting a cosmology of "leaps" was entirely political, and so were Lenin's reasons for following him in this respect.

> As long as Plekhanov considered the concurrence, sequence and concatenation of historical events alone, revolutions and upheavals were bound to remain what they actually are, namely, contin-

---

81. *Dialectics of Nature,* trans. C. Dutt, p. 26. Hegel's thesis that changes remain purely quantitative until they surpass the "measure" of an object, at which point a qualitative "leap" occurs, is found in *Wissenschaft der Logik,* pp. 343–46; *Science of Logic,* pp. 333–36. The *"vice-versa"* which has puzzled commentators is based on Hegel's words: "But we have seen that the alterations of being in general are not only the transition of one magnitude into another, but a transition from quality into quantity and *vice versa"* (*Logik,* 1: 383; *Science of Logic,* p. 370). Engels failed to justify it in his own interpretation.

82. "Here, as in natural science, is shown the correctness of the law discovered by Hegel (in his 'Logic'), that merely quantitative differences beyond a certain point pass into qualitative changes" (*Cap.* 1: 309). A footnote refers to the molecular theory of modern chemistry as developed by Laurent and Gerhardt. In a letter written to Engels on June 22, 1867, Marx also refers to the qualitative leap in a quantitative series.

gent and unforeseeable occurrences. Only the cosmological doctrine of leaps allowed him to establish the inevitability of political revolutions by some kind of cosmic decree and natural necessity.— The law of the interpenetration of opposites is "cosmologized" for the same reason: "A universe brimming over with strife, conflict and contradiction offers self-evident advantages for a social and political theory based on the concept of class antagonism and class struggle."[83]

Thus the two men who restored Hegel's dialectic to Marx's theory were, by a perverse paradox of fate, also responsible for its development toward a homogeneous materialist system.

Yet it took a different kind of mind to complete this development. Engels had first attempted to streamline Marxist dialectic into a "scientific" system. Yet he had been too close to Marx's original vision and had perhaps remained too imbued with the spirit of Hegel's philosophy to reduce the dialectic to a unified, scientific theory. Stalin came better prepared for the task of reducing the dialectic to a cosmic system. Unencumbered by Marx's "spirit" or by a thorough acquaintance with Hegel's thought and endowed with an orderly schoolmaster's mind, he felt but little empathy with the unpredictable novelty of a dialectic of freedom. If dialectical developments were "necessary," as Marx's theory claimed they were, there was no good reason to keep politics apart from a deterministic but fully dialectical cosmology. Hence Stalin uninhibitedly proceeded to homogenize history and nature. Significant for his attitude is that he restored the law of the transition from quantity to quality to the primary position it had held for Engels and from which Plekhanov (followed by Lenin) had removed it. To Stalin the qualitative leap constituted the essence of the evolutionary process of nature. Since he equated the increasing complexity of this process with *progress,* the dialectic would now apply to nature and society *in the same way.*[84] Thus Marx's dialectic was converted into an all-

83. Z. A. Jordan, *The Evolution of Dialectical Materialism,* p. 204.

84. "The dialectical method therefore [*i.e.,* on the basis of this law] holds that the process of development should be understood not as movement in a circle, not as a simple repetition of what has already occurred, but as an inward and upward movement, as a transition from an old, qualitative state, as a develop-

comprehensive theory of evolution of which the revolutionary praxis presents but a particular facet. Only with Stalin does the "monist view" of reality fully conquer Marxist thought. While in previous positions idealist considerations kept interfering with the professed materialism, Stalin at last attempted an entirely homogeneous description of reality. Yet what Marxist theory gained in coherence it lost in revolutionary power. By subjecting human initiative to the same necessity that rules the material world, Stalin diluted revolutionary action into dialectical determinism.

In retrospect we notice in the development of Marxist theory an increasing tendency to impose unity upon a dualist mode of thinking. This was mostly attempted by eliminating the "idealist" factor in favor of the "naturalist" one. If the attempts had ever completely succeeded (Stalin came close to success) the dialectic would have been converted into the unchanging law of a system of nature. But it is most doubtful whether such a "naturalist" dialectic could still fulfill the purpose for which Marx devised it—namely, to understand the social-economic development of history *in such a way* that we gain a *certain* knowledge of the future as well as of the *means* to hasten its coming. The dialectic then becomes a purely empirical, descriptive method. It must be allowed that such an interpretation had some antecedents in Marx himself. *The German Ideology* describes the historical method as follows: "Empirical observation must in each separate instance bring out empirically and without any mystification and speculation, the connections of the social and political structure with production" (*MEGA* 1[5]: 14; *Coll. Works* 5:35). Philosophy can merely sum up the general results arising from the actual developments. The dialectic is thereby reduced to a mere method of inquiry[85] or a mode of exposition applied to historical

---

ment from the simple to the complex, from the lower to the higher" (*Dialectical and Historical Materialism*, p. 9).

85. Engels's controversial reading is entirely consistent with that interpretation: "The process is a historical one, and if it is at the same time a dialectical process, this is not Marx's fault. . . . Marx does not dream of attempting to prove by this [the negation of negation] that the process was historically necessary. On the contrary: after he has proved from history that in fact the process has

and scientific data.[86] It allows no *certain* predictions about the future development of ongoing historical processes. Yet, clearly, Marx and his followers did make such predictions and made them on the basis of the dialectic itself. Dühring touched a sensitive spot when he wrote that Hegel's negation of negation must serve as midwife to deliver the future from the womb of the past.[87] Mikhailovski revived this objection when he questioned whence Marx derived the certainty of future "events" that allowed him to describe them in the present tense. Lenin, in his polemical *What the "Friends of the People" Are* (1894), ridicules the questioner but offers no answer.[88]

Marxists never accepted the reduction of the dialectic to an expository device or a mere method of inquiry and they vigorously denounced Edward Bernstein and all later revisionists who preferred to dump the cumbersome method. They rightly felt that only the dialectical method gave them their unshakable confidence in the outcome of the revolution. In a unique way, the dialectical method incorporates the negativity of man's social experience and, with it, the need for change, as an essential movement into the analysis itself. But its ability to do so also defines its limits, for change and negativity are exclusive charac-

---

partially already occurred, and partially must occur in the future, he then also characterizes it as a process which develops in accordance with a definite dialectical law. That is all" *(Werke* 20: 124–25; *Anti-Dühring*, p. 147).

86. A useless one at that, we might add. For the law of transformation from quantity into quality is so imprecise that one may well wonder what we could possible learn from it. "The proposition 'Nature proceeds in leaps' may be suggestive but has no specific content. Irrespective of whether we assert or deny it, it does not seem to entail any experiental implications or involve any difference capable of verification" (Z. A. Jordan, *The Evolution of Dialectical Materialism*, p. 202).

87. Eugene Dühring, *Kritische Geschichte der Nationalökonomie und des Sozialismus,* 3d ed. (1879), p. 486.

88. *Collected Works,* 1: 168–74, in a commentary on both Marx's famous text on the expropriation of the expropriators and Engels's defense of it against Dühring. One must keep in mind that this is a very early work and that Lenin later shifted his position with respect to Hegel and, consequently, with respect to Engels's reading of Marx. Mikhailovski, enjoyed the dubious honor of having been attacked during his lifetime by Marx (in a letter), Plekhanov *(The Monist View of History),* and Lenin.

teristics of the social experience. In the physical sciences the dialectical method, even when used only as a heuristic device, seriously risks distorting the research. A dialectical schema imposed upon a subject matter without intrinsic necessity will at best be useless, and at worst invite the scientist to abandon the specific principles of his discipline.

Though the dialectic constitutes the most formal part of Marx's theory, it most clearly discloses its underlying assumptions. Here, above all, the missing premise reveals more than the stated conclusion. Marx postulates the loss of an original sociocultural unity and the necessity of its eventual reintegration. This assumption which directs the dialectical process is not a logical principle. But neither is it a moral ideal. It consists, rather, in a historical condition that demands to be changed, not in the name of a moral imperative, but of an intrinsic social necessity. The entire problem of Marx's dialectic revolves around the nature of this assumed necessity. Is it based upon empirical observation? If so, the question returns whether historical evidence ever warrants absolute predictions. If the necessity follows from an a priori principle, we wonder whence it derives in a theory that lacks the dynamic teleology of Hegel's Spirit. Yet Marx's dialectic is clearly more than the heuristic device to which many commentators, Marxist and other, have frequently reduced it. Though the dialectic that underlies his critique of society mostly assumes its premises, it is precisely in doing so that it clearly reveals Marx's fundamental insight: a society divided within itself cannot survive and must, through its demise, lead to a new integration.

4
Economics as Sociocultural Activity

THE SOCIAL ASSUMPTION OF THE CLASSICAL ECONOMISTS

While the tendency in the modern age has been to emancipate itself from any other functions of the cultural process, Marx's theory aims at reintegrating economic activity with the overall process of socialization. For him that activity, from the elementary satisfaction of physical needs to the complexity of modern market operations, forms an integral part of man's sociocultural development. No stage is purely "natural." Primary needs may be physiological and the *means* to satisfy them technical, but the satisfying activity itself is intrinsically social. Human beings have always and everywhere gathered their food in common, built their shelters together, and taken their meals in company. Moreover, all economic activity begins with the cultural act of tool-making: "Only with the first product that is used for new production—even if it consists merely of a stone thrown at an animal in order to kill it—the real process of labor begins" (*MEGA* 2³: 87).

It is important to remember this while reading through an oeuvre the major part of which consists of economic analyses. Marx's insistence on scientific rigor in these analyses should not obscure the fundamental link he establishes between the nature of economic production and all other activities of the producing society. Economics for him forms part of the more comprehensive class of specifically human, sociocultural behavior. Rather than to physical anthropology, it belongs to the social sciences, the *Geisteswissenschaften*.

Of course, economics had been a "social" science from the beginning. Yet classical economists, while well aware of the social nature of economic value (defined by the amount of labor a *particular society* spends in manufacturing it), nevertheless tended to treat it as a "natural" rather than as a social attribute. For them the social quality emerges later, with the division of labor. As social structures grow more complex, the essentially "natural" (physiological and technical) satisfaction of needs comes to depend more and more upon an intricate system of social exchange. At the same time the production process itself, in their view, remains oriented toward the satisfaction of *particular* rather than social needs. With Locke, the classical British economists continued to assume the existence of a preestablished harmony between the common good and private interests. Both theories (the physiocratic as well as the classical) and the practice of liberal capitalism entrusted the realization of the common good to the unrestricted, universal pursuit of private interests. Society as such ceased to be an object of moral concern. Beyond the family and the immediate circle of acquaintances the social came to be circumscribed almost entirely by the economic.

Marx's own theory was, of course, diametrically opposed to such a view. But ever since he had read Engels's "Outline of Political Economy" (1844), he had known that an economic system, once established, cannot be simply dislodged by a better one. If production relations form the basis of the socialization process, then every existing system has a certain immanent necessity, reflected in its institutions and its theories, which protects it against assaults from without. Until its own internal conflicts have sapped its force, no revolutionary action or theory can replace it. Only because the capitalist system was nearing its natural end could new theories emerge and revolutionary action become effective in hastening its demise. Even after its death capitalism would leave behind a complex social structure and an advanced technology of production. Hence the most productive ideas for understanding the present and planning the future would be found not among utopian dreamers but among the theoreticians of the current system. So it was to the classical economists rather than to their social critics, such as Sismondi and his school, that Marx resolutely turned. He needed insight rather than sympathy of ideas.

However one judges Marx's relation to the classical tradition—as a logical conclusion or as a new beginning—there can be little doubt that he developed his own theory within the classical framework. Smith and Ricardo would have had no trouble understanding it and would, most likely, have regarded it as a controversy within their own school of thought. More consistently than the British economists Marx adopted the basic principle that all economic value is made up of labor. He ironed out its ambiguities, explained its apparent exceptions, and excised its unwanted accretions (such as the equation of value with price). But he also transformed the principle from within. What had been a purely technical device for determining cost, a criterion for measuring and homogenizing a qualitative variety of goods, Marx converted into *the* primary economic fact.[1] He drew the conclusion—one that Smith and Ricardo would have unhesitatingly repudiated—(that since labor is the sole source of economic value, any separation between the production of value and its appropriation is intrinsically contradictory. Above all, Marx showed the historical roots, and hence the relativity, of a system of exchange of which they had never questioned the permanent durability. To them, economic history essentially meant the preparation and development of capitalism—all the rest was relegated to prehistory. To Marx, capitalism presented one system of production among others, one not derived from any permanent concept of human nature but grown out of particular historical conditions and bound to develop, to wither, and to die along with those conditions. To define them and to forecast their impact upon the life of the system—that is what Marx saw as his task with respect to classical economy. Capitalist economy had reduced economic productivity to a fetishist pursuit of exchange value. Marx attacked this abstraction. But he did so on the basis of the very economic principles in which it was rooted. Not surprisingly, Marx's own theory, restricted as it is to economic production, shares some of the liabilities of the classical economic theory. We shall see how specifically his concept of

1. Cf. Claudio Napoleoni's preface to Marina Bianchi, *La teoria del valore dai classici a Marx* (Bari: Laterza, 1972), p. xii.

social praxis remains caught in the inter-individual relations of an economic structure conceived primarily as a "natural" appropriation of nature.

From a modern perspective, it is difficult to see the need for the classical concept of value, let alone to grasp its full significance. Fortunately, it is not my task to justify either one. A few remarks about its historical origins suffice. Since the end of the eighteenth century the labor theory of value had come to be accepted in some form or other by most prominent economists. But the concern with value goes back to the medieval Schoolmen who, much as Ricardo and Marx, regarded it as the reflection of man's productive activity in the produced object. In the sixteenth and seventeenth centuries a different, strictly mercantile view emerged, as value came to be identified with market price. The emphasis upon exchange was to remain, yet the identification with market price proved to be unsuitable for the new economic reality. By the end of the seventeenth century the search for a more internal, more subjective definition of value had begun. At first it settled upon a rather tentative, purely empirical connection between value and labor. Thus, John Locke wrote in his famous *Treatise* that "labor makes the far greatest part of the value of things"—a statement for which he was undeservedly acclaimed as the first classical economist. But in this early reference to labor as a source of value, exchange value was no more than a quality derived from use, while for the classical economists it was a whole new entity created by a different sort of labor.[2] Missing was the idea that abstract labor could produce abstract (i.e., exchange) value.

Above all, the concept of profit had not been adequately developed. Profit was thought to consist either in some kind of wages paid by the capitalist to himself for whatever supervisory function he exercised or, more cynically, in an undue exploitation of the buyer in the exchange transaction itself ("profit on alienation"). The idea that profit is made first and foremost in the production itself, so obvious to us, was virtually absent from

2. Ronald L. Meek, *Studies in the Labor Theory of Value,* 2d ed. (New York: Monthly Review Press, 1975), p. 22.

seventeenth-century thought. Yet this idea more than any other determined the classical labor theory of value. Since profit on capital could be earned on *any kind* of production, it came to be included in Adam Smith's triad of natural cost determinations: rent, profit, and wages. At this point, however, the question returns: why was the notion of value not dropped after the one of "natural price"—that is, cost price—had emerged?—why was the vague one still needed, when the more precise one was available?

Why indeed, since the classical economists themselves commonly identified value with natural price? Questions of this kind also troubled the young Marx, who at first rejected the classical concept of value. Ronald Meek is among the few who have tried to answer them, in his *Studies in the Labor Theory of Value.*

> To the economist of the early eighteenth century, interested mainly in the average prices of the relatively small group of goods produced on a capitalist basis and sold under competitive conditions, a cost of production theory of value might suffice, since the constituents of the "natural price" could plausibly be conceived as independent factors. But as the sphere of operation of capitalist commodity production extends, and the prices of more and more foods are revealed as being "subject to law," the constituents of the "natural price" can no longer legitimately be treated as independent determinants of the values of such goods, since they will themselves evidently be partly dependent upon their values.[3]

Slowly and almost reluctantly, Marx accepted the new idea that value consists entirely of labor.

THE CLASSICAL THEORY OF VALUE

In the Paris Manuscripts Marx hailed Adam Smith as the father of economic history who internalized, in human labor, the source of value which before had been buried under the gold-and-silver fetishism of mercantilist theory. But the principle that all value originates in the human subject also foretold the eventual restoration of control over the production to the producing

3. Ibid., p. 32.

subject. Surprisingly enough, at the time when he held these opinions Marx still refused to equate value with labor. Following Engels's "Outlines of a Critique of Political Economy," he considered "value" to be merely a confused and confusing expression for price. In his notes on James Mill (1844), he criticizes Ricardo and Mill for taking only the cost of production into account for the determination of value. Yet in another respect he already anticipates his later theory of value. The actual value, reflected in the market price, stand "in no necessary relationship" to the cost of production (*MEGA* 1^3: 530; *Coll. Works* 3: 211). Other elements than cost, such as competition, supply, and demand, also affect prices. Only when supply and demand balance each other does cost determine price, i.e., value. In *The Holy Family* he still objects to equating value simply with cost, but freely uses the term *value* for actual price: "Value is determined at the beginning in an apparently rational way, by the cost of production and its social usefulness. Later it turns out that value is determined quite fortuitously and does not bear any relation to either the cost of production or social usefulness" (*MEGA* 1^3: 203; *Coll. Works* 4: 32). In *The German Ideology* we notice a significant change. In one passage he bases the price upon the cost of production while in another he equates that cost with labor. A new insight is emerging: though prices fluctuate under the impact of supply and demand, those fluctuations clearly revolve around the axis of the production cost. In *The Poverty of Philosophy* Marx finally accepts Ricardo's principle of value.[4]

In the subsequent years Marx moved away from the classical theory with his distinction between value and price. The last struggle with Ricardo's theory that resulted in this distinction appears in the notes for the historical chapters of his projected opus on capitalist economy, in Engels's preface to *Capital* 2, announced as *Capital* 4 and finally published by Karl Kautsky under the title *Theories of Surplus Value*. Reporting in detail Marx's confrontation with classical economy, to which *Capital* often

4. On this development, see Ernest Mandel, *The Formation of the Economic Theory of Karl Marx* (New York: Monthly Review Press, 1971), p. 45. Also, Jerrold Seigel, *Marx's Fate: The Shape of a Life* (Princeton: Princeton University Press, 1978), chap. 10.

merely alludes, these notes are indispensable for understanding the development of the concept of value. The British economists had felt no need to justify a concept that so clearly determined the social dynamics of their age. With critical penetration, Marx exposes the historical assumptions of their view. Value does not emerge as a primary category before exchange has come to determine all economic activity. Until goods are produced *in order to* be sold, they may be useful or even indispensable and, in that sense, "valuable," but their economic status is not defined by their quality of being exchangeable for other objects or for the abstract symbol of all possible use objects. Only when the production of exchange commodities of indifferent use has become the sole objective of the economic process, does the concept of value begin to function. John Locke had equated economic value with productive labor, while the Mercantilists and Physiocrats had established exchange as a primary economic goal. Adam Smith united both elements in a coherent economic system which, because unlimited exchange had become an attainable economic goal, assumed *all* labor to be potentially productive. This, according to Marx, constitutes the most significant discovery in economic theory, yet one in which the eventual downfall of the system is implicit.[5]

Early in *The Wealth of Nations* Adam Smith presents his two well-known definitions of value. According to the first, the value of a commodity consists in the labor time needed to *produce* it. This definition, it should be repeated, does far more than restate what Locke had written in the *Treatise*. It constitutes a radical attempt to transcend the empirical level altogether. What matters here is no longer the *quality* (the observable element) of the work—whether it produces immediately consumable goods (as "productive labor" had meant to the Physiocrats), or whether it produces *new* products (it may contribute to the improvement of

5. "The problem of value and its determination is *the* problem of classical economy and it is its only problem, for it knows no other system than that of exchange. Hence the problem of exchange receives absolute significance for it and presents itself, at least implicitly, as a problem of the possibility of the economic in general." Michel Henry, *Marx: Une Philosophie de l'économie* (Paris: Gallimard, 1976), 2: 142.

an existing commodity)—but whether the work contributes to the production and is measurable in time. The definition formally expresses the highly socialized method of capitalist production. This is how Smith himself understood it, for his discussion of value directly follows from the principal insight of his erudite work: the unique significance of the division of labor in capitalist society. That a given quantity of labor can be exchanged for another (the essence of value in the classical theory) is due to a radical division and quantification of labor. How much labor a product embodies determines its place in the system of production.

Yet after this revolutionary beginning Smith changes his perspective from production to exchange, and value now becomes the labor time needed to *buy* a product. In principle this second definition need not conflict with the first, since the labor time that "commands" a certain product stands in a direct relation to the time required to produce it. But in the capitalist economy these two quantities, thought to be directly related, are by no means equal, for the exchange value of a product clearly exceeds the wages paid for producing it. It contains, besides the value for which wages were paid, an additional unpaid value. Labor time actually spent on production does not determine the price and since value, according to the second definition, consists in the price, the principle value = labor changes its meaning altogether. Nor is this change due to a mere inconsistency in Smith's presentation, but rather to a fundamental ambiguity in the capitalist economy itself, where labor is not merely the source of all value but an exchange product as well. From the capitalist's point of view, the *purpose* of the production process is not to exchange some commodities for others, but rather to sell more value than he has purchased. The second definition, then, describes a specific historical situation—the accumulation of capital—and presupposes a particular historical condition—the existence of wage labor. Wherever labor can be bought on the market like any other commodity and can be made to produce more than its cost, the question of how much labor has been embodied in a particular product matters less than how much new labor it commands. In the second definition, the generation of surplus value appears to be intrinsically connected with the production of value. The two definitions are not necessarily incompatible. As Ronald Meek puts it:

> According to his [Smith's] way of looking at it, a commodity acquired value because, *but not necessarily to the extent* that, it was a product of social labor. In order to find out how the extent of its value was regulated, Smith believed, one must first find out how its value ought properly to be *measured*. And the measure of its value, in Smith's opinion, could not be ascertained by looking at the conditions of its production.[6]

Indeed, that measure can be found only in the process of exchange. Here lies the origin of Smith's concept of the "natural price"—that is, the price determined by wages, rent, and average profit. At first sight this concept may seem entirely foreign to the value = labor principle. It consitutes, in fact, a supreme though unsuccessful attempt to save it. For it forces the unpredictable effects of supply and demand on market price within the iron rule of cost determined by labor time. Since competition drives the market price invariably back to the natural price in which living and stored-up labor play a determining role, the value of a product still consists in the labor invested. But there remains one basic problem: Smith has simply identified with labor what is in fact no more than a somewhat arbitrary *compensation* for it based upon the price of the laborer's means of subsistence. What determines the price of these means of subsistence? If Smith had answered this question, the second definition would have exposed the discrepancy between the value of a product according to the first definition—that is, the labor incorporated in it—and the price—that is, the "value" according to the second (the labor it commands). If the price sets the value, then inevitably the process of exchange itself becomes a source not only of labor (as Smith's first definition states) but also of value.

Ricardo perceived the ambiguity, if not the full inconsistency,

6. Meek, *Labor Theory of Value*, p. 63.

of Smith's second definition and eliminated it. The amount of labor a product can "command" in the market should not enter into a discussion of its value.

> If the award of the laborer were always in proportion to what he produced, the quantity of labor bestowed on a commodity, and the quantity of labor which that commodity would purchase would be equal, and either might accurately measure the variations of other things; but they are not equal, the first is under many circumstances an invariable standard, indicating correctly the variations of other things; the latter is subject to as many fluctuations as the commodities compared with it.[7]

The value of a product consists exclusively in the labor time it took *to produce it*. No "value" whatever is created in the exchange process. Thus with one stroke Ricardo cleared up all the obscurity surrounding Smith's concept of value. Unfortunately, he overlooked the more basic question which had been at the root of Smith's ambiguity: *why* can products be exchanged for a greater quantity of labor than they incorporate? The exchange between living labor and wages (which incorporate a certain amount of objectified labor) is by no means a discrepancy between equal values, as Ricardo assumes. Smith was far more conscious of the unique character of wage labor; and it is precisely in order to justify the fact that capital (i.e., dead labor) can purchase a greater quantity of labor than it returns in wages that he devised his second definition of value. By equating the value of labor itself with the wages the worker receives for it, Ricardo suppresses the idea of surplus value that had started emerging from his polemics with Smith. With him also the concept of natural price—that is, the cost of a product in capital and wages, plus an average profit—invalidates the primary notion of value. The cost price, he argues, represents the "real value" of a product, and whatever affects the cost affects the value. Having thus equated value with price, Ricardo has no choice but to identify the emerging notion of surplus value with profit. To be sure, price *reflects* value, but, Marx objects, the two may never be

7. David Ricardo, *Principles of Political Economy and Taxation* (1817) (London: Everyman's Library, 1929), p. 7.

equated. The transformation of value into price allows a wide margin for variation, since the price reflects not actual labor time but an average based upon the distribution of the total capital among the various branches of production (*Werke* 26²: 24–31; *TSV* 2: 30–37). Thus Ricardo has in fact added to Smith's confusion by raising to a primary principle (value = price) an error that Smith had committed only "after first abandoning his correct conception of value and substituting for it a view which is evoked by, and arises from the phenomena of competition" (*Werke* 26²: 233; *TSV* 2: 235).

Ricardo's equation of value with natural price is also responsible for his theory of rent, on the refutation of which Marx spent so much time and energy. According to Ricardo, rent is essentially relative. It represents the difference between a given field or mine and the least productive field or mine that can be profitably exploited only when the rent equals zero. The existence of an absolute rent—that is, a rent on *any* productive property regardless of its productivity—would mean that the products of mining industry and agriculture would yield a constant surplus (the amount of the rent) beyond the average profit that is a normal part of the cost price. Such an extra profit without extra labor would undermine the fundamental principle of classical economy, that the value of *all* products is determined entirely by the quantity of labor invested. Ricardo escapes this predicament by his thesis of differential rent: rent is excess profit yielded by products grown or mined in property more productive than the one in which *market price = cost price = 0*. Marx refutes the basic premise of this argument by showing how Ricardo has committed an illegitimate conversion of the resolution from value into cost price (i.e., wages and profits). Since value turns into cost, Ricardo assumes that whatever forms no part of the cost price (the rent) can be no part of the value.

His factual error rests upon the more fundamental but equally erroneous assumption that the value principle is universal rather than historical. Ricardo fails to take into account that precapitalist conditions of production, dating from an age in which landownership was the principal source of wealth, continue to exist side by side with the capitalist economy. Capitalism inherited a system of absolute rent that is incongruous with its own principle of value. Ricardo's lack of historical perspective leaves him no other way of justifying such an unorthodox source of "value" (actually, profit) for which no one had worked than attributing it to the greater profitability of some agricultural and mining capital than other agricultural and mining capital. The difficulty of the "excess" of agricultural and mining profits over average profits in industry vanishes as soon as we take into account the fact that "average profit" itself is established only in capitalist production (*Werke* 26^2: 389; *TSV* 387). The existence of absolute rent is a matter of historical fact, however uncomfortably it may sit with the capitalist theory of profit. Nor does it in any way threaten the principle of labor = value. For the fertility of nature does not constitute *value:* it merely creates the *conditions* for the constitution of value. The labor = value principle remains unaffected by the more or less profitable conditions in which the labor is performed. It does not postulate a fixed amount of profit for an identical quantity of labor, but rather an identical amount of value in one area for an equal amount of labor spent in another area.[8]

Ricardo's theory labors under yet another inconsistency—which again jeopardizes the notion of surplus value. He continues to uphold Smith's ambiguous distinction between fixed and circulating capital. To Smith, *fixed* capital (that is, instruments of production), in contrast to circulating capital (consisting in materials and wages), meant capital that is not totally transformed and consumed in one production cycle.[9] In this purely material distinction "fixed" refers to a property of the objects themselves. Instead of reshaping the distinction in accordance with the formal principle of value, Ricardo merely restricted circulating capital to the wages laid out in the production, since the transformation of wages is clearly of a different nature than that of primary materials. But this halfhearted attempt to surpass Smith's purely material distinction created a new problem, for those primary materials that are wholly con-

8. Marx has pointed this out with great clarity in the conclusion of his chapters on differential rent in *Capital* 3 (*Werke* 25: 755; *Cap.* 3: 746).

9. *The Wealth of Nations,* 2, chap. 1, cf. *Werke* 24: 198 ff.; *Cap.* 2: 197 ff.

sumed in each cycle belong neither in circulating nor in fixed capital. Marx therefore dropped Ricardo's inadequate compromise in favor of the formal distinction between *constant*—that is, not self-expanding—and *variable*—that is, self-expanding—capital. What matters in the production process is not which part of capital "circulates," but which part converts a given value into a self-expanding value. Only wages belong in the latter category, and they alone, therefore, constitute "variable" capital (*Werke* 24: 221; *Cap.* 2: 219). Ricardo's presentation conflicts with his own fundamental principle that labor alone constitutes value. Once again, Marx notes, only an inconsistency in Ricardo's elaboration of the value principle has held back the notion of surplus value (*Werke* 24: 226; *Cap.* 2: 223).

Marx pruned the labor theory of value of all its wild branches until it came to mean a single thing: the value of a product consists in the average amount of labor time that a given society spends on its production. Not the wages paid for the labor, nor the "natural" or the market price, but labor itself in the abstract form of average *labor time,* constitutes value in a capitalist economy. Marx thereby brought out the two principal features of the concept of value that had not clearly emerged in classical economy: its sociocultural quality and its subjective origin. The average time for producing a commodity (its value) depends entirely on the conditions (not only the technical, but, even more, the social ones prevailing in the producing society). Even more important is the principle, implicit in the classical theory, that value is determined by time, "the measure of life itself" (*MEGA* 2³: 46), and hence by a subjective norm. Inconsistently, the thorough objectification that rules the capitalist economy totally betrays this subjective quality of the producing act by submitting it to objective temporal quantification. It thereby reduces labor to a common denominator and enables it to enter the exchange market on the same basis as any other commodity. Instead of being treated as the source of all value, labor acquires an objective value coefficient of its own, subject to the market laws of supply and demand, regardless of the value which itself creates.

This economic objectivism became and remained the principal object of Marx's critique. Labor, the subjective source of all

value, is treated as an object of value. An economic system dominated by this inversion resists being integrated with the overall
socialization process. It constantly undermines the socializing
tendencies of all other activities. As we shall see, precisely this
point separates Marx's integral concept of economic activity as
part of a single process of socialization from the one prevailing
in capitalist practice and theory. To understand all its implications we must first consider the principle of surplus value which
directly follows from the conversion of labor into the source of
value. One inevitably entails the other.

Marx did not discover the notion of surplus value for which
he is commonly credited. Already in the preface to *Capital* 2
Engels denounced this mistaken attribution. "The existence of
that part of the value of products which we now call surplus-
value had been ascertained long before Marx. It had also been
stated with more or less precision what it consisted of, namely of
the product of the labor for which its appropriator had not
given any equivalent. But one did not get any further" (*Werke*
24: 23; *Cap.* 2: 15). Ricardo, for instance, held a theory of surplus value but never accepted the conclusion, inescapable by his
own theory, that this surplus value consists in surplus *labor*. Only
an anonymous pamphlet published in London in 1821 clearly
stated this: "Whatever may be due to the capitalist . . . he can
only receive the surplus labor of the laborer" (*Werke* 24: 19; *Cap.*
2: 11). At the crucial moment Smith and Ricardo failed to intro-
duce the notion of *surplus labor,* which alone could have justified
the emergence of a surplus value. It is with that notion that
Marx completed the value = labor theory.

One could safely claim, I think, that outside the strictly Marxist ambit no living economist accepts Marx's value theory. Joan
Robinson, an uncharacteristically sympathetic critic, expresses
the basic objection of many contemporary economists: "The
concept of value seems to me to be a remarkable example of how
a metaphysical notion can inspire original thought, though in
itself it is quite devoid of operational meaning."[10] This criticism
includes, of course, Marx's predecessors, the Physiocrats and the

10. Joan Robinson, *An Essay on Marxian Economics,* p. xi.

Classicists. Comparing their concerns with those of non-Marxist economists of our own time, we note a preoccupation with concepts and with what the Schoolmen would have called "essences" that is entirely absent in our contemporaries. The older approach always started with a search for the *source* of economic value. For the Physiocrats value originated in agricultural labor only—for Smith in "productive" labor, for Ricardo and Marx in all labor that contributes to the cycle of production and exchange. Rather than engaging in such speculative issues, modern economists prefer to concentrate on the *functioning* of the economic process. The relations and equations which at the beginning of this century took the place of definitions and concepts initiated a reform at least as radical as that of the "Luther of modern economy."

Marx prepared this trend by *intrinsically* connecting the various phases of the economic cycle (production-circulation-consumption-reproduction). Yet his theory remains embedded within the classical concepts. Even his principle that only labor creates value is, in the end, largely a matter of definition. No one can quarrel with the claim that raw materials possess no value by themselves or that capital without labor remains sterile. But most economists today would feel that to conclude from this that value equals labor is not very helpful for understanding the economic process, even though it may be consistent with one's definition of value. For contemporary economists a definition proves its usefulness only by its ability to clarify necessary economic functions. One such function consists in establishing prices. According to Marxian and classical theory, a price must be proportional to value—that is, to the amount of labor invested. But since the proportion of capital to labor varies with technical conditions in each branch of production, while competition tends to establish an equal rate of profit, prices do not uniformly reflect the total amount of labor invested in different products. Marx was aware of the problem and repeatedly referred to it in his controversies with Ricardo's school. But it renders the labor theory of value useless in determining the price in a free-market economy. Indeed, the theory fully applies only to a planned economy that rigorously excludes all competition. In an economic system that *imposes* its prices in strict accordance with labor, no other "factors of production"[11] are needed, since the value of the other factors is exclusively determined by the labor invested in them. But to the question of what enters into the pricing of a commodity on the open market, the value = labor theory offers no helpful answer.

But for Marx's purpose—understanding the nature of the capitalist process—it was essential to keep the concept of value independent from that of price. For the very fact that value which precedes price does not determine it, reveals much about the nature of capitalist production where labor power itself has become a market commodity that produces more than it costs. To draw attention to this discrepancy Marx had clearly to distinguish concepts which classical economy unquestioningly assumed. A simple comparison, then, of Marx's categories with the functional concepts of current economic theory misrepresents the nature of Marx's enterprise. His purpose was not to offer an alternative theory modeled after the classical one, but to criticize the very foundations of classical economy and to expose its inconsistency both in practice and in theory. Above all, he wanted to show what consequences would inevitably follow from this inconsistency. The value = labor principle cannot consistently define the relations between various functions of capitalist economy, for such an economy prevents it from operating consistently. In itself the claim that the principle works only in a rigorously directed labor economy constitutes no criticism, because from Marx's point of view the capitalist economy is indeed inconsistent.

Marx intended to reveal the internal conflicts of the capitalist economy and to prove how they would eventually destroy it. Yet to do so he did not have to show that the inconsistencies in the classical theory are logical flaws, but rather that they are unsuccessful theoretical attempts to justify the very real conflicts of a historically developed economic practice. All economic catego-

11. The expression appears in Joseph Schumpeter's *History of Economic Analysis* (New York: Oxford University Press, 1954), p. 559, which opposes its pluralism to the monolithic labor = value theory.

ries define a particular, historical position of production relations. Value itself, the central concept of the science of his time,
was by no means the "essential," universal category of production as such. This awareness of the historical character of value
distinguishes Marx from all his predecessors. Nothing could be
more mistaken, then, than to label him as a classical "value"
philosopher. Though he operated within the framework of
value theory, Marx was in fact the first to question that theory.
He did so by showing both its historical origin (thereby relativiz-
ing it) and the inconsistencies in the factors that had given birth
to it. We now turn to this historical critique of the capitalist
concept of value.

MARX'S CRITIQUE OF THE CONCEPT OF VALUE

For Marx, the concept of economic value symbolizes a particular
stage of economic production that is riddled with inner conflicts
and condemned to die of its own contradictions. He describes it
as "not only the most abstract . . . but also the most universal
form taken by the product in bourgeois production and thereby
giving it its special historical character" (*Werke* 23: 95; *Cap.* 1:
81). For Adam Smith and his followers, the creation of value was
an attribute of labor *as such*. Smith's position appears clearly in
his theory of reproduction of capital. Arguing from his thesis
that all newly created value can be resolved into profits, rents,
and wages, Smith concludes that the reproduction of capital
does not constitute a "fourth element" next to the others, but
exists only as part of them. Smith knew, of course, that the part
of the production that goes toward the restoration of the consumed capital should not be included in the annual revenue.[12]
For the modern reader, the question of whether production
must be resolved into three or four elements appears to be
mainly semantic and certainly void of practical significance: no
capitalist will ever fail to subtract the consumed portion of his
constant capital from his revenue. Yet Marx devoted hundreds

12. *The Wealth of Nations*, vol. 2, chap. 2. Cf. Marx's reference in *Capital* 2
(*Werke* 24: 364–65; *Cap.* 2: 364–65).

of pages to the interpretation of Smith's position. The reason for
his inordinate attention lies in its historical assumptions.

> Adam Smith identifies the production of commodities in general
> with capitalist commodity production; the means of production
> are to him from the outset "capital," labor is from the outset wage-
> labor. . . . In short, the various factors of the labor process—both
> objective and personal—appear from the first with the marks
> characteristic of the period of capitalist production. [*Werke* 24:
> 387–88; *Cap.* 2: 388]

An essential characteristic of one particular mode of production—that labor can be frozen and stored away from the worker
in order to be released at the appropriate time for the creation
of new value—appears most obviously in the reproduction process. Smith, for whom the creation of value is a natural and
hence universal characteristic of all labor, cannot properly cope
with the strange fact that labor, the sole source of value, under
certain conditions becomes alienated from the laborer. Smith
correctly describes the initial situation. Capitalist value consists
indeed of paid and unpaid labor, and hence all newly produced
value is *resolved* into wages and revenue (i.e., profit and rent).
But it does not follow that therefore wages and revenue are the
sole components of all value produced. They represent merely the
newly created value, not the *entire value* active in the production
process.

Similarly, a fallacy of conversion lies at the root of Ricardo's
uncritical acceptance of the production of surplus value as a
"natural" effect of labor. By converting the basic capitalist principle, value = labor, into labor = value, Ricardo, along with the
entire classical school, has made labor, the source of all value,
into a value itself. To avoid, then, the circular argument that the
"value" of labor consists in the amount of labor needed to produce it, Ricardo simply equates it with the wages paid for it.
Hence the value of a day's labor consists in the wages allowing
the worker to buy the products he needs to support himself and
his family. Such an equation leaves out of consideration the
length of the working day, the nature and intensity of the work,
the productivity of the worker. Above all, it fails to explain how

this particular value yields more value than the wages represent. "Ricardo never concerns himself about the origin of surplus value. He treats it as a thing inherent in the capitalist mode of production. . . . Whenever he discusses the productiveness of labor, he seeks in it, not the cause of surplus-value, but the cause that determines the magnitude of that value" (*Werke* 23: 539; *Cap.* 1: 515–16). This leads to the most important distinction in the critique of capitalist economy, the one between *labor* and *labor power*. Wages pay for *labor power*, not for *labor*. They provide the means of subsistence to the worker who produces value, but they do not pay for the value that labor produces. The value of wages definitely does not equal the labor performed for wages.

Far more is at stake than a logical error. The distinction between labor and labor power enable Marx to explain the paradox of classical economy: how within a system based upon the equality of values, less labor (as objectified in wages) can buy more living labor. The value paid for labor power is by no means equal to the *use* to which capital puts this labor power. The equation of labor with labor power functions as the prime mover of capitalist economy. Marx's critique returns to it again and again. In *Capital* he restricts the discussion to the logical issue, but the 1861–62 manuscript which continues the published part of the *Critique of Political Economy* shows the full philosophical consequences of treating labor power, "the force of the living subject" (*MEGA* 2³: 36), as a market commodity. Labor power, the subjective source of all exchange value, is a social reality that cannot be measured by so-called natural needs. That capitalist exchange reduces the cultural to the natural symptomatizes its dehumanizing tendencies.

> Since the measure of life itself is time as, for instance, weight is the measure of metals, the labor time required to support a worker during an average day would be the daily value of his labor power in order to enable it to reproduce one day into another or, what is the same here, in order to preserve it under identical conditions. These conditions, as we have pointed out, cannot be circumscribed by natural needs but only by those needs as historically defined in particular cultural conditions. [*MEGA* 2³: 46]

If economic exchange were to be ruled by the creative activity of the living subject, wage labor would disappear from the market. Use would cease to be subordinate to exchange value.

In the final analysis, then, the problem of capitalist economy consists in the opposition between a process of socialization ruled by man's culture-creating activity and a process of objectification dominated by the drive to produce a maximum quantity of exchange value and the need to reduce the value-creating force to a physical level of existence. By adopting labor time as its measure, it homogenizes it into quantified units of value; but it also reduces the subjective source of value itself to an objective commodity. It is not the identical quality of all labor that homogenizes values, but rather the commodity market that equalizes all human labor.

> When we bring the products of our labor into relation with each other as values, it is not because we see in these articles the material receptacles of homogeneous human labor. Quite the contrary; whenever, by an exchange, we equate as values our different products, by that very act, we also equate, as human labor, the different kinds of labor expended upon them. [*Werke* 23: 88; *Cap.* 1: 74]

To remedy this situation it is not sufficient to abolish wage labor, as long as one continues to measure labor by a single time unit. Marx attacked the Gotha Program for its proposal to grant each worker in the future exactly as much labor value as he himself had contributed. "Here [in the postcapitalist system of distribution] obviously the same principle prevails as that which regulates the exchange of commodities, as far as this exchange of equal value" (*Werke* 19: 20; *Critique of the Gotha Program* in *Sel. Works* 2: 23). Labor cannot be equalized. Not only does one kind of labor differ from another, but even when two workers perform identical tasks, one exerts himself more, or suffers more easily from fatigue, or requires more to support his family. Hence an equalizing "that recognizes no individual endowment or family circumstances is, in fact, a right of inequality." Such a policy may be necessary during the period immediately following the overthrow of the capitalist economy, but it cannot be the ideal of a society where labor is "not only a means of life, but life's prime want" (*Werke* 19: 21; *Sel. Works* 2: 24). Yet as long as the value standard prevails, the abstraction of value will require the further abstraction of labor.

Marx's critique of mathematical equality in social distribution, however brief, is crucial to understanding his attempt to reintegrate the sphere of economics with social life as a whole. In attacking the abstraction of economic value, he in fact denounces the independence of the economic sphere itself. His theory, accepted early on, that economic systems have an inherent necessity which cannot simply be "tampered with," by no means implies, as it did for the classical economists, that therefore these systems remain entirely beyond human reach. The particular error of capitalist society is precisely that it has allowed its system of economic production to follow its course independently of all other interests and concerns. Once this position has been adopted, no "reforms" will remedy its inherent defects. Marx's critique of the economic system *is* at the same time his critique of the society that has allowed its independence. The concept of productive activity that guides his *Critique of the Gotha Program* goes to the heart of Marx's conception of culture, more so than his occasional discussions of literature and the arts. A reunited society integrates all productive activity: none of it is allowed to descend to the low level of "merely making a living" and none, however speculative or artistic, remains detached from economic productivity.

It is from this broader social perspective that we must read Marx's controversial theory of the "contradictions" which, according to his argument, will eventually cause the collapse of the capitalist system. Of the several conflicting tendencies to which Marx refers in various places we shall consider only the three that appear in *Capital* 3. First and foremost, capitalism suffers from a fundamental conflict between the increasing socialization of productive methods and the persistence of an anarchical and haphazard system of private appropriation. The methods of production and even the structure of investment have moved ever further from the individual enterprises of liberal capitalism. The emergence of large stock companies, Marx predicted, would eventually abolish the last remnant of private initiative.

> The capital, which in itself rests on a social mode of production and presupposes a social concentration of means of production and labor power, is here directly endowed with the form of social capital (capital of directly associated individuals) as distinct from private capital, and its undertakings assume the form of social undertakings as distinct from private undertakings. It is the abolition of capital or private property within the framework of the capitalist production itself. [*Werke* 25: 452; *Cap.* 3: 436]

However, the distribution of this social production process continues to be directed by private interests without any regard for the needs of society or, for that matter, of the production process itself. Recent developments appear to confirm at least part of Marx's prognosis. Sectors of vital importance to the well-being of society and, it would seem, of the production process itself, such as public transportation, are neglected, while others, even when their products are proven to be harmful and of no direct benefit, continue to expand.[13] Want and plenty coexist in ever sharper contrast.

The inevitable trend toward socialization of private industry contains "a self-dissolving contradiction" insofar as the takeovers by gigantic stock companies inaugurate an expropriation process through which all means of production will eventually cease to be privately owned.

> Expropriation extends here from the direct producers to the smaller and the medium-sized capitalists themselves. It is the point of departure for the capitalist mode of production, its accomplishment is the goal of the production. In the last instance it aims at the expropriation of the means of production from all individuals. With the development of social production the means of production cease to be means of private production and products of private production, and can thereafter be only means of production in the hands of associated producers, i.e., the latter's social property much as they are their social products. However, this appropriation appears within the capitalist system in a contradictory form, as appropriation of social property by a few. [*Werke* 25: 455–56; *Cap.* 3: 439–40]

13. Cf. Ernest Mandel, *Marxist Economic Theory* (New York: Monthly Review Press, 1968), pp. 170–71.

Marx prophesies that the conflict between inevitable socialization and the goals of private profiteering leads to an ever greater neglect of the common good, and eventually to a violent revolt of the dispossessed.

Marx was not alone in attributing a self-destructive tendency to the capitalist system. Social critics of very different intellectual allegiances have equally noted the conflict between its founding principles and its internal dynamism. According to Jacques Ellul, the system has developed a technical automatism which it is no longer able to assimilate. The built-in drive toward profit prevents it from developing a mode of distribution able to absorb the abundance which its social technique of production generates. The cycles of overproduction and unemployment endanger the very functioning of the system. "The simple fact is that liberalism permitted the development of its executioner, exactly as in healthy tissue a constituent cell may proliferate and give rise to a fatal cancer."[14] The efficiency and rationality characteristic of a capitalist method of production conflict with its exclusive pursuit of profit. In an efficient economy, profit should be only *one* of the determining factors. Since the capitalist system can no more abandon the primacy of the profit motive which stimulates its operation than it can reduce the rational efficiency of its production methods, the system itself is bound to suffer major problems. With Marx, Ellul considers the principal threat to a capitalist economy the very method to which it owes its greatest triumphs. Yet for him communism itself appears as merely a more advanced phase of the same independent economic process, "an epiphenomenon of technical development, a phase of the painful marriage of man and technique."[15] Both systems will be overtaken by the technological process that brought them to prominence. The ownership of the means of production ceases to be a central issue once technical efficiency rather than the social system of distribution comes to determine the entire economy. Marx himself foresaw that technical progress (automation) would eventually create conditions in which

14. Jacques Ellul, *The Technological Society*, trans. John Wilkinson (New York, Alfred Knopf, 1964), p. 200.
15. Ibid., p. 290.

the value = labor theory on which his own theory rested would cease to be operative. We shall postpone the discussion of these complications.

But the second "contradiction" of capitalism indirectly hints at them. It results from the capitalist tendency to expand production by means of mechanization rather than labor, in order to increase the surplus value. But a decline in the proportion of labor to capital entails a proportionate reduction of the sole factor that produces surplus value. Marx has formulated this in his so-called law of the declining rate of profit. Since the life source of capitalist economy consists entirely in the surplus value it generates, capitalists constantly attempt to increase the rate of surplus labor and to reduce that of socially necessary labor (the amount of labor equivalent to the value of the wages). Yet to decrease the rate of wage labor is also to increase the organic composition of capital—that is, the proportion of capital to labor. Hence *by reducing labor time, capital also dries up its sources of surplus value.* "It presses to reduce labor time to a minimum, while it poses labor time, on the other side, as sole means and source of wealth" (*GR* 593; NIC 706). Thus the goal of the capitalist drive also marks the end of capitalist development and "causes its own dissolution" (*GR* 588; NIC 700).

We find this argument first in the *Grundrisse*. But Marx gives it more technical precision in the famous three chapters (13, 14, 15) of *Capital* 3 on the declining rate of profit. Here Marx ascribes the increase of the rate of constant capital with respect to variable capital to "a tendency towards absolute development of the productive forces, regardless of the value and surplus-value it contains, and regardless of the social conditions under which capitalist production takes place" (*Werke* 25: 259; *Cap.* 3: 249). Yet to the extent that capital increases the productivity of labor, it lowers the proportion of labor to capital, and even though a higher investment of capital may yield more profit, the profit *rate* declines. The growth of constant capital in relation to variable capital necessarily leads to a gradual fall of the general rate of profit, so long as the rate of surplus-value or the intensity of exploitation of labor by capital remains the same (*Werke* 25: 222; *Cap.* 3: 212). The tendency of a capitalist economy toward unlimited expansion, regardless of the yield of surplus value, conflicts with the tendency to preserve and increase its profit. "The contradiction of the capitalist mode of production . . . lies precisely in its tendency towards an absolute development of the productive forces, which continually come into conflict with the specific conditions of production in which capital moves, and alone can move" (*Werke* 25: 268; *Cap.* 3: 257). This contradiction would already have resulted in the collapse of capital "if it were not for counteracting tendencies, which have a continuous decentralizing effect alongside the centripetal one" (*Werke* 25: 256; *Cap.* 3: 246).

Unfortunately, Marx does not evaluate the nature and impact of those counteracting tendencies, and thus fails to provide his law with the precision needed for scientific prediction. Contrary to what is often claimed, he does take the rising productivity of mechanized labor into account. But, he assumes, the increase in surplus value thus obtained will be more than offset by the fact that less actual labor is employed, the sole source of surplus value. At least in *Capital* 3 this assumption remains wholly unproven. One passage in the *Grundrisse*, however, compares the additional value generated by the mechanization of labor with the loss of surplus value resulting from a decrease of living labor in the production.

Firstly: The increase in the productive force of living labor increases the *value* of capital . . . because it diminishes *necessary* labor, hence, in the same relation as it diminishes the former, it creates *surplus labor*, or, what amounts to the same thing, surplus value. . . . *Secondly:* The surplus value of capital does not increase as does the multiplier of the productive force, i.e., the amount to which the productive force increases; but by the surplus of the fraction of the living work day which originally represents necessary labor, in excess over this same fraction divided by the multiplier of the productive force. . . . *Thirdly:* The larger the surplus value of capital *before the increase of productive force*, the larger the amount of presupposed surplus labor or surplus value of capital; or, the smaller the fractional part of the working day which forms the equivalent of the worker, which expresses necessary labor, the smaller is the increase in surplus value which capital obtains from the increase of productive force. Its surplus value rises, but in an ever smaller relation to the development of the productive force. Thus the more developed capital already is, the more surplus labor it has created, the more terribly must it develop the productive force in order to realize itself in only small proportion, i.e., to add surplus value—because its barrier always remains the relation between the fractional part of the day which expresses *necessary labor*, and the entire working day.[*GR* 245–46; NIC 339–40]

The preceding argument results in a more restrictive conclusion than the "law" of the declining rate of profit. It states that it becomes ever more difficult to increase surplus value by means of mechanization as the actual labor time decreases, until at a certain point no more increase is possible. It has, of course, long been known that profits decline beyond a certain amount of capital investment. But Marx fails to answer the question of why a capitalist should want to expand his enterprise beyond the point where a higher capital investment no longer increases a profitable production.[16] To make his argument conclusive, Marx should have proven the *necessity* of unlimited expansion. The argument in *Capital* 3 undoubtedly assumes such an expansion, because Marx refers to the difficulty created by ever-increasing production in a limited consumer market. But neither here nor in the "crises" argument (our third "contradiction") does he prove this necessity.

Another counteracting tendency which Marx fails to take into account consists in the reduction or elimination of competition that follows the introduction of monopoly capitalism. If a small number of producers control the entire industry, they are in a comfortable position to raise prices whenever profits go down. Such interventions render the law inoperative in much of the modern economy.[17] Even more fundamentally, modern econo-

16. Cf. Joan Robinson, *An Essay on Marxian Economics,* pp. 37–38.
17. The impact of monopolistic capitalism upon the rate of profit decline has been competently argued in Paul Baran and Paul Sweezy, *Monopoly Capital* (New York: Monthly Review Press, 1966), pp. 78–82. They replace the "contradiction" of declining profit rate by the tendency of monopoly capital to produce more surplus value than consumption and investment outlets to absorb it (ibid., p. 113).

mists question Marx's assumption that the increase or decrease of living labor decisively determines the rate of profit. By all appearances this rate has remained relatively constant since his day, despite an unprecedented economic expansion, a continuing decline in actual labor time (through ever-growing mechanization), and an enormous increase in real wages. Does this not force us, Habermas wonders, to consider the work incorporated in rationalization as an *additional source of value*, though one that depends on productive labor of the first order (i.e., actual labor)?[18] Such an interpretation clearly conflicts with Marx's reading of the classical value = labor theory. Yet in a well-known passage of the *Grundrisse*, Marx himself projects economic conditions in which that theory will no longer unequivocally apply.

> To the degree that large industry develops, the creation of real wealth comes to depend less on labor time and on the amount of labor employed than on the power of the agencies set in motion during labor time, whose "powerful effectiveness" is itself in turn out of all proportion to the direct labor time spent on their production, but depends rather on the general state of science and on the progress of technology, or the application of this science to production. . . . As soon as labor in the direct form has ceased to be the great wellspring of wealth, labor time ceases and must cease to be its measure, and hence exchange value (must cease to be the measure) of use value. *The surplus labor of the mass* has ceased to be the condition for the development of general wealth. . . . The free development of individualities, and hence not the reduction of necessary labor time so as to posit surplus labor, but rather the general reduction of the necessary labor of society to a minimum, which then corresponds to the artistic, scientific etc. development of the individuals in the time set free, and with the means created, for all of them. [*GR* 492–93; NIC 705–06]

In contrast to the familiar succession of ever more severe crises through which the capitalist system grinds to permanent incapacitation, Marx here entertains the possibility of a gradual phasing out of a system that has rendered itself superfluous. In a purely technological society, labor ceases to be the principal

18. *Theory and Practice*, p. 228.

source of wealth and, concomitantly, exchange value loses its independent status. In this scenario of the future, change results not from the failure of capitalism but from its technological success. The "powerful effectiveness" of the technique is out of all proportion to the direct labor spent on production. Since the production of surplus value by means of surplus labor practically vanishes, revolutionary action loses its purpose. Marx did not pursue this line of thought.[19] If he had, it might have changed his entire political program.

Periodic crises due to overproduction or underconsumption create a third conflict in capitalist economy. Economic crises were, of course, well known to the classical economists, yet for the most part they rejected the idea of an absolute limit to consumption. Their general attitude is well expressed in "Say's law" (which in fact was first formulated by James Mill), according to which a society can always consume as much as it produces, since the value of all commodities combined equals the combined incomes of those who contributed to their production. Say and his followers admitted that overproduction might occur in some sectors. But it would automatically be compensated by an inadequate production elsewhere, and supply and demand would soon restore the balance. Marx attacks this principle in a number of passages, often without naming Say (for whom he felt nothing but contempt). He points out how it neglects the discrepancy in time and space between production and consumption. With even less justification it assumes that each producer is compensated according to his contribution and is thereby qualified to buy his share of the total productive output.[20] Against such uto-

---

19. Raya Dunayevskaya regards Marx's reliance on technology for the solution of social conflict as one of the reasons why he later abandoned the entire structure of *Grundrisse* and started anew in *Capital. Philosophy and Revolution*, p. 70.

20. Before Marx, the Swiss economist Sismondi had expressed concern about a limited consumption in an ever-expanding capitalist economy. "[All the modern economists] know perfectly well, that in a private fortune, the most important fact to consider is the income, and that by the income must be regulated consumption or expenditure, or the capital will be destroyed. But, as in the fortune of the public, the capital of one becomes the income of another, they have been perplexed to decide what was capital, and what income, and they have

pian expectations Marx emphasizes the severe restrictions which the creation of surplus value imposes upon the purchasing power of the producers. The consumer power of a bourgeois society "is determined neither by the absolute productive, nor by the absolute consumer power, but by the consumer power based on antagonistic conditions of distribution, which reduce the consumption of the bulk of society to a minimum varying within more or less narrow limits" (*Werke* 25: 254; *Cap.* 3: 244). If in some way labor would not be prevented from consuming the entire amount of value it produces, no accumulation of capital would ever take place.

Meanwhile, Marx himself did not always give its due weight to the enormous problem of adequate consumption in an economy which he assumed to be undeviatingly headed for continued accumulation of capital. In discussing enlarged accumulation in *Capital* 1, he simply assumes that the increased production can also be absorbed by the producing community. Even in *Capital* 2, where he compares the department of production with that of consumption, he never mentions the intrinsic limitations of the consumer market. His complex diagram of accumulation shows no awareness of the important distinction that he clearly stated in the quoted passage of *Capital* 3. Rosa Luxemburg has shown in detail how in his diagram Marx takes production and realization to be aspects of the same process that expands year after year, regardless of the limits set to consumption by the "antagonistic conditions of distribution."[21]

---

therefore found it more simple to leave the latter entirely out of their calculations. By neglecting a quality so essential to be determined, Say and Ricardo have arrived at the conclusion that consumption is an unlimited power, or at least having no limits but those of production while it is in fact limited by income" (*Nouveaux principes d'économie politique* (1827), 2d ed., vol. 1, p. xiii, trans. in M. Mignet, *Political Economy and the Philosophy of Government* [London, 1867], p. 120).

21. Rosa Luxemburg, *The Accumulation of Capital* (New York: Monthly Review Press, 1968), p. 367. Of course, confronted with an inconsistency of this scope, we do well to keep in mind that the so-called third section of *Capital* 2 consists of an incomplete set of notes of which Marx had informed Engels that it was "very much in need of revision." He first confronted the question of reproduction in the analyses of Smith's and Ricardo's systems that appear in the first volume of the *Theories of Surplus Value*. The argument bogs down from the start in Smith's

Remarkably enough, the same diagram that accommodates unlimited bourgeois consumption does not include trade with precapitalist societies. Of course, Marx was well aware of the need for a capitalist economy to conquer new markets, as the final chapter of *Capital* 1 on colonialism clearly shows. Yet the diagram of *Capital* 2 does not include them. Nor does his theory of economic crises which, as a result, remains defectively incomplete.

> A crisis could only be explained as the result of a disproportion in various branches of the economy, and as a result of a disproportion between the consumption of the capitalists and their accumulation. But as matters stand, the replacement of the capital invested in production depends largely upon the consuming power of the non-producing classes; while the consuming power of the workers is limited partly by the laws of wages, partly by the fact that they are used only as long as they can be profitably employed by the capitalist class. [*Werke* 25: 501; *Cap*. 3: 484]

Various interpretations have been given of Marx's theory of crisis, ranging from simple underconsumption due to lack of purchasing power (Luxemburg) to overproduction resulting from monetary effective demands (Mandel). But the ground of all real crises consists in what Marx, in a note found after his death, referred to as the conflict between the need to pay adequate wages in order to maintain purchasing power, and the tendency to keep wages down in order to create a maximum of surplus value (*Werke* 24: 318; *Cap*. 2: 316; also *Cap*. 3: 484).

Since Marx formulated his crisis theory, state governments appear to have acquired sufficient control over the productive forces at least to prevent them from following their course straight to disaster. Legislative assemblies now establish the general conditions of production and exchange, while the executive branch actively interferes to stimulate or slow down production whenever the economic conjuncture reaches the danger point.

---

murky reflections on the sources of the money supply for an expanded reproduction. After more than a hundred pages of mostly circular discussion, Marx gives up on Smith's problem. He returns to it in the second volume, but with no greater success.

We have ceased to consider economic developments processes beyond the reach of human intervention. Even the most dogmatic free-trader is not likely to repeat today what the president of the Board of Trade told the British House of Commons at the beginning of World War I: "No government action could overcome economic laws and any interference with those laws must end in disaster." Since World War II the state has become industrial society's principal employer and has thereby assumed the role of a supreme manager who, by means of tax policies, public works, and defense contracts, directs economic developments with a strong hand. This repolitization of the economy has in fact transformed the entire production system from within.

One cannot but wonder how Marx would have formulated his crisis theory if he had foreseen the present political control over the accumulation of capital and the growth of the market. Orthodox Marxists tend to answer that the new scenario makes no difference, since political measures can merely "postpone" the final crisis. But if they would do so indefinitely, they would nevertheless render Marx's argument purely hypothetical. More to the point, Habermas replies that political control can permanently circumvent an economic collapse, but that the unlimited economic growth, essential to capitalism, must result in serious ecological, anthropological, and international imbalances.[22] Such consequences would undoubtedly follow from an unbridled pursuit of exchange value. The question is, however, whether unlimited growth is truly essential to the capitalist system and whether a shift in emphasis from the production of exchange to use value would destroy the operational coherence of the capitalist system. Much here depends on the limits of the concept "capitalism." Why should uninhibited growth and the uncontrolled production of exchange value be more essential than so many other past characteristics which the current economic system has shed in the course of the last half-century? Can a system be called capitalist only as long as it unrestrictedly produces exchange value by means of surplus labor? By that

---

22. Jürgen Habermas, *Legitimation Crisis*, trans. Thomas McCarthy (Boston: Beacon Press, 1975), pp. 40–44.

definition "capitalism" has already ceased to exist. Our current economic system has little more in common with the earlier stages of capitalism than free exchange, wage labor, and a production system that is partly homogenized by time measurement.

The concepts that figure so prominently in the classical theories—value and especially its equation with labor—have all but vanished from today's textbooks in economics. The "capitalism" that Marx attacks refers to a complex nineteenth-century situation. Early "capitalism" certainly did not define itself by the exclusive pursuit of exchange value, or even by the equation of value with labor. Marx rightly objected to the lack of historical perspective among the classical theorists who treated economic categories as eternal concepts. Yet did Marx draw all the conclusions from his historical principle? Need a "capitalist" economy be linked to a value = labor theory? Did Marx himself not foresee the day when there would be no more proportion between "the powerful effectiveness" of future technology and the amount of labor employed in directing it? Have the emerging economic conditions which are rapidly turning this vision into a reality created a new economic species? The deemphasis of actual labor unquestioningly constitutes a drastic change in the functioning of our economic system. But, then, was the advent of industrial capitalism a lesser innovation? That capitalism will cease to exist in its present form is not an especially noteworthy fact. Whether we shall continue to refer to our economy as "capitalist" is a semantic question the answer to which depends on rather arbitrarily set terminological limits.

The preceding questions are not meant to deny the existence of internal conflicts in the economy of our day. The resolution of past tensions has created new ones. Our present concern is merely with the interpretation of Marx's "contradictions." Earlier I have shown that they are not logical contradictions. But neither are they purely economic in nature. The simple fact, obscured by nineteenth-century economic dogma, is that all significant economic changes have been achieved by deliberate, human intervention. The so-called economic conflicts result, in fact, from the simultaneous adoption of contrary principles.

Though economic systems have a logic of their own, they vary from physical and biological systems in that they are man-made. Economic trends result, in the final analysis, from human choices. Of course, contradictory and mutually exclusive trends, if left to follow their course, may well destroy the entire system within which they exist. But in man-made systems this remains a hypothetical argument, since the trends can be stopped or the system altered.

Yet objections such as the preceding are themselves based upon an abstraction. For economic systems are never purely economic: they are rooted in social structures. This means that even the most technical factor in the production process has a social origin and a social effect. It also means that in the end all major economic change involves social action. Marx's entire critique of classical economy is based on this insight. Yet to substantiate it he had to show that capitalist economics was by no means the universal, scientific system for which the classicists presented it, but a historical synthesis based on the social assumptions of a particular epoch. While acquitting himself of this task, Marx came to adopt the language of his antagonists and to discuss economic "contradictions" as if they had the same inevitability as incompatible chemical elements. Thus his discussion of capitalist economy all too often leave the impression that the system will destroy itself, as if its internal conflicts alone were sufficient to abolish it. But such a presentation of the economy as a closed system conceived after the model of physics and chemistry conflicts with Marx's fundamental thesis: the intrinsic connection between the economic and the social.

Neither Marx's social theory nor his revolutionary activity would make sense if he had not been convinced that social structures—including the "fundamental" relations of production—can be changed only by social action. Such action, of course, does not move in a vacuum, as utopians assume; it is solidly anchored in the life conditions of a society. Hence a bourgeois society can be changed only *within the conditions* created by its capitalist economy. But the developing economy is not the principal agent of change. Society itself is. In reading through the volumes of *Capital* the reader may feel too often that the projected changes are to result automatically from the existing economic conditions, as if capitalism would collapse by its own momentum and would, with equal necessity, give birth to a communist society. Such an economic determinism remains incompatible with Marx's basic thesis.[23] It also, of course, conflicts with historical fact. Not a single communist revolution has taken place in those economically advanced societies where the economic "contradictions" were most acute. All of them occurred in economically underdeveloped countries under the direct impact of social factors.[24] In no instance did the revolution follow directly from the economic conditions. The critical issue in the end is not so much the internal logic of the economic system as the *relation between the social and the economic spheres.* In presenting them as intimately united, Marx's theory is diametrically opposed to any economism. The critical question concerning Marx is how he conceived this union. Is the economic the condition of the social? Or does the social depend upon the economic in a unilateral, causal way? This is what we must now investigate.

THE ECONOMIC AND THE SOCIAL

Marx clearly perceived the intrinsically social nature of economic activity. Production is social even in its primitive forms.

> Individuals producing in society—hence socially determined individual production—is, of course, the point of departure. The individual and isolated hunter and fisherman, with whom Smith and Ricardo begin, belongs among the unimaginative conceits of the eighteenth-century Robinsonades.... The more deeply we go back into history, the more does the individual and hence also the producing individual, appear as dependent, as belonging to a

23. Ernst Bloch refers to it as the new "opium for the people" (*Das Prinzip Hoffnung,* p. 229).
24. Robert Tucker has shown how, with the major exception of the Cuban, all revolutions have been set off on the occasion of a world war, usually even without the existence of a so-called revolutionary situation. In some cases a national resistance movement staged a social coup (Yugoslavia, China, Vietnam, Albania); in others, a victorious country imposed a new social-economic system upon another through military intervention (Eastern Europe, Mongolia). Robert Tucker, *The Marxian Revolution* (New York: Norton, 1969), pp. 130–71.

greater whole: in a still quite natural way in the family and in the family expanded into the clan; then later in the various forms of communal society arising out of the antitheses and fusions of the clans. Only in the eighteenth century, in "civil society," do the various forms of social connectedness confront the individual as a mere means towards his private purposes, as external necessity. [*GR* 5–6; NIC 83–84]

Production is always "production at a definite stage of social development—production by social individuals" and always occurs in a cooperative complex (*GR* 6, 8; NIC 85, 86). This social view of production had directed Marx's theory from the beginning. Already in the Paris Manuscripts he described production as an essentially social exchange between man and nature.[25] In *The German Ideology* he defined the nature of the production through the form of social cooperation (*MEGA* 1[5]: 19; *Coll. Works* 5: 43). In his first analytic survey of the capitalist economy, "Wage Labor and Capital" (1849), Marx again emphasizes the social quality of the production process:

> While producing, men are not only in relation to nature. They produce only if they cooperate in some fashion and exchange their activities. In order to produce, they establish between themselves precisely determined contacts and relations: their contact with nature, that is production, takes place only within the framework of those social contacts and relations. [*Werke* 6: 403; *Sel. Works* 1: 89]

A cotton-spinning jenny is a machine for spinning cotton which becomes capital *only in certain relations:* "Torn from these relationships it is no more capital than gold in itself is money or sugar the price of sugar" (*Werke* 6: 407; *Sel. Works* 1: 89). Even labor power, the main source of production (*GR* 325; NIC 422), becomes a source of value only to the extent that labor is socially integrated. By itself labor is no more than "the manifestation of

25. "Just as society itself produces *man as man,* so is society produced by him. Activity and enjoyment, both in their content and in their mode of existence, are social: *social* activity and *social* enjoyment. The *human* aspect of nature exists only for *social* man. . . . Above all we must avoid postulating 'society' again as an abstraction vis-à-vis the individual. The individual *is the social being*" (*MEGA* 1[3]: 116; *Coll. Works* 3: 298).

a force of nature, human labor power" (*Werke* 19: 15; *Gotha Program* in *Sel. Works* 2: 18). In individual isolation labor power can create use, but not exchange value. The dependence of capitalist production on a specific social structure appears most obviously in the central concept of value. To consider a commodity a value is by definition to consider it under the aspect of crystallized social labor. "To stamp an object of utility as a value is just as much a social product as language" (*Werke* 23: 88; *Cap.* 1: 74. Also, *Werke* 16: 123; *Wages, Price and Profit* in *Sel. Works* 1: 418). What makes productive forces *economically* productive is not so much physical power as social organization. "Machinery is no more an economic category than the bullock that drags the plough. Machinery is merely a productive force. The modern workshop, which depends on the application of machinery, is a social production relation, an economic category" (*Werke* 4: 149; *Coll. Works* 6: 183).

Yet the social structure underlying the capitalist economy subordinates all other relations to efficient modes of cooperation in the production of material objects, reducing them to "material relations between persons and social relations between things" (*Werke* 23: 87; *Cap.* 1: 73). Labor must be shorn of all specific qualities in order to function as social labor in a capitalist economy. It must be reduced to an abstract form of production "in a given state of society under certain average conditions with a given social average intensity and an average skill of labor employed" (*Werke* 16: 125–26; *Sel. Works* 1: 420). Human labor thereby becomes a mere function of time. "Time is everything; man is nothing; he is, at the most, time's carcase. Quality no longer matters. Quantity alone decides everything" (*Werke* 4: 85; *Coll. Works* 6: 127). Differences in exertion or skill vanish in the abstractly egalitarian demands of a market that buys and sells units of labor time. All concrete features of precapitalist labor, both the social and the individual, must make room for the abstract purpose of creating exchangeable time value. Capitalist labor becomes social labor by means of a homogenizing quantification (*Werke* 13: 19; *Critique of Political Economy*, p. 32). Its social quality derives neither from the internal dynamics of labor nor from social planning, but solely from the external demands of economic exchange and from the division of labor it imposes.

As a general rule, articles of utility become commodities only because they are products of the labor of private individuals or
groups of individuals who carry on their work independently of
each other. The sum total of the labor of all those private individuals forms the aggregate labor of society. Since the producers do
not come into social contact with each other until they exchange
their products, the specific social character of each producer's labor does not show itself except in the act of exchange. In other
words, the labor of the individual asserts itself as a part of the
labor of society, only by means of the relations which the act of
exchange establishes directly between the producer and, individu-
ally, through them, between the producers. [*Werke* 23: 87; *Cap.* 1:
73]

The satisfaction of private needs and the pursuit of particular
interests does not result in a genuine "community of needs," as
the classical economists implied. True, exchange transactions in
which each arrives at his end by using the other as a means
create a reciprocity of self-interest and service of others, as Hegel had asserted in his theory of civil society. But, Marx replies
in the *Grundrisse*, "generality of self-seeking interests" generates
neither equality nor true freedom. The worker is *compelled* to
produce: his product does not benefit him directly, but only
after having passed through an exchange process over which he
exercises no control and in which only part of the produced
value returns to him. This, we may recall, is the very definition
of what Marx in his early writings had described as "alienation."

> The social character of activity as well as the social form of the
> product, and the share of individuals in production here appears
> as something alien and objective, confronting the individuals, not
> as their relation to one another, but as their subordination to rela-
> tions which subsist independently of them and which arise out of
> collisions between mutually different individuals. [*GR* 75; NIC
> 157]

To understand the full context of Marx's critique we must,
once again, consider the changes that took place in social structure during the eighteenth century, specifically the constitution
of the so-called civil society (*bürgerliche Gesellschaft*), a realm of
interindividual transactions relatively independent of the political sphere. Distinctions between the state and other forms of

society had, of course, existed long before. Grotius had distinguished *societas*—that is, a group of families loosely united and living together—from the union of free men juridically united to protect an order of mutual support. Pufendorf had added a moral dimension to this juridical order. In England the concept of an order of right independent of the king's sovereignty, first recognized in the Magna Charta, had crystallized around the right of property. With the upsurge of capitalism, the content of the "civil society" had become more and more exclusively economic, while its significance had come to exceed that of the state. In his essay on the *History of Civil Society* (1767) Adam Ferguson even claimed that the state had developed out of the need to organize property relations.

Ironically, it was the great continental admirer of British social philosophy who would first raise his voice against this conception. Rousseau never stopped praising Locke and his liberal followers while mounting an all-out attack upon the subordination of the public order to private interests. In his *Discourse on Inequality* he challenges the very basis of the current contract theory: that a relation based upon private interest can ever be truly social. All activity inspired by motives of economic profit disrupts social harmony. Once *social* inequality is accepted in principle, *natural* inequality turns into an instrument of social domination. This, according to Rousseau, occurs when private property is born. A "civil society" driven by cupidity and ambition can hardly improve man's original social status.

> Free and independent as men were before, they were now in consequence of a multiplicity of new wants, brought into subjection, as it were, to all nature, and particularly to one another; and each became in some degree a slave even in becoming the master of other men: if rich, they stood in need of the services of others; if poor, of their assistance; and even a middle position did not enable them to do without one another.[26]

What emerges is in fact "le plus horrible état de guerre"—the *bellum omnium contra omnes* of Hobbes's state of nature perpetu-

26. *The Social Contract and Discourses*, trans. G. D. H. Cole (London, New York: Everyman's Library, s.d.), p. 218.

ated after the political contract and sanctioned by law. The legality of this contract rests on "precarious and false titles," invented by the rich and the powerful to support their dominion over the poor. Rousseau's *Discourse* anticipates Marx's critique of politics as the legitimation of a ruling class: "The different forms of government owe their origin to the differing degrees of inequality which existed between individuals at the time of their institution."[27] Once they are in power, governments produce further inequality: "Political distinctions necessarily produce civil distinctions."[28] Whatever political order would emerge from this state of affairs was certainly not due to a preestablished harmony between private interests and social well-being. To be more than a state of nature confirmed by law, a society must first overcome the "natural" inclinations of its members. Our present societies for the most part still hold on to an inequality established in the natural state. In *Emile*, Rousseau, generally known as the rhapsodist of precivilized nature, does not hesitate to call good only those social institutions which best strip man of his nature. A person does not become truly civilized until he *relates* to others and thereby *relativizes* his individual existence.

Rousseau's warnings against the assumption of a natural harmony never gave pause to the economists of the following decades. Only one tested them against his own expertise and found them true. In his *Nouveaux principes d'économie politique* (1811), his countryman Simonde de Sismondi denounces the uninhibited rule of the economic in society: "All the modern economists, in fact, have allowed that the fortune of the public, being only the aggregation of private fortunes, has its origin, is augmented, distributed and destroyed by the same means as the fortune of each individual."[29] They confuse income with capital. For the state to let itself be guided by the exclusive pursuit of capital is to deprive a large part of its citizens of even the most common necessities of life—as the condition of England proves. "The mass of the nation here, no less than philosophers, seems to

27. Ibid., p. 230.
28. Ibid., p. 231.
29. *Nouveaux principes*, 2d ed. (1819), 1: xiii, trans. M. Mignet in *Political Economy and the Philosophy of Government* (London, 1847), p. 120.

forget that the increase of wealth is not the end in political economy, but its instrument in procuring the happiness of all. I sought for this happiness in every class and I could nowhere find it."[30] Yet neither Sismondi nor Rousseau come up with serious alternatives. Especially not Rousseau, who appears to have been totally obtuse regarding the realities of the economic process and who, in *Julie, ou la nouvelle Héloise,* proposes a return to a patriarchal, rural existence. Yet the same Rousseau never questioned the independent existence of a self-contained social sphere for the pursuit of private interests. Only the social theorist Carl Ludwig von Haller, who influenced (though mostly in a negative way) Hegel's *Philosophy of Right,* questioned the independence itself. The conservative von Haller attributed all evils of the French Revolution to the illegitimate transference of the Roman concept of *societas civilis* to the modern state. By means of this egalitarian concept, the revolutionaries had abolished all political rank and structure—and, simultaneously with them, all order.

Hegel agreed on the recent origin of an egalitarian sphere of "needs." Yet, with more confidence in the modern development, he ascribed the existence of such a sphere not to political naïveté, but to the emancipation of the state from its material basis. In the still economically undeveloped German *Länder,* the *societas civilis* had, until recently, remained united to the *res publica.* Even at the time of Hegel's writing the term "bürgerlich" had not yet acquired the more narrowly social-economic connotations of the English "civil society" or of the French adjective "bourgeois." Hence, in setting up the *bürgerliche Gesellschaft* as a separate sphere of private economic interaction, Hegel had to justify his innovation in reference to the only "society" his contemporaries recognized—the state. He therefore presented all social relations established through the pursuit of private ends as intrinsically connected with the sphere in which citizens explicitly assert that the attainment of the common good is the ultimate purpose of society: "Individuals in their capacity as burghers in this State are private persons whose end is their own

30. Sismondi, *Nouveaux principes,* trans. Mignet, p. 114.

interest. The end is *mediated* through the universal which thus *appears* as a *means* to its realization."[31] The state constitutes the substance and truth of right and civil society, which remain essentially subordinate to its ideal purpose.

This was the very thesis which Marx attacked in his first major writing after the doctoral dissertation, the unfinished *Critique of Hegel's Philosophy of the State* (1842–43) (*MEGA* 1¹: 401–553; *Coll. Works* 3: 3–129). In contrast to Hegel's lofty political theory, the state, according to Marx's *Critique,* functions merely as the mask of the common good that at once hides and legitimates the strictly private interests of economically powerful individuals and groups. Hegel's *Philosophy of Right* had idealized this social mirage of the asocial civil society by absolutizing the historical separation between a real yet private economic sphere and an illusory social-political one. But the state is more than a harmless illusion. Having no longer a content of its own, it is forced to draw its substance from the sphere which alone contains whatever social reality there is—civil society. The state then officially sanctions the private interests of that society and dignifies them with a legal status. Modern society has reversed the situation of the Greek *polis* and the Roman Republic, where the *res publica* gave content to the private lives of its citizens (*MEGA* 1¹: 438; *Coll. Works* 3: 32). Hegel's description reflects the fundamental dualism of society in the modern age: social on the ideal level of the state, individualist on the real level of civil society. One is the spiritual realm of history; the other the physical world of necessity. As a spiritual being, man defines himself through free relations with others; as a natural being, through a necessary interaction in the appropriation of nature. Only a bond of logic unites the two.[32] Marx rejected this dualistic interpretation of society both in fact and in principle. The division of society into two levels is more apparent than real. Even less can it claim an ideal legitimacy. A society such as the Greek *polis* genuinely uni-

31. *Grundlinien der Philosophie des Rechts,* para. 187. *Hegel's Philosophy of Right,* trans. T. M. Knox (New York: Oxford University Press, 1967), p. 124.

32. Cf. Umberto Cerroni, *Società civile e stato politico* (Bari: DeDonato, 1973), pp. 51–60. Also, the valuable introduction to Joseph O'Malley's translation of Marx's *Critique of Hegel's Philosophy of Right* (New York: Cambridge University Press, 1970).

fies private and public interests, while the present one merely covers its contradictory reality with an ideal appearance of political unity. In his *Philosophy of Right* Hegel had given meaning to a new historical experience. He had thematized the intensive social exchange that he saw emerging at the end of the eighteenth century. It was a largely nonpolitical, supranational exchange. Yet, in Germany at least, it had received little official recognition. It is a credit to Hegel's historical insight that he immediately detected the independent status and different orientation of this new "society." Yet to be part of the only officially recognized social structure, it had to remain fundamentally subordinate to the state. Such an integration was consonant with Hegel's early political ideal of the Greek *polis*, which he had adapted but never abandoned. But no form of modern society could ever develop into one that had the common good itself as object, least of all the purely economic civil society. At best, economic activity could serve as a first step toward genuine, social living. In the classical tradition the economic stood at the opposite end of the political sphere, and Hannah Arendt has rightly pointed out that the term *political economy* would have had no meaning for the ancients, since economics dealt with the strictly private business of running one's own estate *(oikos)*, while politics was concerned with the affairs of the state *(polis)*. Hegel continued to recognize that distinction, despite the increasing difficulties he experienced in squaring it with the reality of modern life. In order to integrate civil society with the realm of the common good, he had to give it a legal and corporate underpinning.

> The society would not be civil if it were not juridically, ethically, and politically ordered and coordinated. The notion which Hegel mentions here with regard to the exercise of law is at the same time the notion of civil society itself. In Hegel it preserves—beyond the new, now constitutive and private juridical element—yet the ancient structures of the ethical and the political, even if they are reduced to the police and restricted within the corporations.[33]

33. Manfred Riedel, "Der Begriff der 'Bürgerlichen Gesellschaft' und das Problem seines geschichtlichen Ursprungs," in *Studien zu Hegels Rechtsphilosophie* (Frankfurt: SuhrKamp, 1969), p. 160. My translation.

Marx wrote out of a very different experience. By the middle of the nineteenth century it had become quite clear, even in Germany, that political power was no longer the determining factor of society. Private interests played an increasingly decisive role and the state itself had come to depend on them. For all its rhetorical claims to restore the unity and harmony of the Roman Republic, the French Revolution had succeeded in creating political equality only by ignoring existing social oppositions. The political emancipation had merely given them free rein. Von Haller was right: with equality came the loss of political order and structure. The hierarchical vacuum left by the abolition of the political structures of the ancien régime had immediately been filled by an economic order that used political power for its own ends. Marx had first observed the reality of the new politics when, as a young reporter, he covered the debates on the punishment for wood theft in the Prussian legislative assembly. By draconian laws, including capital punishment, the Junkers used the law to protect their own landed property. This abuse of political institutions for private gain alerted Marx to the real source of power. But he would not grasp its full significance until, some two years later, he started studying the British economists.

In the British writings all pretense of pursuing the common good for its own sake had been abandoned. Smith and his followers conceived of society according to a model devised for satisfying "natural" needs. It is not objective reason that forms the basis of society, as Hegel thought, but the rationalization of subjective desire. What distinguishes man from the animal and enables him to build a society is "a certain propensity in human nature . . . the propensity to truck, barter, and exchange one thing for another."[34] Society itself consists of the interindividual relations created by these economic transactions. "Every man lives by exchanging, or becomes in some measure a merchant and the society itself grows to be what is properly a commercial society."[35] The self-interest upon which this system is based is all

---

34. Adam Smith, *An Inquiry in the Wealth of Nations*, bk. 2, chap. 1.
35. Ibid., 1:4.

to the good, because in it "nature" provides man with an innate and infallible guide toward private and public well-being. Virtue itself follows the course of self-interest. Hence there remains no reason for separating economic activity from the "ethical substance," as Hegel had still done in his theory of the state: ethics and self-interest function in perfect harmony. Smith's rule provides welcome moral support to a society of hard-driving commercial entrepreneurs: "In the middling and inferior stations of life, the road to virtue and that to fortune, to such fortune, at least as men in such stations can reasonably expect to acquire, are, happily, in most cases very nearly the same."[36]

Smith's ethical principles, hardly different from those of the Utilitarians whom he fought all his life, consist in a mild hedonism tempered by a psychology of delayed satisfaction. Yet this worldly wisdom is inspired by an almost supernaturally optimistic belief in the course of nature as a guide to ultimate personal and social success. By means of free competition, the invisible hand of an unknown Providence distills society's well-being out of the selfish behavior of its members. Smith overcomes the traditional distinction between a state of nature and a social state. While rationally attending to the satisfaction of their natural needs, men attain at the same time the highest social objectives. The juridical structure of society simply supports the economic process. Aside from its most important task, the protection and legislation of property, it defends the system against external threats, it regulates trade and money supply, it opens up new markets and new resources which individuals, left to themselves, might not be able to explore. In thus relegating the political realm to a purely subsidiary function, Smith and his followers completed a century-old development in social theory from rationality to functionality. The functional view controlled economic life, both in theory and in practice, all through the nineteenth century, and to a great extent continues to do so today.[37]

36. *A Theory of Moral Sentiments* in *Works*, ed. S. Stewart (London, 1811–12, [1963]), 1: 101.

37. "National economy operates with a reduced anthropology that regards man as an egocentric individual whose existence is not ordered by reason, but

With respect to the social assumptions of the British economists, Marx adopted the same complex attitude with which he
confronted their economic theories. He fully accepted them as
expressing the reality of their time, but a reality which, far from
being universal, as Smith thought, results from specific historical
conditions that will eventually also cause it to perish. Smith and
his followers correctly understood that the power of modern
society, including the political power, rests on an economic basis.
Civil society does not simply exist next to the state, as Hegel
presented it; the economic production determines the entire
social quality of life. Yet this is neither a "natural" condition, nor
a desirable one: its unprecedented, exclusive orientation toward
the satisfaction of particular needs prevents the present social-
economic reality from constituting a genuinely social order.

A CRITICAL CONCLUSION

Harking back to an older tradition, Marx, from his earliest writings on, sought to establish a society that would reintegrate individual needs with social concerns. To reunite the economic with
the social was, he announced in the tenth thesis on Feuerbach,
the object of his "new materialism" (*MEGA* 1^5: 534; *Coll. Works* 5:
5). Marx distinguishes *immediate* or *physical* relations from *mediate*
or *species* relations. The former are directly determined by physical needs or drives, such as hunger, thirst, sexual desire, while
the latter, on the basis of physical objects, relate persons *to one
another*. All economic transactions other than the simplest forms
of exchange in a primitive society, constitute *mediate* or *species*
relations. Instead of directly connecting objects with physical
needs, the exchange process mediates them first through the

---

receives its coordination from the impulses of instinctive nature. . . . This abandoning of reason lowers man to the status of a 'natural' being—a fact that since
Bacon has been celebrated as progress, because it is connected with the hope that
by conforming to the motions of nature we shall control it and thus attain full
autonomy. National economy even though it deals with problems of behavior
has been restricted to an epistemological position modeled on the positive sciences" (Lothar Kramm, *Die politische Wissenschaft der bürgerlichen Gesellschaft*
[Berlin: Duncker & Humblot, 1975], p. 126 [my translation]).

abstract generality of exchange value "in which all individuality and peculiarity are negated and extinguished" (*GR* 75; NIC 157). In the capitalist system this exchange value has reached a state of independence that allows it to connect commodities with one another, while bypassing the social totality (the herd, the city, the state) that in earlier social systems mediated the economic relations among individuals (*GR* 763; NIC 881–82).[38] Social relations, then, differ essentially from instinctive cooperation such as we find in gregarious animals. In fact, they are so far from being natural that many individuals, though physically belonging to the group, are excluded from a positive relation to its mediating totality—for example, slaves in the ancient city-state, serfs and persons of low birth in the feudal community, and proletarians in the bourgeois society.

As early as the Paris Manuscripts, Marx had claimed that in his productive activity man "treats himself as the actual, living species, because he treats himself as a *universal* and therefore a free being" (*MEGA* 1³: 87; *Coll. Works* 3: 275). Man is the only animal that views the species as its *own* being and produces accordingly. Marx had taken the concept of *species*-being from Feuerbach, for whom it had the abstract, ideal meaning of a being that in its individual existence remains intrinsically related to its biological species. Yet Marx gave the concept a less biological interpretation. In August 1844 he wrote to Feuerbach: "The unity of man with man, which is based on the real differences between men, the concept of the human species brought down from the heaven of abstraction to the real earth, what is this but the concept of *society*!" (*Werke* 27: 425; *Coll. Works* 3:354). In society human beings consciously express the communal being that the species represents biologically.

In his later writings Marx defines this social relation in a more concrete way. Thus in the *Grundrisse* he develops it as an interconnection of needs:

> [Individuals] are not indifferent to one another, so that individual
> B, as objectified in the commodity, is a need of individual A, and

38. The significance of this social totality in Marx's thought has been demonstrated by Anthony Cuschieri in a doctoral dissertation, "The Philosophical Foundations of Marx's Social Philosophy" (McMaster University, 1979).

vice versa; so that they stand not only in an equal, but also in a social, relation to one another. This is not all. The fact that this need on the part of one can be satisfied by the product of the other, and that each confronts the other as owner of the object of the other's need, this proves that each of them reaches beyond his own particular need etc. as a *human being,* and that they relate to one another as human beings, that their common species-being [*Gattungswesen*] is acknowledged by all. [*GR* 154; NIC 263]

Increasingly Marx emphasized the historical differences in the individual's relation to his social totality. In an unfinished draft for an introduction to *Critique of Political Economy* (later published as the beginning of *Grundrisse*) he shows how, the further we move into the past, the more the individual experiences himself as part of a greater totality. Not until the emergence of the eighteenth-century "civil society" does social connectedness appear as mere means toward the attainment of individual goals. Paradoxically, "the epoch which produces this standpoint, that of the isolated individual, is also that of the hitherto most developed (from this standpoint, general) social relations" (*GR* 6; NIC 84).

Such a view reversed the traditional hierarchy of social and private interests. The period which preceded the rise of capitalism had integrated all private activity with the attainment of a universal good.

Economics is still a branch of ethics. The activity and interests of the individual are subordinated and made to conform to the end of "common good." The social order is seen as a well-articulated "organism" whose parts contribute, in different ways, to the common goal. All human activities are treated as part of a single system, the nature of which is determined by the spiritual duty of humanity.[39]

Whereas the social had traditionally ruled private interest, including the right of property, from the eighteenth century on, first in England and Holland, then in France, and gradually all over western Europe, private interest came to dominate. The

---

39. Lucio Colletti, *From Rousseau to Lenin* (New York: Monthly Review Press, 1972), p. 201.

pursuit of personal gain which hitherto had been tolerated mainly within the limits of a feudal or national society (even during the Mercantilist epoch), emancipated itself from all social restrictions. It now was thought to pave the shortest road to general enrichment and universal happiness. Even the vices of self-interest would turn into social virtues, Mandeville had cynically maintained. Adam Smith softened the expression—the exclusive pursuit of private interest is not always "vicious"—but did not challenge the priority of private interest. Nor could he have challenged it, as long as he continued to accept that the primary function of the state consists in the unconditional protection of individual rights—life, liberty, and property. Foremost among them was the right to acquire property. It made economic activity self-sufficient independently of its contribution to the common good. Since the successful individual clearly benefited from his economic transactions, it was assumed that society as a whole could not help but reap equal benefits from a universal pursuit of private interests. The relation between individual and society was conceived in technical terms, as a well-oiled mechanism that performed best when least tampered with. The new state of affairs has been expressed with classical precision in R. H. Tawney's *The Acquisitive Society:*

> Modern societies aim at protecting economic rights, while leaving economic functions, except in moments of abnormal emergency, to fulfill themselves. The motive which gives color and quality to their public institutions, to their policy and political thought, is not the attempt to secure the fulfillment of tasks undertaken for the public service, but to increase the opportunities open to individuals of attaining the objects which they conceive to be advantageous to themselves. If asked the end or criterion of social organization, they would give an answer reminiscent of the formula of the greatest happiness of the greatest number. But to say that the end of social institutions is happiness, is to say that they have no common end at all. For happiness is individual, and to make happiness the object of society is to resolve society itself into the ambitions of numberless individuals, each directed toward the attainment of some personal purpose.[40]

40. R. H. Tawney, *The Acquisitive Society* (New York: Harcourt, Brace & World, 1920), p. 29.

Marx criticized the social structure of this modern age with unprecedented perspicacity. Did he himself succeed in achieving a new synthesis between the social and the economic spheres? His critique of classical economy entails a new relation between the two. Yet his continued insistence on the *primacy* of the economic with respect to all other activity prevented him from entirely fulfilling the promises held in his early writings. In those early writings he had criticized economic conditions in the name of politics: the social prevails and *determines* economic production. Over the years Marx came to accept more and more the classical economist view that the instrumental relation to nature functions as the *basis* of all social structuralization.[41] Thus in the preface to the *Critique of Political Economy* he strongly emphasized the fundamental character of the economic over all other spheres. Moreover, he regarded the social structure of this economic activity as primarily defined by the technical demands of production. This was an unexpected development, since Marx's theory had begun as a reaction against the instrumentalist view of human activity. In the early Paris Manuscripts he had widened the scope of productive activity far beyond the utilitarian (and, hence, instrumentalist) restrictions of the British economists. For the young Marx this activity had adopted the meaning of a *total expression* of man.

Trained in the school of Fichte and Hegel, Marx had begun by emphasizing man's creative powers. Yet, understanding the crucial significance of economic production in modern society, he had turned to the classical economists. He had immediately criticized the lack of historical perspective as well as the misplaced social pretensions of their theories. But he had not questioned their assumption that economic production constitutes the primary sphere of life. Indeed, the *primacy* of this sphere which in the classical theory had remained implicit, he gradually developed into a full-fledged theory. The base-superstructure scheme tended to isolate the instrumental aspect of the productive act from its total social and cultural context.[42] When Marx declared that production relations are prior to other social and cultural

41. See also Hannah Arendt, *Between Past and Future* (New York: Penguin Books, 1977), pp. 78–79.
42. What Habermas has called *communicative action*, through which we struc-

relations and are determined mainly by the forces of production, he in fact subordinated all other aspects of human activity to the instrumental one. *Wage Labor and Capital* provides the *locus classicus*:

> The social relations within which individuals produce, the social relations of production, are altered, transformed, with the change and development of the material means of production, of the forces of production. The relations of production in their totality constitute what is called the social relations, society, and moreover, a society at a definite stage of historic development. . . . [*Werke* 6: 408; *Sel. Works* 1: 91]

Unquestionably, forces of production and relations of production go hand in hand in Marx's view, but at least in the quoted text, the latter are subordinated to the former. No overarching social structure unites and directs technology and social engineering toward a common goal.

Marx's emphasis upon the determining role of the means of production in the process of socialization, if consistently maintained, would result in a heavy dependence of social structures on advancing technology. At least once Marx admitted as much. In the passage of the *Grundrisse* quoted above, technical progress virtually eliminates the need for social revolution or even social reform. Technology is known to be a notoriously poor community builder. Because it requires malleable human collectivities, it breaks down the existing natural ones. Upon contact with technique, a social complex usually turns into an inorganic mass. The true community depends upon a stable relation between man and his environment. Once this relation is subjected to abstract decisions, its stability becomes disturbed and its social structures destroyed.[43] The point here is not to question the intervention of social technology—that intervention has become an irreversible fact—but to question its aptitude for building genuine social bonds. Nor do I charge Marx's theory with technical-economic "determinism." What "determines" religion, cul-

_____

ture our social relations, remains secondary to the simple act of technical control over nature. Jürgen Habermas, *Knowledge and Human Interest*, p. 53.

43. Jacques Ellul, *The Technological Society*, pp. 49, 207, and 215.

ture, and morality are not the *material means* of production, but the *relations* of production. Nor do these relations function unilaterally like environmental factors in materialist systems. For Marx, the determined feeds back into the determining Whether such a presentation of culture is adequate will be investigated in the next chapter. But clearly it is not economic determinism. Our present criticism bears only on the fact that Marx *singled out economic relations of production* (which are, of course, social relations, though of a very limited kind) *from the social complex as a whole as being more fundamental,* and that his work displays a *tendency* to regard these relations as being primarily determined by the *means* of production. The tendency never hardened into an "economic" theory. Again and again Marx backed away from a view which he rightly regarded as a threat to his fundamental social critique. Yet the ambiguity remains one of the divisive issues in the interpretation of his work. I cannot claim to have resolved it. But from the preceding discussion, as well as from the second chapter, it should appear that any reduction of Marx's theory of society to a technical-economic determinism is wrong; yet it should also be obvious that this theory placed an emphasis upon the role of economic production which may have been justified in the period of early industrial capitalism but no longer corresponds to contemporary social structures.

5
The Uses of Ideology

MARX'S CONCEPT OF IDEOLOGY

No aspect of Marx's work has more profoundly affected the modern mind than his critique of ideology. Friends and foes alike have, often unwittingly, spoken Marx's language in interpreting arts and letters and have adopted his standards in judging the overall drift of our culture. The critique of bourgeois ideology has united Marxists of contrary persuasions in a rare unanimity. While Marx's economic projections may have lost much of their credibility after having been repeatedly adjusted to ever-new recoveries of the capitalist economy on its purported road to decline, his evaluation of the bourgeois superstructure has gained greater acceptance. In fact, there seems to be an inverse proportion between one and the other. The less the economic development of bourgeois society followed the course of Marx's predictions, the more its cultural attitudes seemed to justify his critical judgment; the less people were inclined to dispense with the benefits of a capitalist economy, the more they found its culture "alienating." Thus the attention shifted from Marx's critique of economy to his critique of capitalist ideology. This development is all the more striking in that the concept of ideology has for the most part remained undefinably vague and has left countless conflicting interpretations in its wake.

Though Marx dealt with the critique of ideology directly only once, there can be little doubt that the subject always occupied a significant place in his thought. To capture its full meaning requires, of course, far more than an attentive reading of *The German Ideology*, a work in which he was above all concerned to settle his account with the Hegelian Left. Equally important for understanding Marx's evaluation of culture is his earlier discovery of the notion of praxis. Nor did his critique confine itself to the term *ideology*. After his polemics with the Young Hegelians, the term *ideology* receded almost as suddenly as it had risen to prominence. But the *concept* reemerges in the opposition of structure to superstructure in the preface to the *Critique of Political Economy*. Even that expression sets no limits to the discussion. Assumptions and casual remarks made in the later writings on economics and politics significantly contribute toward Marx's overall critique of culture. Moreover, the interpretation that Engels initiated during Marx's lifetime constitutes, in this instance, an indispensable though not always reliable aid to understanding that critique.

The Young Hegelian critique of Hegel's philosophy defines the conceptual framework within which Marx first learned to think about the relation between reality and idea. It is useful to remember this well-known fact at the outset of a discussion of Marx's views on the status of ideas. For though he soon left the Young Hegelian camp, Marx never abandoned the question of how ideal structures intrinsically relate to what we uncritically call "the real."

In the complex story of the Left Hegelian movement[1] we must again recall the crucial impact of Feuerbach's critique. Feuerbach rejected what he considered to be the basic principle of all speculative idealism: that the ideal and the real can ever coincide in the realm of pure thought. Spirit to him is not the ultimate synthesis but merely a dialectical antithesis of nature. The encounter between mind and nature occurs exclusively on the level of sense perception, the one and only locus of the identity of the ideal and the real. Marx soon became aware of the latent idealism of this "materialist" interpretation. In assuming the existence of a fundamental harmony between the sensuous consciousness and nature, Feuerbach uncritically adopts an idealistic thesis which even Hegel felt had to be proven. Moreover, the materialist idea of all-comprehensive matter is as spec-

1. For its influence on Marx, cf. Auguste Cornu, *Karl Marx et Friedrich Engels*, vols. 1–2 (Paris, 1955), and Sidney Hook, *From Hegel to Marx* (Ann Arbor: University of Michigan Press, 1962).

ulative as the idealist idea of pure Spirit. Both exist independently of living praxis. In the first three "Theses on Feuerbach," Marx settles his account with Feuerbach and all other theoretic materialists. A practical materialism must incorporate the active element (what idealists call "spirit") as well as the passive (determinist) one. Man *produces* his own life through his "sensuous human activity." Theoretical problems are rooted in practical attitudes:

> The question whether objective truth is an attribute of human thought—is not a theoretical but a *practical* question. Man must prove the truth, *i.e.*, the reality and power, the "this-sidedness" of his thinking in practice. The dispute over the reality or non-reality of thinking that is isolated from practice is a purely *scholastic* question (Thesis II). [*MEGA* 1⁵: 534; *Coll. Works* 5: 3]

The age-old question of whether thinking and reality "correspond" to one another cannot be answered outside the active encounter of theory with praxis. In contrast to Hegel, Marx sees the subject as exercising its active role in the objectification process primarily in the *practical* order of production. Hence the subject is never single but always social, and never "truthful" when only contemplative. Truth is constituted in praxis. This, and not the activist anti-intellectualism, is the real thing meaning of the much abused eleventh thesis: "The philosophers have only *interpreted* the world in various ways; the point is to change it" (*MEGA* 1⁵: 535; *Coll. Works* 5: 5). Theory itself forms part of a larger, practical consciousness which assigns it its specific function. Such were the ideals that brought Marx to the question of ideology.

The term *ideology* was shrouded in ambiguity when Marx first encountered it. He compounded the problem by using the term in more than one sense. Yet whatever the precise meaning of *ideology* in his work may be, there can be no doubt about the underlying principle: ideas express and are conditioned by the fundamental structure of society. At least in *The German Ideology* a second, critical principle is added: ideological complexes hide their social dependence behind a semblance of autonomy, which makes them *appear* different from what they *are*. Neither one of these principles was new, but they had never before been associated with the term *ideology.*

When in 1796 Destutt de Tracy first used the word *idéologie* in a paper read at the Institut National des Sciences et des Arts, newly erected for promoting the "scientific" (in contrast to the "metaphysical") knowledge of man, he certainly had no form of consciousness in mind that needed a social critique. The new science which the French nobleman and recent convert to the republican cause was about to develop on the basis of Condillac's sensationalist theory of man would itself provide a critical understanding of ideas.[2] True, the *idéologiste* made no distinction between "true" and "false" ideas: his attention focused entirely on their beginnings in sensation. In principle he was critical only of any claims for innate or infused ideas. But in exposing these uniformly humble origins, he would also break down the barriers of social prejudice. More and more, Destutt came to attribute prejudice to class interest, thus moving in the direction of Marx's later critique of ideology.[3] Meanwhile Destutt's new "science" itself was not free of prejudice. Critics have charged that it merely rationalized the cultural assumptions of the postrevolutionary bourgeois elite. Indeed, it was precisely this connection with the political legacy of the revolution which discredited the new scientists with Napoleon. By an ironical turn of fate, he accused them of the same kind of abstract speculation that had moved them to dismiss metaphysics. Gradually Napoleon's contemptuous term *idéologue* came to refer to intellectuals who, oblivious of empirical realities, endlessly disputed abstract concepts. The road was clear toward a critique of ideology that would expose the illusions and unexpected presuppositions of particular "ideologies."[4]

2. Destutt traces *idea* to its Greek root *eidein* ("to see") and declares, "L'idéologie est une partie de la zoologie." Destutt de Tracy, *Elements d'idéologie. Première partie: Idéologie proprement dite,* ed. with introduction by Henri Gouhier (Paris: Vrin, 1971), p. xiii.

3. Emmet Kennedy, *A Philosophe in the Age of Revolution: Destutt de Tracy and the Origins of "Ideology"* (Philadelphia: The American Philosophical Society, 1978), p. 206.

4. Marx alludes to Napoleon's usage in *The Holy Family* (*MEGA* 1³: 299; *Coll. Works* 4: 123). The German philosopher F. H. Jacobi wrote in 1806 to a French

Marx borrowed from both traditions, but the negative meaning dominates. In an article in the *Rheinische Zeitung* he wrote: "let us take the world as it is, let us not be ideologists" (*MEGA* 1¹: 341; *Coll. Works* 1: 317). At the same time the young Marx shows little patience for what he considers to be Napoleon's global rejection of philosophical ideas as "ideology." When, in the Rhineland Diet debates on wood theft, one deputy invoked the free will of private persons, Marx wrote in the *Rheinische Zeitung*: "How are we to understand this sudden rebellious emergence of ideology, for as far as ideas are concerned we have before us only followers of Napoleon?" (*MEGA* 1¹: 286; *Coll. Works* 1: 244). Marx's own rejection of ideas for being "ideological" is clearly more qualified. After some initial hesitation he settles upon a social meaning: ideas are ideological when, in a seemingly universal and disinterested manner, they actually represent the interests of a particular segment of society.

Of course, Marx had not been the first to retrace ideas to their social-historical origins. In France the search for an ulterior basis of ideas may be traced back to Rousseau and Montesquieu. In his *Discourse on Inequality*, Rousseau had suggested that a society's modes of satisfying its material needs determines its cultural progress and political institutions, while Montesquieu, in *The Spirit of the Laws*, had assumed that a fundamental, "geographical" level of material wants and needs determines political systems. The two theories, though considerably different in other respects, had made a common impact upon the French philosophy of progress. No longer was the human mind considered the leading principle of cultural development. Civilization had its roots in the structure created for satisfying physical needs of society. Thus the historian Raynal assumed a direct connection between artistic development, social mores, and *economic* struc-

---

correspondent: "Intelligence is extinguished once the heart dries up. A Frenchman of note told me in Berlin that in his country all manifestations of this sort of stupidity are designated by the generic term idéologie." *F. H. Jacobi's auserlesener Briefwechsel*, ed. Friedrich Roth (Leipzig, 1825), 2: 380. I owe this reference to Xavier Tilliette: "De l'idéologie comme philosophie à l'idéologie comme idéologie," in *Démythisation et idéologie*, ed. Enrico Castelli (Paris: Aubier, 1973), p. 455.

tures. Condorcet clearly anticipates Marx's schema of culture with his thesis that material needs provide the real stimulus to mental achievements. Condorcet placed history on a physiological basis, while attempting to perserve the autonomy of the mental processes originating on this basis. But whereas Condorcet's historical determinism had remained vague in its causal explanations, that of his student Destutt de Tracy was very precise.

For Destutt the question of determinism had been settled by his master. The only remaining task was to define the ultimately determining factor. He attributed an absolute primacy to economic conditions. Moral virtue as well as cultural development result, not from geographic causes, as Montesquieu had assumed, but from economic ones.[5]

In Germany the quest for the origin of ideas had taken a somewhat more ideal turn. According to Herder, each people expresses permanent truths in its own historical form and construes them into unique cultural complexes. Through the national spirit *(Volksgeist)* history shapes each people's culture into an original, unrepeatable totality. Hegel had pruned Herder's theory of its romantic nationalism, but only to emphasize all the more the link between culture and ethical structure. Man's universal, rational nature concretizes itself in the ethical totality of the state. Yet the actual consciousness of an individual or a group never coincides with that total object of consciousness which is the Objective Spirit itself. No group or individual can ever fully internalize what has been called the Objective Spirit's "superexistence."[6] Hence the possibility of an alienated consciousness (discussed in chapter 1) but also of an "ideological" consciousness. The spiritual objectivity defines the limits within which a particular culture or a group within that culture thinks. Its assumptions, principles, and values are seldom subjected to critical scrutiny, and its operates largely as an unconscious (and therefore all the more powerful) source of individual or group consciousness. The development of thought, religion, and aesthetic creativity in a particular culture, then, is largely deter-

5. *A Commentary and Review of Montesquieu's Spirit of Laws,* trans. William Duane (Philadelphia, 1811; reprint 1969).
6. Nicolai Hartmann, *Das Problem des geistigen Seins,* 1933.

mined by the hidden assumptions of the society that gave birth to it.

Gradually it became clear to Hegel that the neoclassical ideal of *polis* which had inspired his theory of the Objective Spirit was no longer adequate for an interpretation of the modern national culture. The nation was obviously not the single source of its members' artistic, religious, and cultural life, as the Greek *polis*, his early model, had been. But he nevertheless continued to regard those highest expressions of the Spirit as available to the individual through the mediation of the national state.

After Herder and Hegel had shown the social connections of ideas, a mere analysis of the theoretical arguments alone was no longer sufficient for adequately evaluating an intellectual position. A critical understanding required an investigation of its historical origins as well as of the social assumptions of its proponent. Now as long as conflicting parties belonged to the same social universe they rarely questioned the intellectual foundations of each other's beliefs. Hegel himself, though he had laid the groundwork for a social interpretation of culture, never felt it necessary to set up one contemporary social body in opposition to another, as he had done in comparing one past civilization with another. To him the nation-state still presented the same undivided unity it had provided since the beginning of the modern age. Loyalty to a common fatherland overruled the very real struggle between opposite interest groups. Here, as in other instances, Hegel had couched revolutionary principles in traditional beliefs.

Marx applied those principles to a very different social condition. After the succession of social revolutions and counterrevolutions in France and the unprecedented economic expansion in England, the collapse of the social hegemony of the national state had become inevitable. What Marx's contemporaries witnessed was the beginning of a clash between social groups that occupied conflicting positions in a gigantic, supranational economic network. The state still symbolized universal unity, but more and more it had come to represent and legitimate the needs of a single class. It no longer dispensed the spiritual nourishment that had united other social groups in the past. Each group now attempted to present its particular interests as universal. One class succeeded in imposing its own, at least externally, upon the state as a whole. But its rule was no longer internally accepted by all citizens. Members of other groups regarded political government as the rule of another group.

By combining the notion of class with that of ideology Marx unified what had hitherto been considered the unfocused prejudices of diverse, ill-defined groups.[7] He thereby gave the idea of group thinking a more solid footing. He had already used the concept of class in his 1843 "Contribution to the Critique of Hegel's Philosophy of Right." But in *The Holy Family* he first applied it to the social conditioning of ideas. The issue rose in a polemic over Bruno Bauer's theory of a self-developing universal consciousness. To Bauer's idealist theory Marx opposed his own notion of a class consciousness reflecting class interests. Identical social conditions generate different modes of consciousness as they affect different classes: "The propertied class and the class of the proletariat present the same human self-estrangement. But the former class feels at ease and strengthened in this self-estrangement, it recognizes estrangement *as its own power* and has in it the semblance of a human existence. The latter feels annihilated in estrangement; it sees in it its own powerlessness and the reality of an inhuman existence" (*MEGA* 1^3: 206; *Coll. Works* 4: 36). As each class evaluates the impact of the prevailing social-economic conditions, it universalizes its private interest in a general theory. It is precisely for not recognizing this fragmentation of one "humanity" into different interest groups that the leaders of the French Revolution failed to emancipate society as a whole. "Every mass-type 'interest' that asserts itself historically goes far beyond its real limits in the 'idea' or 'imagination' when it first comes on the scene and is confused with *human* interest in general. This *illusion* constitutes what Fourier calls the *tone* of each historical epoch" (*MEGA* 1^3: 253; *Coll. Works* 4: 81). The ideas of the French Revolution represented the interests of the ruling class, the bourgeoisie. In spite

7. On this and on the development of social determination from Herder to Hegel, Karl Manheim's *Ideology and Utopia* (1929; rpt. 1963) remains the outstanding study.

of its phrases about human equality, the Jacobine rhetoric mainly served the purposes of the ascending bourgeoisie. Ideas alone *make* no history, except the history of ideas. They "can never lead beyond an old world order but only beyond the ideas of the old world order" (*MEGA* 1³: 294; *Coll. Works* 4: 119). What Bauer considered to be the failure of the ideas of the French Revolution—namely, that they were appropriated by private interests—belongs to their very nature. Only those who know ideas for what they really are, representations of class interests, know how to use them. Marat, Robespierre, and Saint-Just fell victims to their own ideas because they failed to perceive their class-relatedness. In this early discussion the term *ideology* has an essentially negative connotation. It refers to a basically false and deceptive mode of consciousness. This derogatory meaning persists throughout the crucial passage of *The German Ideology*, even though the method of interpretation set up in this work no longer requires it.

In *The German Ideology* the division of labor plays a decisive part in the origin and nature of ideas. Only after a society had properly distributed its material tasks is enough leisure available for culture to develop. Already in the Paris Manuscripts Marx had written, "The care-burdened, poverty-stricken man has no sense for the finest play" (*MEGA* 1³: 120; *Coll. Works* 3: 302). But the balance between a division of labor required for the creation of leisure and a destructive fragmentation of life imposed by a ruthless pursuit of economic profit is precarious. Marx had added, "The dealer in minerals sees only the commercial value but not the beauty and the specific character of the mineral." Once the division of labor sacrifices the unity of life to utilitarian efficiency, it excludes the very possibility of an integrated culture. Thought then degenerates into ideology, art into formalism, science into scientism. Indeed, the very concept of culture as a realm of values independent of social-economic structures, into which man "withdraws" from his daily occupations, could emerge only in a compartmentalized society. The dualism between a corporeal and a mental realm, which permeates modern culture, directly results from the capitalist separation of bodily and mental labor.[8] The proudly proclaimed autonomy of bourgeois thought mainly reflects the isolation of the thinkers from the real, active life of material production. "Thoughts and ideas acquire an independent existence in consequence of the personal circumstances and relations of individuals acquiring independent existence. We have shown the exclusive, systematic occupation with these thoughts on the part of ideologists and philosophers, and hence the systematizaton of these thoughts, is a consequence of the division of labor" (*MEGA* 1[5]: 414; *Coll. Works* 5: 447). All philosophical and theological systems were born in the thin air of a culture that had set itself apart from praxis.

Social determination constitutes a primary factor in Marx's theory of ideology. Yet it becomes a controversial one only by the addition of a second feature: the basically derivative quality of all thought complexes. The description of ideas in *The German Ideology* as "reflexes and echoes" of the real life practice of active men (*MEGA* 1[5]: 16; *Coll. Works* 5: 36) drastically changes the relation between theory and practice from what it was in the earlier writings and even, I believe, in the "Theses on Feuerbach."[9] Ideas now are no longer *mediated* by social structures: they *directly reflect* those structures which, in turn, reflect the conditions of the material production process. The problem with such "derived" mental constructs is that they lose the critical and revolutionary powers with which Marx had earlier endowed

8. As early as *The German Ideology*, Marx pointed at the split in bourgeois culture. Yet, being more interested in the social-economic aspects of the division of labor, he did not develop it. Members of the Frankfurt School made it into a major theme of their critique. Both Horkheimer and Adorno wrote against the existence of a separate sphere of culture. Herbert Marcuse also stressed the separateness of culture in a capitalist society: "Culture means not so much a better world as a nobler one: a world to be brought about not through the overthrow of the material order of life, but through events in the individual's soul. Humanity becomes an inner state. Freedom, goodness and beauty become spiritual qualities." "The Affirmative Character of Culture" (1937), in *Negations*, trans. Jeremy Shapiro (Boston: Beacon Press, 1968), p. 103.

9. On this and other internal grounds, I am inclined to place the "Theses" before *The Germany Ideology*.

them when he called philosophy "the spiritual weapon" of the proletariat (*MEGA* 1¹: 620; *Coll. Works* 3: 187). Ideas that are "necessary sublimates of their material, empirically observable, materially preconditioned life process" (*MEGA* 1⁵: 15; *Coll. Works* 5: 36) could hardly serve as weapons in the creation of a new social system: they merely reflect and legitimate the existing one. Marx now replaces the dialectical interaction between forms of consciousness and social relations by a one-directional, causal link between relations of production and ideas. But, it should be noted, unlike nineteenth-century materialists, he does not derive *the conscious from the unconscious.* Productive activity itself is already a form of conscious activity. The distinction, then, is not between physical reality and immaterial consciousness, but between conscious activity and the rationalization of it.[10] Yet overreacting to the purely speculative theories of the Hegelians, Marx unhappily reduces the practical activity which involves man directly with the physical world to a "materially preconditioned life process." This basically conflicts with his earlier thesis that philosophy cannot be abolished but must be realized (*MEGA* 1¹: 613; *Coll. Works* 3: 181). Once thought has lost its independence, it can no longer set up ideals and goals to *realize.*

What Marx writes about the derivative status of ideas must be qualified by the immediately following distinction between *ideologies* and other complexes of thought, particularly scientific theories. An ideology is not merely dependent: it is illusory as well because of its "semblance of independence" (*MEGA* 1⁵: 16; *Coll. Works* 5: 37).[11] It is, in short, a mode of thought that misunderstands its own origin. This additional characteristic distinguishes religious beliefs, moral and legal codes, even philosophical systems from the positive sciences and any critique of ideology based on them. Scientific theory differs from "speculation" as real knowledge differs from "empty talk" (*MEGA* 1⁵: 16; *Coll. Works* 5: 37). If ideas were only "sublimates . . . of the material life process," such a distinction would lose its meaning; for a

10. Shlomo Avineri, *The Social and Political Thought of Karl Marx,* p. 67.
11. Engels used the formula "false consciousness" in his 1894 letter to Franz Mehring (*Werke* 39: 97; *Sel. Corres.,* p. 434).

"scientific" mode of awareness would be as much a "sublimate" and "reflex" as an ideological one. The difference between the awareness of its social, economic origin of one and the absence of such an awareness in the other does not make the former less a "reflex" of material life processes. The question of truth could hardly be raised in either case.

The German Ideology is a complex book, the thesis of which cannot be pinned down by any single interpretation. Still another element appears that is hard to reconcile with either the derived character of ideas or a basic distinction between theory and ideology: the status of language. All modes of consciousness trace their roots to man's practical need to communicate. Any intellectual discourse, however abstruse, has developed out of the common language of daily living. "Language is practical, real consciousness that exists for other men as well and only therefore does it also exist for me; for language, like consciousness, arises only from the need, the necessity of intercourse with other men" (*MEGA* 1⁵: 20; *Coll. Works* 5: 44). Through language individuals universalize their relations, thus laying the foundation for culture. But if all conscious activity is and remains linguistic, then inadequate modes of thinking consist, in the final analysis, of linguistic deviations. To detach thought from language, or either of them from the practical activity of life, distorts the entire perspective of thinking. Yet this is precisely what philosophy does.

> Language is the immediate actuality of thought. Just as philosophers have given thought an independent existence so they were bound to make language into an independent realm. This is the secret of philosophical language, in which thoughts in the form of words have their own content. The problem of descending from the world of thoughts to the actual world is turned into the problem of descending from language into life. [*MEGA* 1⁵: 424; *Coll. Works* 5: 446]

Each class naturally attempts to turn communication into a tool for imposing its own ideas upon other classes. The class that effectively rules succeeds in presenting its particular use of lan-

guage as the only correct one. But, in itself language is neither ideological nor derived: it belongs to the *basis* of all social relations.[12] Endowed with a structure of its own, it does not "reflect" reality, it *expresses* and *represents* it.
The linguistic symbolization transforms any *direct* relation into an indirect *representation*. To speak is to speak *about* something and hence to transfer the subject from the realm of immediate experience to the more abstract universe of discourse. The basic autonomy of this linguistic symbolization process distinguishes a genuine language from the nondiscursive signs by means of which, as far as we know, animals communicate. No truly discursive structures are "derived" from any previous ones. Language first and foremost conditions *itself:* it never "reflects" existing social conditions without providing at the same time a structure for transforming them.[13] All social action operates by means of signs ruled by a syntax from which it draws both its structure and its meaning.[14] This holds true on any level of discourse—scientific or ideological. Thus, also from a linguistic point of view, the distinction between theory and ideology loses much of its significance. An ideological discourse that interprets itself without regard for its social origin does not thereby lose its practical effect or turn into an "illusion." Since Weber and Tawney we have become aware of the enormous impact of such purely "ideological" discourse as theological doctrines. Developed without any concern for social-economic relations, their real influence has nevertheless surpassed that of economic theories. One may well wonder whether Marx's own theory owes its present success as much to its scientific as to its holistic and, in that respect at least, quasi-theological character.

12. Stalin reminded Soviet Marxists of this in his essay on linguistics: "Language is not a product of one or another base, old or new, within the given society, but of the whole course of the history of society and the history of bases throughout centuries. It was created not by any class, but by all society, by all classes of society." *Marxism in Linguistics* (New York International Publishers, 1951), pp. 10–11.
13. Jean Guy Meunier, "Langage et idéologie chez le jeune Marx," in *Dialogue* 13, no. 2 (June 1974).
14. Fernand Dumont, *Les Idéologies* (Paris: P.U.F., 1974), p. 107.

FROM IDEOLOGY TO SUPERSTRUCTURE

Ideologies are rarely simple concepts. They are mostly general *models* for conceiving the relation between ideal structures and the practical, everyday conditions of existence. The closer those structures come to being comprehensive world views, the more they tend to be unquestioned assumptions and the less obviously they display their social-economic roots. It is precisely their uncritical acceptance that renders universal world views such unassailable fortresses. More than anything else, then, the critical self-understanding of a culture requires insight into the relations between society and its various levels of discourse. *The German Ideology* was among the first writings to focus attention on these relations. Yet it left a number of crucial questions unanswered. In what specific manner does an ideology reflect a particular state of society? Can the distinction between ideological and other modes of thought be consistently maintained? Will the society of the future be free of ideologies? Instead of answering those questions in his later writings, Marx merely changed his perspective. In the preface to the *Critique of the Political Economy,* he refers to all thought complexes that play no direct role in the production process as "superstructures." Although Marx continued to distinguish ideology from science, as the following passage from the preface illustrates, the term *ideology* more and more tends to broaden its meaning.

> In considering such transformations a distinction should always be made between the material transformation of the economic conditions of production which can be determined with the precision of a natural science, and the legal, political, religious, aesthetic or philosophical—in short, ideological forms in which men become conscious of this conflict and fight it out. [*Werke* 13, 9; *Sel. Works* 1: 363]

Marx always felt that there was an essential difference between philosophy, law, morality, and religion, on the one hand, and scientific or critical investigation, on the other. He certainly intended to distinguish the two within the superstructure. But he shifted the emphasis from the polemical term *ideology,* denoting an intrinsically deceptive form of consciousness, to the more neutral term *superstructure*. This, however, aids us little in defining the nature of this social determination. *That* mental phenomena are socially determined is certain. *How* this social determination affects their autonomy remains obscure. As long as the precise impact of production relations upon the intrinsic quality of ideas (their truth or falsity) is not established, the entire concept of ideology remains unclear and the distinction between an ideological and a scientific superstructure, unjustified.[15]

Chapter 2 has acquainted us with the general idea of superstructure. The discussion that follows will be restricted to those intellectual and aesthetic parts of the superstructure to which the term *ideology* is most often applied. At once we notice, however, that Marx uses the two terms for different purposes. While *ideology* deflated the claims of a false consciousness, the base-superstructure model serves to establish an order among various kinds of conscious activities, regardless of their truth or falsity. In that sense at least, it fulfills a more vital function in integrating all social activity. Superstructure possesses none of the negative connotations inherent in the term *ideology* as Marx first used it. It provides no criterion for distinguishing a scientifically correct from an inadequately justified, or even from a false, superstructure. Nor does it provide any assistance for aesthetically evaluating art and literature or for comparing the scientific merits of one theory with another. Earlier we drew attention to the relation of mutual dependence that exists between basis and superstructure. A purely economic interpretation of artistic or scientific developments is clearly inadequate, since various aspects of "high culture" play themselves a role in directing that *basic* activity. Not much can be learned about the Renaissance from a study of the economy of northern Italian cities unless one takes into account how spiritual developments participated in shaping that economy. Repeatedly in his later years Engels reacted against an economist interpretation of culture. We recall his well-known admonition to Joseph Bloch:

> According to the materialist conception of history, the *ultimately* determining factor in history is the production and reproduction of real life. Neither Marx nor I have ever asserted more than this.

15. Jan Plamenatz, *Man and Society* (London, 1968), 2: 330.

Hence if somebody twists this into saying that the economic factor is the *only* determining one, he transforms that proposition into a meaningless, abstract, absurd phrase. [*Werke* 37: 963; *Sel. Corres.* p. 394]

A few weeks later, in a letter to Conrad Schmidt, Engels again stressed the mutual influence of economic and other social developments. But, most importantly, he insists on the relative independence of various spheres of the superstructure as they follow their own internal determinations. Law, for instance, must not only "correspond to the general economic condition," it must also be an "internally coherent expression which does not, owing to internal conflicts, contradict itself" (*Werke* 37:491; *Sel. Corres.*, p. 399).

Hence an ideological system depends as much, if not more, upon its *own* past tradition as on the particular social-economic conditions in which it develops. An economically backward country, such as Germany was at the beginning of the nineteenth century, nevertheless succeeded in playing a leading part in philosophy and literature.

If Luther and Calvin "overcome" the official Catholic religion, or Hegel "overcomes" Fichte and Kant, or Rousseau with his republican *Contrat social* indirectly "overcomes" the constitutional Montesquieu, this is a process which remains within theology, philosophy or political science, represents a stage in the history of these particular spheres of thought and never passes beyond the sphere of thought. [*Werke* 39: 97; *Sel. Corres.*, p. 434]

One wonders how much, under these restrictions, remains of the original principle of "ultimate dependence." What we find instead is an evolution toward internally coherent systems that follow their own laws yet still remain connected within one social-economic unity. Marx referred to the social-economic structure as a base, and Engels, in spite of all his later qualifications, continued to use that term, because it holds the elementary conditions of all social life. Being dependent upon this primary structure, all in some way reflect its impact.

Such a thesis considerably differs, of course, from the kind of economic determinism that often passes for a Marxist theory of culture. Marx has written enough about the various sociocultural spheres for us to ascertain that he never accepted any one-directional influence of the base upon the superstructure. Unlike his immediate followers, he remained aware of the dialectical, and hence mutual, character of this influence. Thus, when Marx wrote that without industry there would have been no science (*MEGA* 1⁵: 15; *Coll. Works* 5: 36), his followers interpreted this to mean that industrial technology belonged to the base while natural science belonged to the theoretical superstructure. But such a reading contradicts Marx's persistent concern to keep the theoretical and practical aspects of praxis united. Without the theoria of science, practical technology would simply not exist. The cases of art, morality, and religion are more complex, yet not essentially different. If art consisted in detached, esoteric achievement as it is often presented in modern aesthetics, it would exclusively belong to the superstructure. But Marx never subscribed to such a purist theory of art. He considered all fully *human* production to be inherently aesthetic. For him, quite naturally, man "forms objects in accordance with the laws of beauty" (*MEGA* 1³: 89; *Coll. Works* 3: 277). Even when, through social circumstances, he ceases to produce aesthetically, his activity is still guided by the kind of imaginative projection that characterizes human production. "What distinguishes the worst architect from the best of bees is this, that the architect raises his structure in imagination before he erects it in reality" (*Werke* 23: 193; *Cap.* 1: 178). Even morality and religion are called "particular modes of production" that fall under its general law (*MEGA* 1³: 115; *Coll. Works* 3: 297).

Unfortunately, Marx failed to define the nature of the base impact. Nevertheless, the quoted passages effectively exclude any mode of conceiving its relation to the superstructure whereby economic production becomes separated from other sociocultural activities. Detached from its superstructure, the base immediately turns into the kind of objective hypostasis that Marx had ruled out when he opposed his own notion of praxis to materialist determinism. Once praxis ceases to unite all levels of human production, it no longer accomplishes what it was meant to do—namely, to reintegrate man's social activity. However we distinguish the various levels of socialization, we should never separate them into closed compartments. For this reason Marx's undeveloped ideas are preferable to Engels's elaborate descriptions of the mutual causal impact of base and superstructure. Engels disrupted the unity of praxis which continued to guide Marx's reflections. He thereby reduced its "base" part to an objective datum hardly different from Feuerbach's "Nature." The objectivist reduction appears in the tendency that began with Engels to equate the base with the material forces of production rather than with the productive forces in their total (i.e., also spiritual) social context. For Marx, base and superstructure are different functions of one praxis. Hence the base is constituted by the same individuals who think, imagine, and play—in one single process of socialization. "The same men who establish their social relations in conformity with their material productivity, produce also principles, ideas and categories, in conformity with their social relations" (*Werke* 4: 130; *Coll. Works* 6: 166). Material productivity can by no means be reduced to material forces of production. Those "forces" are themselves the outcome of a total social activity, as is indicated in a phrase preceding the quoted passage. "These definite social relations are just as much produced by men as linen, flax, etc."

Michel Henry has shown how Marx recognizes only one praxis rather than two different kinds of activity, one of which produces economic objects and the other ideas and artifacts. "The relation that gives rise to the ideology does not move from classes or conditions of production to ideas: it originates in what grounds *both* classes and ideas. One and the same source . . . produces conditions of production, classes and ideas."[16] The distinctions are rooted in the *intrinsic* differences that distinguish various kinds of activity, not in different origins. Material production presents praxis in its more immediate activity, while ideas and aesthetic activity, *because of their reflective nature*, belong to the mediate part of praxis. In the latter, man becomes reflectively, theoretically, or aesthetically aware of the processes in which he is already engaged on an immediate level. One cannot exist without the other, since both are different aspects of one

16. Michel Henry, *Marx*, 1: 415.

praxis, just as thought is the *idea of the body* in Spinoza's philosophy. Marx asserts the need to keep reflection intrinsically united with economic production, not to derive one from the other. Only in the questionable passages from *The German Ideology* on the genesis of ideas ("reflexes and echoes of this [material] life process") does he appear to propose a *causal* relation between material and spiritual production. In the light of Marx's overall discussion, however, an ideology (in the original, pejorative sense) is not an idea that fails to recognize its causal dependence on material production, but a reflective content that has become unduly abstracted from the totality of praxis.

Engels's valiant efforts to reunite base and superstructure by a mutual causality fail to undo the effect of having first separated them. His exclusive use of the category of causality is indicative of this separation. And since causality requires a beginning, the architectural model according to which the base must remain first assumes the importance of an axiomatic principle. It prevents Engels from explaining satisfactorily how a social process can take place simultaneously in base and superstructure. Marx, on the contrary, regards the two spheres as *intrinsically* united. For that reason the base-superstructure model alone cannot account for a crucial element in his theory: the internal coherence of all social activity. The conclusions of our analysis force us to accept, beside the vertical, architectural model of society, an organic one that is far less in evidence but may have influenced Marx's theory even more deeply. Recent commentators have rightly drawn attention to this second model.[17] The vertical model appears clearly in the preface to the *Critique of Political Economy* but also seems to have inspired the first part of *The German Ideology* and has left traces in some of the historical works. The organic model dominates the economic writings and, I believe, most of Marx's historical analyses. It integrates the various processes of socialization without reducing them to one another. Before discussing the compatibility of the two

17. Most explicitly by Melvin Rader, *Marx's Interpretation of History* (New York: Oxford University Press, 1979), but much of the groundwork toward an organic concept of society had been done already by Bertell Ollman.

models, we must briefly establish first that the organic concept, until recently unrecognized, truly exists. American scholars have made a convincing case for it.[18] What follows has profited from their research.

The passages in Marx that support an organic conception are numerous and extend over his entire writing career. Not surprisingly, the early *Critique of Hegel's Philosophy of the State* bears the imprint of Hegel's organic theory of the state. "It is a great advance to consider the political State as an organism and therefore to look upon the variety of authorities no longer as something inorganic, but as a living and rational differentiation" (*MEGA* 1^3: 411; *Coll. Works* 3: 11). Marx here accepts the organic concept, but he goes on to criticize Hegel for not being sufficiently specific about the particular nature of the state organism, what distinguishes it from an animal organism. Hegel simply applies the general idea to "the specific idea of the organism of the State" (*MEGA* 1^3: 414; *Coll. Works* 3: 14). Did Marx maintain this organic conception throughout his later work? Implicitly, yes. To what extent he continued to adhere explicitly to it is less obvious. Of course, Marx held that the cycles of the economic activity, production-circulation-consumption, are interconnected with one another as moments in an organic process. But the real question at hand is whether that economic production processs itself is *organically integrated* with other sociocultural activities. The social nature of production, discussed in chapter 4, implies that all social relations determine every branch of human activity, including that of economic production. (We also pointed out some inadequacies in this position!) In one passage of his *Theories of Surplus Value*, Marx explicitly states this total impact.

> Man himself is the basis of his material production, as of any other production that he carries on. All circumstances, therefore, which affect man, the *subject* of production, more or less modify all his functions and activities, and therefore too his functions and activities as the creator of material wealth, of commodities. In this re-

18. Besides Rader and Ollman, William L. McBride and Michael Harrington should also be mentioned.

spect it can in fact be shown that *all* human relations and functions, however and in whatever form they may appear, influence material production and have a more or less decisive influence on it. [*Werke* 26¹: 260; *TSV* 1: 288]

Indirectly and facetiously, Marx makes the same point in his "Apologist Conception of the Productivity of All Professions": even the criminal profession is productive and influences all aspects of society, including law and poetry (*Werke* 26¹: 363–64; *TSV* 1: 387–88). Once, in the significant preface to *Capital*, Marx refers to society as "an organism capable of change, and . . . constantly changing" (*Werke* 23: 16; *Cap.* 1: 10).

Granting the existence of an organic conception of society, we must investigate whether it is compatible with the vertical model and, more specifically, with a permanent priority of the economic factor vis-à-vis all others. That a *permanent* subordination is compatible with an organic model seems to defy prima facie empirical evidence. To compensate for lack of empirical support, Melvin Rader distinguishes the "causally dominant" rule, permanent privilege to the social-economic sphere, and the "dominant among the effects," which varies from one historical epoch to another. Thus the heart, he claims, is "the most determinant of all the bodies," while mental activity is more dominant among the effects. In the same way, the feudal system of production was the dominant cause in medieval society, while the Church was the dominant effect. But this falls far short of a proof. True enough, to any organism certain functions are more vital than others. But the issue is not whether the production process is a vital one (the fact that all other processes depend on it does not make it *more* vital), but whether the production process enjoys a *lasting* priority over all others.

There appears to be only one method capable of combining the organic with the architectural model, and that is the dialectic. Melvin Rader has correctly perceived the need for a dialectical synthesis, but I doubt whether he has grasped its full implications. Hegel also maintains a hierarchy in his dialectic of society: family and civil society remain subordinate to the state. Marx, in his early critique on Hegel's theory of the state, while preserving the dialectic, inverts the hierarchy; the basic social activity occurs in civil society, the realm of economic transactions. The state merely gives a semblance of universality to these social-economic relations and provides them with a legal sanction. Though Marx later abandoned the Hegelian concept of society, he retained its two principal features, namely, the (inverted) hierarchical structure of the political and the economic realm, and the dialectical quality of the relation between the two. Now the latter may seem to guarantee the kind of mutual determination an organic theory of society requires. But *only* if the dialectic itself is adequately founded. As we saw in the third chapter, however, without its spiritual teleology the dialectic is bound to remain a purely heuristic device or, as in "orthodox communism," a dogmatic presupposition.

At any rate, no dialectic can allow any moment of society to exercise an *absolute* superiority over all others, since all remain subordinate to a higher principle of coordination. Hence, in order for the dialectic to reconcile the base-superstructure model with an organic concept of society, the primacy of the base must first be redefined as a relative one. The simple priority of cause over effect should give way to that of the more elementary (in the sense of providing the basic conditions for survival) over the less elementary. Of course, there is also the priority of the more immediate over the more reflective. But even here we should refrain from *assuming* that fundamental, immediate praxis consists exclusively of economic production. When Engels asserts the mutual determination of the various social spheres while at the same time maintaining the ultimate priority of the social-economic, he posits two incompatible theses. Stated in causal terms, the priority of the base cannot be but absolute.

The same problem has been phrased in a somewhat different way. In a genuinely organic concept any part affects society as a whole. It follows that, even if we grant an original priority to the base, the superstructure directly reflects *the social totality* rather than the economic changes. It ideally expresses a social complex in which the economic factor has been assimilated and transformed by various social spheres. Hence, any information about the social-economic conditions alone would provide little assistance in judging the merit or even the social content of a work of art, a moral principle, or a speculative theory.

I do not believe that Marx ever reconciled the architectural-causal interpretation of culture with the more fundamental organic-dialectic one. The tension between the two approaches continues to affect the work of his successors, especially their critique of the arts and sciences.

MARXIST DEVELOPMENTS OF THE CRITIQUE OF IDEOLOGY

That the ideas and values of a period merely mirror the economic interests of a particular class is a thesis that, to my knowledge, no serious Marxist thinker has ever held. The objections against such a monolithic interpretation are too substantial. Each culture spawns artists, prophets, and thinkers who, far from expressing the interests of the ruling class, fiercely oppose them. The subculture of groups antagonistic to the ruling class is itself part of the spiritual physiognomy of an age, particularly during a period when a group begins to emancipate itself from social oppression. Thus, when black culture suddenly erupted on the American scene in the late 1960s, a culturally underprivileged group managed not only to be noticed but to leave an impact upon society entirely out of proportion to its numbers.

Nevertheless, the theory shaped by Engels, developed by Plekhanov, and completed by Lenin occasionally approached the simplicity of a mirrorlike reflection. Engels's nondialectical view of knowledge surfaces whenever he raises epistemological questions. "Is our thinking capable of cognition of the real world? Are we able in our ideas and notions of the real world to produce a correct reflection of reality?" (*Werke* 21: 274; *Ludwig Feuerbach and the End of Classical German Philosophy* in *Sel. Works* 2: 370). Any doubts that critical philosophers like Hume or Kant expressed concerning the validity of naive realism are dismissed, with "all other philosophical crotchets," by a mere reference to experiment and industry. For Engels, science and technology have replaced the age-old questions. Once you are able to make the "thing-in-itself," you cannot doubt its existence any more! Engels criticizes Feuerbach for having failed to distinguish mechanistic materialism from Marx's dynamic dialectic. But his own concept of the dialectic is, as we have seen, thoroughly empiricist and nondialectical. The following description may serve as a reminder.

> According to Hegel the dialectical development apparent in nature and history, that is, the causal interconnection of the progressive movement from the lower to the higher, which asserts itself through all zig-zag movements and temporary regressions, is only a copy *(Abklatsch)* of the self-movement of the concept going on from eternity, no one knows where, but at all events independently of any thinking human brain. The ideological perversion had to be done away with. We comprehended the concepts in our heads once more materialistically—as images *(Abbilder)* of real things instead of regarding the ideal things as images of this or that stage of the absolute concept. [*Werke* 21: 293–94; *Sel. Works* 2: 386–87]

Not surprisingly, this kind of "dialectical" materialism eliminated the distinction between nature and history: the laws of motion also rule the course of history (*Werke* 20:11, *Anti-Dühring*, p. 16). Through his productive activity man actively participates in the material process of nature. Engels's materialist interpretation came to dominate Marxist thought, and his polemical *Anti-Dühring* became "the canonical statement of dialectical materialism" (Plekhanov). Yet this position clearly conflicts with Marx's dismissal, at the end of the Paris Manuscripts, of the materialist concept of nature as one more speculative abstraction.

> *Nature as nature*—that is to say, insofar as it is still sensuously distinguished from the secret sense hidden within it—nature isolated, distinguished from these abstractions, is *nothing—a nothing proving itself to be nothing*—is *devoid of sense,* or has only the sense of being an externality which has to be annulled. [*MEGA* 1³: 171; *Coll. Works* 3: 346]

I know of no occasion when Marx retracted or fundamentally deviated from this position. Why, then, did he tolerate the development of Engels's materialist theory during his lifetime? Did failing health during his later years impair his critical capacity? Or did the issue not interest him sufficiently to prompt him to confront Engels with their philosophical differences? Or, most improbably, had he really come to agree with what Engels read him from his *Anti-Dühring*? The history of this strange infiltration of a materialism distinct from mechanism, mainly by gratuitous dialectical assumptions, remains to be written.[19]

Fortunately, Engels's impact upon the notion of ideology is not limited to his dubious materialist interpretation. Far more fruitful is his discussion of the order and connection of ideologies. He regards the state as the first ideology a society creates for the safeguarding of its common interests. The state in turn generates second-level, independent spheres of public and private law. Religion and philosophy emerge "still further removed from the material, economic basis" (*Werke* 21: 302; *Sel. Works* 2: 397). In this presentation of the dialectical interaction between structure and superstructure, especially as expressed in the three letters we discussed in the chapter on history, Engels completed Marx's theory where it needed to be completed, without letting his own materialist theories interfere with the subject.

Even Engels's reductionist interpretation of the dependence of ideological structures upon material production may have had an unintended beneficial side effect: it weakened the connotation of falsehood that had encumbered the term *ideology* since Marx's polemics with the Young Hegelians. Having reduced mental processes to "reflections" of production relations, Engels had no more *adequate* basis for distinguishing the false from the true. Henceforth "ideology" came to mean a socially determined, rather than a false, ideal complex. Engels thus cleared the way for the kind of social critique of culture (rather than only of socially suspicious ideas) which twentieth-century sociology so successfully performed.

More and more Marxists have come to regard ideologies as the common assumptions through which a group or a society conceptualizes the values and beliefs that allow it to operate effectively.[20] Thus, to Louis Althusser, ideology, conceived as a

19. Meanwhile, the reader can profitably consult the first chapter of Z. A. Jordan's *The Evolution of Dialectical Materialism*.

20. Cf. Leszek Kolakowski, *Der Mensch ohne Alternative* (Munich: Piper Verlag, 1960), p. 24.

system of representations (images, myths, ideas), forms an organic and vital part of every social structure.[21] If men are to be formed, to respond to the demands of their conditions of existence, they need to make certain unproven assumptions concerning their relation to society. No society can fully justify the principles by which it operates; most of the time it simply takes them for granted. Nevertheless, in Althusser's view, ideologies differ critically according to the kind of society they legitimate. All traditional ideologies suffer from the perspectival error created by one class that imposes its own views upon all others. Ideologies in a classless society no longer have this problem. But even they inevitably distort the relation between men and their real conditions of existence. While a bourgeois society remains permanently unaware of the ideological nature of its projections, the classless society of the future, though not *actually* aware of its assumptions, can at least in principle scientifically justify them.[22] In the latter case Althusser speaks of a "theoretical ideology." Together scientific theory and theoretical ideology constitute the necessary theoretical apparatus of praxis and, as such, are both justified.[23] Nevertheless, a substantial difference remains: a scientific theory relates each particular aspect of praxis to its origin, while an ideology presents only one stage of

21. *For Marx*, pp. 231–32.

22. I write "of the future" because, according to Althusser, much in the ideology of the present communist societies remains bourgeois, derived partly from their own bourgeois inheritance, partly from a constant exposure to bourgeois influences around them. Thus he rejects such "humanist" concerns as the dignity and free development of the person as bourgeois-oriented. "The themes of socialist humanism . . . are the way the socialists are *living* the relation between themselves and these problems, that is, the *conditions* in which they are posed. . . . However, considered in themselves, these problems are basically problems that, far from calling for a 'philosophy of man' invoke the preparation of new forms of *organization* for economic, political and ideological life (including new forms of individual development) in the socialist countries during the phase of the withering-away or supersession of the dictatorship of the proletariat" *(For Marx,* p. 239).

23. "In its most general form theoretical practice does not only include *scientific* theoretical practice, but also pre-scientific theoretical practice, that is, 'ideological' theoretical practice (the forms of knowledge that make up the prehistory of science and their 'philosophies' " (ibid., p. 167).

that development.[24] The intrinsic limitations of an ideology preclude it from posing the question of truth in its totality.

The "epistemological break" which, according to Althusser, fundamentally separates ideology from scientific theory raises serious difficulties. What is the state of the unproven axioms of science? Are they scientific or ideological? The history of science consists of a succession of assumptions at one time believed to be self-evident or scientifically justified and later demoted to a nonscientific status, if not positively proven to be false. How can any theory remain without unproven assumptions? Philosophers of science today, more modest in their claims than their nineteenth-century predecessors, do not know what to do with Althusser's distinction. For the same reason, the claim made for the concept of theoretical ideology is impossible to substantiate, since no ideology can ever fully justify its assumptions. Nor can a theory that remains part of a *living practice*, ever with scientific exactitude chart the course of its future development. By its very nature action moves beyond the given, and hence beyond the known. However much it may be defined by existing social-economic conditions, inasmuch as it is a project oriented toward the future it will transform these conditions as much as it transforms itself, and it will do so in unpredictable ways. A theory that situates itself *within* a development can never exhaustively comprehend that development. Althusser has misstated the problem. Having first taken the concept of ideology out of the narrow true-or-false debate by describing it as the cultural assumptions a society needs to make in order to maintain its vitality, he then inconsistently falls back upon the traditional distinctions between theory and ideology, or between true and false ideologies. Once one accepts the integration of theory and practice in a united world-view, such distinctions cannot be consistently maintained. As Louis Dumont writes:

> Any ideology is a social set of representations—certainly a very complex affair. The fact that one particular representation in that set is judged as true or false, rational or traditional, scientific or not, is irrelevant to the social nature of the idea or value. For

24. Ibid., p. 167.

example: that the earth revolves around the sun is, I take it, a scientific statement, but it is admitted by most of our contemporaries without their being able to demonstrate it. Moreover, even for those who are able to do so, this statement is part of their world view, together with many other statements they cannot demonstrate. As such, it may be legitimately be taken as an integral part of the ideology as a whole. . . .[25]

In a later essay[26] Althusser softens the distinction between theory and ideology. Marx's separation of structure and superstructure, he now admits, is itself no more than a "topographical metaphor," a "descriptive" theory that actually remains on a representational level and merely *initiates* a genuine theory. A scientific critique must *show* how an ideology is integrated with the economic production system, rather than dogmatically assert that it "reflects" that system. Ideology fulfills an essential function in the cycle of economic reproduction. The reproduction of labor power requires not only physical procreation but also a renewal of the "submission to the rules of the established order, i.e., a reproduction of submission to the ruling ideology for the worker, and a reproduction of the ability to manipulate the ruling ideology correctly for the agents of exploitation and repression."[27] In this view, ideology creates the appropriate disposition for providing a new generation of labor power. Althusser eliminates the last traces of a "reflection" theory in favor of an indissoluble, active union between what Marx called structure and superstructure. This appears clearly in the case of the state. More than a mere political power that sanctions existing social structures, the state provides, via the educational system, the communication media, the Church and the family, an ideological apparatus that actually *creates* the mentality needed for preserving and expanding the existing system of production.

One might, of course, object that church, family, and communication media do not always function as state apparatuses. They may do so in a country where the boundaries of the state

25. Louis Dumont, *From Mandeville to Marx*, p. 17.
26. "Ideology and Ideological State Apparatuses," in *Lenin and Philosophy*, trans. Ben Brewster (New York: Monthly Review Press, 1971).
27. Ibid., pp. 132–33.

coincide with those of the nation and, roughly speaking, with those of the entire culture. But in a culturally pluralistic society, ethnic, religious, and communicative structures display a far greater independence with respect to the state. Even in France the church of the last hundred and fifty years can hardly be called an apparatus of a state to which it stood in almost constant opposition. Those inaccurate generalizations should not obscure the merit of Althusser's attempt to rescue the notion of ideology from the wasteland of "illusory" consciousness. For Marx's negative reading—"exactly like the theoretical status of dreams among writers before Freud"[28]—Althusser substitutes his own positive one, grounded in what he claims to be the undeveloped theory of Marx's mature works. An ideology does not consist in a group's imaginary representation of the real conditions of existence, but in its imaginary representation of its *relation* to those conditions. As such, it never *directly reflects* the economic production process, but expresses how the members of a particular group or society pre-reflectively *feel about* this relation. The language of causality used in Marx's early theory must give way to that of structural description.

> What is represented in ideology is therefore not the system of the real relations which govern the existence of individuals, but the imaginary relation of those individuals to the real relations in which they live. If this is the case, the question of the 'cause' of the imaginary distortion of the real relations in ideology disappears and must be replaced by a different question: why is the representation given to individuals of their (individual) relation to social relations which govern their conditions of existence and their collective and individual life necessarily an imaginary relation?[29]

I must confess that I do not see how Althusser answers that question at all satisfactorily. But at least he eliminates the simplistic answer suggested in *The German Ideology*, that an alienated society *directly* reflects itself in a distorted consciousness.[30] Althusser attempts to preserve the original character of mental

28. Ibid., p. 159.
29. Ibid., p. 165.
30. Of course, Marx and Engels themselves abandoned this simplistic view. According to the preface to the *Critique of Political Economy*, the relations that

processes by means of a more comprehensive concept of praxis. The realm of pure ideas, the object of a philosophy of culture, disappears into praxis, but praxis itself ceases to be purely economic. No ideology exists that is not rooted in praxis; no praxis exists that is not cultural (hence ideological) as well as economic. Ideas and productive activity become fully integrated with one another.[31]

That ideologies are illusions or distortions without intrinsic truth had been denied by Marxists before Althusser, most emphatically by Karl Korsch in his influential *Marxism and Philosophy.* Far from being illusions which, unlike social and political structures, have no direct footing in reality, ideologies, according to Korsch, command an unparalleled power in the dynamics of social life. A critique of society, then, should not be restricted to economic theories and political institutions: it should include the theoretical forms of consciousness as well. In fact, only the active intervention of consciousness can convert a critique of capitalist economy into a theory of social revolution. If consciousness and the material conditions of production are truly interdependent, as they ought to be in a *dialectical* theory, *all* forms of consciousness, including the "higher" ideologies, count and must be reckoned with. "They must be criticized in theory and overthrown in practice, together with the economic, legal and political structures of society and at the same time as them."[32]

Marx's distinction between a social-economic structure and an ideological superstructure has often led to the conclusion that economic concepts contain more truth than ideologies. But this inference does not follow. No concepts have been more subjected to Marx's critique than the categories of capitalist economy. Value, for instance, is as questionable as any philosophical concept ever was. The dynamic core of reality, praxis, includes *all forms of consciousness,* even the ones more remote from the

---

structure the process of production determine the modes of thinking only in the last instance.

31. Ibid., pp. 169–71.
32. *Marxism and Philosophy,* pp. 96–97.

actual process of production and its social structures. On the one side, all theory, including Marxist theory, belongs as much to the superstructure as what have been traditionally called "ideologies" do. All remain subject to the same constant critique of the praxis. The critical principle, the essence of Marx's concept of history, must be applied to the Marxist conception of history itself.[33]

Korsch's radically dialectical interpretation of praxis goes beyond anything Marx ever wrote, and probably ever meant. Lukacs, who wrote his *History and Class Consciousness* at the same time, independently reached a very similar conclusion. Yet he placed even more emphasis upon the need to integrate all theory with praxis. Against the idealism latent in all pure theories Lukacs cites Marx's Theses on Feuerbach. In his reading, the critique of the first thesis applies to so-called scientific Marxism as much as to the materialism of Marx's own time: "The chief defect of all materialism . . . is that the object, reality, what we apprehend through our senses, is understood only in the form of the *object* of *contemplation,* but not as sensuous *human activity,* as *practice,* not *subjectively.*" Any theory that isolates nature from living praxis is materialist. Its speculative detachment reflects industrial man's inability to take an active and conscious part in the productive process: a social-economic system over which the worker has no control has reduced its producers to passive onlookers.[34] But the same separation of thought from reality has come to prevail in scientific Marxism. In its abstract frame of thought it is no longer evident how thinking could ever correspond to reality. All attempts to connect one with the other are made on the basis of the relations of consciousness to itself. A

33. Ibid., p. 102.
34. "As labor is progressively rationalized and mechanized his lack of will is reinforced by the way in which his activity becomes less and less active and more and more contemplative. The contemplative stance adopted towards a process mechanically conforming to fixed laws and enacted independently of man's consciousness and impervious to human intervention, *i.e.,* a perfectly closed system, must likewise transform the basic categories of man's immediate attitude to the world" (*History and Class Consciousness,* p. 89).

genuine theory of praxis must stress, as Marx did, the intrinsic bond between consciousness and productive activity. Only in that perspective does the impact of social-economic processes upon modes of thought become more than an unprovable materialist axiom.

All three, Korsch, Lukacs, and Althusser, unanimously reject the structure-superstructure schema as an adequate model for the understanding of ideas. Ideas are not "derived." Fulfilling an essential function of praxis, they must rather be seen as an integral part of it. In defining this function in purely economic terms Althusser reveals what all Marxist theorists (including Korsch and Lukacs) assume: the priority of the economic production in the totality of praxis. The many contemporary social critics who have adopted the concept of ideology rarely accept the priority of the economic production process. All non-Marxists and most Marxists have freed the concept from the negative connotation which it had in *The German Ideology*.[35] Marxist interpreters continue to emphasize strongly the connection of ideology with praxis, and even with class.[36]

In the next three sections we shall trace the development of Marx's theory in three areas crucially significant to the critique of ideology yet never explored by Marx himself. Since the very validity of the theory depends on its applicability to those areas, we cannot pass judgment on one without acquainting ourselves with the others.

35. For Clifford Geertz, ideologies construe disclosure models that represent the social order of a community in order to allow its members to find meaning in their society (*The Interpretation of Cultures* [New York: Basic Books, 1973]). For Gouldner, they provide linguistic maps that guide the members of a community participating in common projects.

36. Cf. Frederic Jameson, *Marxism and Form*. Alvin Gouldner, *The Dialectic of Ideology and Technology: The Origins, Grammar and Future of Ideology* (New York: Seabury Press, 1976), writes: "A fundamental rule of the grammar of all modern ideology was the principle of the unity of theory and practice mediated by rational discourse" (p. 30). According to Terry Eagleton, *Marxism and Literary Criticism* (Berkeley: University of California Press, 1976), ideologies are connected with the social function of the class which gave rise to them, but in order to fulfill their social function, they must remain meaningful to other classes as well.

THE MEDIATION OF PSYCHOLOGY

Psychology, particularly psychoanalysis, poses a unique problem to Marxism. Is it part of the ideology of a bourgeois society or of the "science" that exposes the self-deception of such an ideology? Clearly Marx did not confront the issue. The science of psychology was still in its infancy and psychoanalysis arrived long after his death. But the nature of Marx's critique inevitably raises the question of whether that critique would accept or even require the mediation between the social-economic determining relations and the individual. Until well into the twentieth century Marxists never seriously considered the problem, though some statements made by Engels suggest that he eventually came to realize the weight of the subjective factor in the social determination. As an ardent reader of the literary classics and an admirer of Balzac, Marx was well acquainted with the complexity of personal feelings and behavior. His analysis of Eugène Sue's *Les Mystères de Paris* in *The Holy Family* even shows an awareness of the role of unconscious motives (the fear of incest). But he shows little inclination to investigate such motives beyond the individual's social environment. At least his writings provide no evidence that he ever moved much beyond his early, disparaging judgment on interpretations of human behavior based on unconscious, personal motives of self-interest.

> It is well known that a certain kind of psychology explains big things by means of small causes and, correctly sensing that everything for which man struggles is a matter of his interest, arrives at the incorrect opinion that there are only "petty" interests, only the interests of a stereotyped self-seeking. Further, it is well known that this kind of psychology and knowledge of mankind is to be found particularly in towns, where moreover it is considered the sign of a clever mind to see through the world and to perceive that behind the passing clouds of ideas and facts, there are quite small envious intriguing manikins, who pull the strings setting everything in motion. [*MEGA* 1¹: 218–19; *Coll. Works* 1: 171]

In general, then, we can say that for Marx and Engels social conditions adequately define human development and require no further psychological interpretation. "Human beings become individuals only through the process of history" (*GR* 395; NIC 496).

Nevertheless, Engels's theory of the origin of the family, inspired by Marx's own notes, might have led him to accept some of the insights of modern psychology had he been acquainted with them. In his discussion of Morgan's *Ancient Society,* Engels admits that production plays no primary role in the formation of the oldest form of society, whereas sexual relations do. He assumes, rather gratuitously it appears, a period of total sexual freedom at the beginning, a freedom that could be converted into a family-style society only by a process of repression. "Mutual toleration among the adult males, freedom from jealousy, was, however, the first condition for the building of those larger and enduring groups in the midst of which alone the transition from animal to man could be achieved" (*Werke* 21: 42; *Sel. Works* 2: 197). When production begins to determine the shape of society, it imposes its demands by means of an increasingly severe repression. Hence a psychic factor mediates social relations with the production process.

But the most obvious place for introducing the psychic factor is the mechanism through which the ideology of the ruling class is unconsciously transmitted to the members of a society. Both Marx and Engels here simply *assume* the existence of unconscious processes. In fact, Engels explicitly refers to them in a letter to Franz Mehring: "Ideology is a process which is indeed accomplished consciously by the so-called thinker, but it is the wrong kind of consciousness. The real motive forces impelling him remain unknown to the thinker; otherwise it simply would not be an ideological process. Hence he imagines false or illusory motive forces" (*Werke* 39: 97; *Sel. Corres.,* p. 434). This interpretation, of course, corresponds to Freud's concept of rationalization.[37] Marx himself distinguished "the forms of social consciousness" from the conscious ideologies (*MEGA* 1⁵: 16; *Coll. Works* 5: 36). John McMurtry refers to this unconscious a priori

37. Reuben Osborn, *Marxism and Psychoanalysis* (1967) (New York: Octagon Books, 1974), p. 95.

as "historical materialism's version of the collective uncon-scious."[38]

If neglect of the psychological mediation is understandable in Marx and Engels, in their modern followers it is considerably less. For a long time many of them regarded any interpretation of human behavior that was less than totally dependent on social structures as a typical rationalization of bourgeois ideology. Such a simplistic attitude is hardly in keeping with the demands of a radical critique of ideological superstructures. If the impact of class structures is as pervasively repressive as the Marxist cri-tique implies, then patterns of behavior and thought cannot be assumed to reveal themselves without the aid of a method for probing the hidden motives underneath the surface appear-ance. The precise nature of the social-economic determination cannot be established until the social critic understands the mode of transmission.

As far as I know, Plekhanov first paid serious attention to this mediating agency. In *The Development of the Monist View of History* (1895)[39] he allowed the mental states that precede, accompany, and follow social-economic developments a certain degree of independence. This ruled out any *direct* interpretation of mental events through social-economic development. Thus, even an ex-pert knowledge of the economic conditions of France in the eighteenth century sheds little light on the nature of the minuet, a dance which, Plekhanov claims, expressed the psychology of the nonproductive class. "Consequently, in this case the eco-nomic factor is second to the psychological."[40] Of course, the introduction of a psychic factor does not necessarily signal a break in the cycle of economic determinism. In the case of Plekhanov, it fails to do so altogether. In his theory of super-structures, psychology, which precedes the ideologies proper, is "*partly* determined" by the social-economic relations and *partly*

38. John McMurtry, *The Structure of Marx's World View* (Princeton: Princeton University Press, 1978), p. 153.

39. G. V. Plekhanov, *The Development of the Monist View of History* (New York: International Publishers, 1973).

40. *Fundamental Problems of Marxism* (New York: International Publishers, 1969), p. 71.

by the economic conditions themselves.[41] Plekhanov mentions no other factors and insists that individual psychology primarily reflects the psychology of the social class to which the individual belongs. Such a restrictive view deprives psychology once again of the independence it needs to serve as a genuine principle of interpretation in a critique of society.

To be more than ideological the psychological factor must be dialectically, rather than causally, related to the social-economic conditions. Marxists have often enough admitted this in principle but rarely applied it in practice. Wary of granting psychology an independence that would place it outside Marx's cultural pyramid, they have tended to subordinate it to social-economic factors. To some extent their concern is justified. For *by itself* the psychic element can never function as an adequate principle of social critique. The concept of mental health, for instance, if understood as being well adjusted to one's social environment, merely assumes that society itself is healthy. Marxists rightly point out that social health must be previously established if social adjustment is to have normative force. Yet a social theory of culture does not necessarily exclude a relative independence of the psychic factor. Freud himself refers to communal neuroses induced by the social environment rather than by individual disposition. In *Civilization and Its Discontents* he even dealt with the problems that afflict a civilization as a whole and with their social-economic origin. Economic scarcity, in his view, determines both the relations of the members of society and their view of life. Earlier he had written, almost in Marx's own words, that "the motive of human society is in the last resort an economic one."[42] Freud wonders whether the social and economic

41. Ibid., p. 80.

42. *Introductory Lectures on Psychoanalysis*, in *Complete Psychological Works* (London: Hogarth Press, 1967), 16: 312. The basis of civilization consists in man's attempt to exploit the wealth of nature and in the rules by which he adjusts all human relations to this exploitation. "The two trends of civilization are not independent of each other: firstly, because the mutual relations of men are profoundly influenced by the amount of instinctual satisfaction which the existing wealth makes possible; secondly, because an individual man can himself come to function as wealth in relation to another one, insofar as the other person makes use of his capacity for work, or chooses him as a sexual object . . ." (*The Future of an Illusion*, in *Works* 21:5).

benefits that a production-oriented society offers merit the psychological toll—an ever-increasing feeling of guilt and neurotic behavior—they exact. Yet Freud, in contrast to the Marxist view, does not ascribe the ills of society to the capitalist mode of production as such, but to the growing complexity and hence the increasing regimentation of modern society. Nor does he expect much good from large-scale social-economic experiments. Drastic solutions arouse his suspicion, and he merely anticipates increased suffering from a socialization of the means of production. This generally pessimistic attitude of its founder is, according to Jürgen Habermas, the reason why psychoanalysis has never developed into a social theory. Yet without the support of such a theory individual psychology must remain abstract.[43]

In recent years the aversion of Marxist critics to psychoanalytic methods has made room for a tendency to adopt them as an essential part of the critique of ideology. In his *Critique of Dialectical Reason*, Sartre shows how some method is needed to explain the mechanism that transmits the general, social determinations to the individual.

> [Psychoanalysis] is a method that establishes how a child lives his family relations inside a given group. This does not mean that it questions the priority of institutions. On the contrary its object depends on the structure of a particular family which in its own way instantiates the family structure proper to that particular class under particular conditions.[44]

It is of little use to study the effects of the working conditions in a particular society if one neglects the effects of the early, unconscious *living* conditions. The early, personal history of the person is as much part of the *given* past from which he or she

---

43. "The conception of the instincts as the prime mover of history and of civilization as the result of their struggle forgets that we have only *derived* the concept of impulse privatively from language deformation and behavioral pathology. At the human level we never encounter any needs that are not already interpreted linguistically and symbolically affixed to potential action." (Jürgen Habermas, *Knowledge and Human Interests* (Boston: Beacon Press, 1971), p. 285.

44. *Critique de la raison dialectique*, p. 47.

operates as the social-economic conditions into which he or she is born. Yet they are not *independent* of those conditions. For the forces that have shaped the child's unconscious have themselves been shaped by the way in which its parents and educators *lived* the general interests of their class.

Even before Sartre, Erich Fromm had included the methods and conclusions of depth psychology as a necessary factor of interpretation in his critique of bourgeois society. In the first issue of the journal of the Frankfurt neo-Marxist school, he mapped out a program for a science of social psychology that would study the effects upon the child's psychic development of social-economic structures unconsciously transmitted through the family.[45] Over the years Fromm developed this thesis in a number of books, especially *Escape from Freedom* (1941) and *The Sane Society* (1955), which became increasingly critical of ortho-dox Freudianism. The psychological forces that shape a person's character and history are themselves socially conditioned.

> Thus the mode of life, as it is determined for the individual by the peculiarity of an economic system, becomes the primary factor in determining his whole character structure, because the imperative need for self-preservation forces him to accept the conditions un-der which he has to live. . . . Primarily his personality is molded by the particular mode of life, as he has already been confronted with it as a child through the medium of the family, which represents all the features that are typical of a particular society or class.[46]

The family is in fact "the psychic agency of society"[47] that trans-mits the requirements of society to the child. The factors that most profoundly affect the formation of the young individual, the parents' unacknowledged hopes and fears expressed in their methods of child training, bear the imprint of society's demands

45. "Über Methode und Aufgabe einer analytischen Sozialpsychologie," in *Zeitschrift für Sozialforschung* (1932), pp. 28 ff. For the context and significance of Fromm's effort, cf. Martin Jay, *The Dialectical Imagination, A History of the Frankfurt School and the Institute of Social Research 1923–1950* (Boston: Little Brown, 1973), pp. 86–101.

46. Erich Fromm, *Escape from Freedom* (New York: Holt, Rinehart, Winston, [1941] 1955), p. 33.

47. *The Sane Society* (New York: Holt, Rinehart, Winston, 1955), p. 79.

and expectations. Allegedly "innate" drives and instinctual needs are developed in the course of man's adaptation to his social environment. Each society creates its own psychic attitudes and needs.

Freud's theory, with its heavy stress on the Oedipus complex, reflects the patriarchal attitude of the European middle class in the nineteenth century. On the basis of ethnological studies by Bachofen and Malinowski, Fromm concluded that individuals raised in matriarchal societies pass through different stages of development. The narrowness of Freud's social vision, he claimed, distorted his psychological model. Capitalism fosters a possessive, hoarding mentality, fixated on the anal stage of development. Its demand for economic productivity overemphasizes the need for paternal authority. Emotional fulfillment is subordinated to goal-oriented productivity and acquisitiveness.[48] Psychoanalysis, then, needs to be complemented by a critical theory of society. Unfortunately, Marx never developed the psychological "substructure" needed for a fully credible critique of culture. The emergence of culture requires a more sophisticated psychology than the existence of such instinctive cravings as hunger, thirst, and sexual gratification from which Marx deduces the entire process.

> Marx had underestimated the complexity of human passions. He had not sufficiently recognized that human nature has itself needs and laws which are in constant interaction with the economic conditions which shape historical development; lacking in satisfactory psychological insights, he did not have a sufficient concept of human character, and was not aware of the fact that while man was shaped by the form of social and economic organization, he in turn also molded it.[49]

Fromm was not alone in noticing this serious deficiency in Marx's critique of society. In the same first issue of the Frankfurt *Zeitschrift* in which he had published his essay, Horkheimer had

---

48. That Freud was not aware of the limitations imposed by our own type of society is contradicted by his own very severe critique of its repressive mentality in *Civilization and Its Discontents*. Yet Fromm concentrated more on the early works, all the more so since he rejected the theory of the death instinct presented in the later ones.

49. *The Sane Society*, p. 230.

argued that without the aid of psychology it is impossible to understand the fact that ideas, institutions, and even social structures survive long after they have ceased to be useful in the production process—a social phenomenon that Marx had observed but never justified.[50]

A few years later Marcuse attempted an even more daring synthesis of Marx and Freud in his *Eros and Civilization*. Unlike Fromm, Marcuse viewed Freud's theory as radically critical of capitalist society. The universal claim for happiness underlying the psychoanalytic pleasure principle directly conflicts with the condition of a society whose very structure prohibits emotional fulfillment.

> The social content of Freudian theory becomes manifest: sharpening the psychoanalytical concepts means sharpening their critical function, their opposition to the prevailing form of society. And this critical sociological function of psychoanalysis derives from the fundamental role of sexuality as a "productive force"; the libidinal claims propel progress toward freedom and universal gratification of human needs beyond the patricentric-acquisitive stage.[51]

In Marcuse's judgment, revisionist interpretations (such as Fromm's) have softened the critical impact of Freud's theory. By rejecting the death instinct they negate the actual presence of a destructive society, while by denying the sexual nature of emotional gratification they refuse to recognize the individual's unmitigated claim to happiness. Thus they have turned Freud's implicit critique of society into a method for capitulating to its demands. From that limited perspective a neurosis is nothing more than the individual's refusal to adjust to the demands of society.

Rejecting such compromises, Marcuse reinstated Freud's theory of the later years and grounded Marx's critique of society in Freud's controversial death instinct. For Marcuse the principle

50. Max Horkheimer, "Geschichte und Psychologie," in *Zeitschrift für Sozialforschung* 1, 1/2 (1932). My attention was drawn to this article by Martin Jay in *The Dialectical Imagination*, pp. 100–01.

51. Herbert Marcuse, *Eros and Civilization* (Boston: Beacon Press [1955] 1966), p. 263.

of Eros represents the primeval, constructive impulse in the
building of a culture. When a culture once established inhibits
this impulse, Thanatos, the instinct of death and destruction,
gains the upper hand. By concentrating exclusively on material
production bourgeois civilization has emptied human activity of
its erotic drive. That drive continues to operate only on the
unsublimated level of lust, while Thanatos, equally unsublimated, runs its destructive course through nature and society.
Crude eroticism and brutal productivism complement one another in an increasingly dehumanized society. Freud himself
considerably weakened the impact of his "radically critical theory" by adjusting it to the demands of practical therapy. Protect-
ing his patient against painful conflicts, the therapist adjusts his
claim for total satisfaction in accordance with the reduced possibility of happiness allowed by the prevailing principle of productive performance. Rather than recognizing the patient's real
needs, he merely attempts to bring him to a state where he can
continue to function in the very society that made him sick.
Thus psychotherapy ends up being "a course in resignation."[52]

Marcuse's interpretation of the erotic principle is too utopian
to fit either Freud's fundamental pessimism or Marx's social determinism. Yet he and other members of the Frankfurt School
have rescued psychoanalysis from the repository of bourgeois
ideologies and have fully incorporated it into the critique of
society. Recently more orthodox Marxists have made similar efforts. Louis Althusser also advocates liberating psychoanalysis
from its current function as an instrument of social conformity
and restoring its initial purpose of social critique. Unlike Marcuse, though, he attributes its practical abuse to Freud's scientis-
tic terminology. His biological bias predestined psychoanalysis to
degenerate into an ideology. The humanization process begins
neither with drives nor instincts, but with "the law of culture,"
that is, "the law of language."[53] Language gives *form* to social
structures.

Habermas went further and turned the psychoanalytic princi-

52. Ibid., p. 246.
53. *Lenin and Philosophy*, p. 209.

ple into a critique of Marx's own theory. Fascinated by economic production, Marx failed to recognize ideology for what it essentially is—distorted communication. What Marx overlooked Freud explored: the motivational foundation of communicative action and the consequent emergence of an institutional framework of distorted communication. Because of the intrinsic complexity of processes of communication, no single social measure is guaranteed to clear up distorted communication. The critique remains basically an interindividual task. Institutional reform should support it, but as Freud wisely cautioned, such reform should never take the form of worldwide social experiments.

> Within the premises of Freudian theory, the natural basis neither offers a promise that the development of the productive forces will ever create the objective possibility for completely freeing the institutional framework from repressiveness, nor can it discourage such a hope. Freud clearly set out the direction of the history of the species, determined simultaneously by a process of self-production under categories of work and a self-formative process under conditions of distorted communication.[54]

Yet Habermas also criticizes Freud's own objectivist model of communicative action, which links what are in fact social-historical processes to a biological theory of instincts. "At the human level we never encounter any needs that are not already interpreted linguistically and symbolically affixed to potential action."[55] Marx rejected such naturalist models from the outset. To him the process of humanization consists not in a natural evolution, but in a dialectical struggle through which an emerging subject attempts to create a distance between itself and its natural environment. Human development progresses not only by simple instinctual satisfaction or frustration but by socialization of primary needs. The true meaning of psychoanalysis lies in its social critique, and here it helps the Marxist search for the social origins of human behavior. It analyzes the individual's attempt to cope with social structures over which he or she exercises little control. With Marx, it assumes that social repression

54. Jürgen Habermas, *Knowledge and Human Interest*, pp. 283–84.
55. Ibid., p. 285.

has distorted communication beyond the patient's capacity of rectification. In his attempt to reestablish, through the psychoanalytic dialogue, communication with society as a whole, the individual incorporates his private history into the more general history of the society to which he belongs. His narrative, however personal, provides information about that society and about the particular difficulties its members experience in relating to it. Thus psychoanalysis fulfills an essential task in the hermeneutics and critique of culture as a whole. The following section should confirm this conclusion.

ART AND THE AESTHETIC DIMENSION OF LIFE

The Marxist approach to art and letters labors under a clouded reputation. A social-economic interpretation of aesthetic achievements is, in general, considered to be unpromising. Very few Marxist critics have been widely accepted (Lukacs being the foremost exception) and even those that have been are suspected of being more concerned with social classification than with analysis or interpretation of individual works of art. Most social-economic studies are helpful in understanding artistic genre and social content but shed little light on the particular structure. In artistic creation man does not simply *re-act* to his social environment: he uses that environment to articulate an inward impulse. Since that inner force directs the creative process, any theory that places the emphasis on man's productive activity risks jeopardizing the specifically aesthetic.

Thus goes the well-known objection. To answer it we must, at our own risk, of course, move beyond Marx's and Engels's random observations on the subject. The sketchiness of their remarks might discourage us from introducing them into the discussion of ideology were it not that art and literature occupy a unique and crucial position in the cultural superstructure. Marx's sporadic observations do not amount to a theory of aesthetics; nevertheless, they reveal a keen awareness of the complexity of the aesthetic process. Most revealing in his early writings is his view of the aesthetic as a universal quality of conscious life. Aesthetic activity is not a pastime left to a few, ideal moments; it forms an integral part of all human activity. The underlying assumption, apparently inspired by Schiller's view in *On the Aesthetic Education of Mankind,* is that aesthetic awareness unifies all other forms of consciousness. Yet in contrast to Schiller, Marx subordinates the play impulse to the productive impulse. Production without play, however, deprives the worker of the aesthetic enjoyment inherent in all truly human activity and returns him to an elementary, exclusively practical relation to nature. Inhuman activity of this kind stunts aesthetic development. "The care-burdened, poverty-stricken man has no *sense* for the finest play" (*MEGA* 1³: 120; *Coll. Works* 3: 302). In contrast, when nature is allowed "to relate itself humanly to a human being" (*MEGA* 1³: 119; *Coll. Works* 3: 300), work awakens all senses. But the eye and the ear can become "capable of human gratification" only in a humanized work-world (*MEGA* 1³: 120; *Coll. Works* 3: 301).

Man is the only animal that produces in accordance with the nature of objects. It is in man's ability to allow the object to follow its own laws of being that, according to Marx, the basic condition of all aesthetics lies. "An animal forms objects only in accordance with the standard and the needs of the species to which it belongs, whilst man knows how to produce in accordance with the standard of every species, and knows how to apply everywhere the inherent standard to the object. Man therefore also forms objects in accordance with the laws of beauty" (*MEGA* 1³: 89; *Coll. Works* 3: 277). This description sounds remarkably "classical." For the Greeks, certainly arts or crafts did not aim at creating something entirely new. They constituted no attempt to change nature, but rather an effort to create in *accordance with* nature. It is precisely because of the essentially subordinate function of actualizing a form which already preexists in matter that the craftsman (and the artist was essentially a craftsman) was not more highly regarded in classical Greek society.[56] The objective nature of the aesthetic experience does not decide the question of whether the aesthetic quality resides, as a natural property, in the nature of things, or whether it is produced by a

56. J. P. Vernant, *Mythe et pensée chez les Grecs* (Paris: 1979), 2: 39–42.

particular attitude in the subject which enables it to *preceive* aes-thetically. While the quoted passage favors rather an objective interpretation, elsewhere Marx appears to hold a more subjective position. Occasionally the two positions are stated in succession, as in the following passage: "just as the most beautiful music has *no* sense for the unmusical ear—is no object for it, because my object can only be the confirmation of one of my essential powers and can therefore only be for me as my essential power is present for itself as a subjective capacity—" (*MEGA* 1³: 120; *Coll. Works* 3: 301).[57]

In considering the more specific, but also more controversial aspects of Marx's theory, we must not lose sight of the primary role which aesthetic creation and appreciation play in his program for a total emancipation. His emphasis on the direct relation between art and its social-economic "basis" may easily obscure his very real aesthetic concerns. In the introduction to the *Critique of Political Economy* he writes that Greek art would not have been possible in the age of automatic machinery, railways, and telegraph. But immediately after this rather trivial remark he cautions against any simplistic, one-directional interpretation of the relation between art and economic production. Classical art continues to inspire long after the Greek *polis* and its economy have vanished. "But the difficulty lies not in understanding that the Greek arts and epic are bound up with certain forms of social development. The difficulty is that they still afford us artistic pleasure and that in a certain respect they count as a norm and as an unattainable model" (*GR* 31; NIC 111). The disappearance of an artistic style (which more *directly* reflects the social structure and technical development of a society) does not mark the end of the masterpieces it has produced.[58]

57. On this question, cf. Edward Swiderski, *The Philosophical Foundations of Soviet Aesthetics* (Boston: D. Reidel Co., 1979), chap. 5.

58. Many studies of Marxist inspiration concentrate on the influence of social and political ideologies upon the emergence of particular aesthetic techniques and styles. In a remarkable monograph, *Aeschylus and Athens* (1941), George D. Thompson has shown the impact of fifth-century Athenian society upon the development of the tragedy. According to Arnold Hauser's study, *Mannerism* (1965), mannerism both expresses an "alienated" society and reacts against it. Lucien Goldman, in *Le Dieu caché* (1955), argues eloquently—though not always

The passage on Greek art clearly does not allow a simple "ideological" interpretation. The highest peaks of aesthetic achievement were reached at a relatively early stage of social development which later, economically more advanced periods appear unable to match. Nor does this passage express a momentary opinion, unprecedented and never reiterated. In 1842 Marx collaborated with Bruno Bauer on a polemical pamphlet, to be published anonymously, on "Hegel's Doctrine of Religion and Art Judged from the Standpoint of Faith" (the title reflects the authors' ironical approach). Later he developed his ideas further in separate essays on Christian art, religious art, and romanticism. All have been lost, but the guiding idea on Greek art may be gathered both from the anonymous pamphlet and from the book excerpts that have been preserved from the period of his writing (spring 1842). According to these sources, Marx argued that monotheism's gigantic projection of the egoistic individual leaves no room for the unselfish ideals of genuine art. It tolerates no pursuit of the purely human. According to an excerpt of Rumohr's *Italienische Forschungen,* Greek art is perfectly intelligible on the sole basis of its natural environment, independently of all religious doctrine. It is, in fact, nothing more than a "Darstellung menschlich schöner Sitten in herrlichen organischen Bildungen."[59] The pamphlet similarly contrasts the aesthetic perfection of the Greeks (based upon the political order of the city-states) with the intrinsically religious art that preceded and followed them. "Religious" art is not fully aesthetic, since it derives from practical needs, and hence, Marx echoes Johann Jacob Grund, *Die Malerei der Griechen,* "can have no end but satisfaction." The opposition between Greek art and "religious" art corresponds to the one between creative activity and what Marx later called fetishist activity. The emphasis of religious art may *seem* to be all on spiritual content, but, relying

---

convincingly—for the role of the new *noblesse de robe* in the origin of seventeenth-century French drama. Studies of this nature constitute a valuable contribution to art history and literary theory, but they do not decide the aesthetic issue proper.

59. Cf. Michael Lifschitz, *Marx und die Asthetik* (Dresden, 1967), p. 63. My interpretation of the early essays follows Lifschitz's study.

heavily on sheer quantity of form and being mainly pragmatic in intent, it misses the disinterested, harmonious self-expression characteristic of genuine art and reflects, in fact, the opposite of a spiritual attitude. As far as we are able to reconstitute them, Marx's views in this early discussion favor an aesthetic humanism that stays clear of sensuous materialism as well as of the symbolic idealism of Christian art. In this latter respect he already differs from Hegel, who considered the appearance of Romantic (i.e., Christian) art a more radical breakthrough of the Spirit. Most interestingly, Marx's early aesthetic reflections set up an ideal of cultural integration that gradually came to dominate his entire work.

Greek art established a permanent *ideal* of humanity; what came later was more a *reflection* of humanity in its actual, historical, existence. Art thus becomes "art production," a particular function in the overall process of production related to, and, to some extent, dependent upon, other functions. "It is even recognized that certain forms of art, *e.g.*, the epic, can no longer be produced in their world epoch-making, classical structure as soon as the production of art, as such begins" (*GR* 30; NIC 110). Art production functions as a part of the production process, while art as *ideal,* though conditioned by a particular state of society, nevertheless transcends its social context altogether. "The charm of their [the Greeks'] art for us is not in contradiction to the undeveloped stage of society on which it grew. It is its result, rather, and is inextricably bound up, rather, with the fact that the unripe social conditions under which it arose, and could alone arise, can never return" (*GR* 31; NIC 111). In one sense, however, this ideal of the past anticipates the future. In the expected communist society social conditions will again allow aesthetic activity to *idealize* all of life. But to do so, art as an individual achievement, as a solo performance of a "unique" creator, must cease to exist. In his attack on Stirner's theory of the "unique" individual in *The German Ideology,* Marx had outlined the essential transformation of the role of art in the society of the future.

> The exclusive concentration of artistic talent in particular individuals, and its suppression in the broad mass which is bound up with

this, is a consequence of division of labor. .... In any case, with a communist organization of society, there disappears the subordination of the artist to local and national narrowness, which arises entirely from division of labor, and also the subordination of the artist to some definite art, thanks to which he is exclusively a painter, sculptor, etc., the very name of his activity adequately expressing the narrowness of his professional development and his dependence on division of labor. In a communist society there are no painters but at most people who engage in painting among other activities. (*MEGA* 1⁵: 373; *Coll. Works* 5: 394]

According to this text, the division of labor prevents art from penetrating all of existence and thereby becoming an ideal of life. In an essay on "Marx on Ideology and Art," O. K. Werckmeister thereby evokes the kind of universal aesthetic attitude that was advocated by Schiller. "In Marx's view art as it existed and still exists belongs to the social condition we must overcome; in its ideological realization the essence of art is alienated from its classical idea as well as from its utopian liberation. In this respect it differs from the other forms of ideology."⁶⁰ But we should keep in mind that this total reintegration of aesthetic activity belongs to, and is conditioned by, the wholly utopian abolition of the division of labor ("to hunt in the morning, fish in the afternoon, rear cattle in the evening") which Marx abandoned in his later writings. Nevertheless, taken together with the introduction to the *Grundrisse*, the passage of *The German Ideology* presents us with something more than what orthodox Marxism has traditionally read in Marx's notes: a critique of the capitalist attitude. Such a critique definitely appears in Marx. But its meaning is not that all art is ideologicaly dependent on social-economic structures, and hence that utilitarian societies are less likely to produce great art. What Marx is saying is more fundamental: art must cease to be one function among others in the social production process. It must cease to be, or at least cease to be limited to, a separate activity in the total productive output of society. Such a liberation entails more than overcoming the capitalist system of production. It calls for a transforma-

60. *Ideologie und Kunst bei Marx u. a. Essays* (Frankfurt: Fischer, 1974), p. 16. The essay also appeared in *New Literary History* 4 (1972–73): 500–19.

tion analogous in the practical order to the (theoretical) end of art in Hegel's aesthetics.

On this radical reintegration of art with the whole of culture, however, Marx has left no more than some sparse notes. They suffice to distinguish art from a mere ideology, but not to define the nature of the aesthetic "ideal," particularly during the period intermediate between the "naive" epoch of our classical past and the anticipated liberation of a remote future. Still, even during the capitalist epoch art does more than "reflect" its particular society: it idealizes, and in doing so sets up new standards which are at least partly opposed to the existing state of society. It may even help to overthrow the society out of which it emerges. Yet certain societies encourage this aesthetic idealization more than others.

As we might have expected after his earlier judgment on the capitalist method of production, Marx considers its influence upon arts and letters to be primarily negative—at least in its present industrial stage.

> Capitalist production is hostile to certain branches of spiritual production, for example art and poetry. If this is left out of account, it opens the way to the illusion of the French in the eighteenth century which has been so beautifully satirized by Lessing. Because we are further ahead than the ancients in mechanics, etc., why shouldn't we be able to make an epic too? And the *Henriade* in place of the *Iliad*. . . . [*Werke* 26^1: 257; *TSV* 1: 285]

Again this text does more than criticize the impact of the capitalist system of production upon aesthetic creation. It explicitly denies the existence of a general parallelism between art and economic production (and thus asserts the opposite of the "ideological" thesis). Even the initial suggestion that the bourgeois attitude discourages aesthetic disinterestedness must be qualified. As we know from the Communist Manifesto, Marx deeply admired the unprecedented cultural achievements of the bourgeois era. Initially, the bourgeois revolution had renewed the arts with fresh, secular subjects, different social ideals, and innovative form experiments. But after three centuries the bourgeois Enlightenment had lost whatever creative impulse it had originally possessed. By Marx's time arts and letters had begun to find their inspiration mainly in opposing the capitalist world-view.[61]

Significantly, Marx criticizes bourgeois culture primarily because of its *attitude*. Being totally involved in "interested" production, it fails to stimulate the disinterested creation of art. That aesthetic integration of the sensuous and the spiritual in which mankind, according to Schiller, finds its moral ideal, does not bloom in the sterile pragmatism of bourgeois culture. Not the economic conditions but the attitudes generated by them weaken the aesthetic impulse. Indeed, at an earlier stage of capitalist society, before the economic factor had absorbed all mental energy, the new social environment of capitalism had opened up unique possibilities for aesthetic expression, evident enough in the artistic flowering of the northern Italian cities in the Renaissance. Yet once attitudes became thoroughly affected by the single-minded pursuit of material gain, even those economic conditions which initially had favored expansion turned into cultural obstacles. Today, more than in Marx's time, art has become an investment, while publishing, increasingly dependent on larger, purely commercial enterprises, has come to be ruled by the laws and methods of the mass market. The artist and the writer are pressured to conform to standards that artistic integrity inspires

61. Adolfo Sanchez states what Marx merely implied: "From the start of the nineteenth century, artists began to develop an awareness that their work could be saved only by breaking with those artistic tendencies, such as neo-classicism, which everywhere stifled naturalness and spontaneity, and which degenerated into a bourgeois academicism. At the same time, artists became conscious of the fact that the prevailing social reality was unacceptable, and took refuge in art as the purest and most adequate means by which to affirm their liberty and individuality in the face of that reality. Romanticism expressed this alienation of artists from bourgeois society. The romantic artist expressed both an attitude of disenchantment with the reality around him and a search for roots outside that reality. He rebelled against the present by taking refuge in the past and by projecting himself into the future. He rebelled against reason because reason was used to justify reality. He exalted his individuality, the unrestrained freedom of his ego, or his radical isolation, thus expressing his opposition to the prosaic and banal reality which harassed his existence. With capitalism, everything became abstract and impersonal, and the romantic, by unleashing an internal, subjective volcano, attempted to reclaim everything vital and personal." Adolfo Sanchez Vazquez, *Art and Society: Essays in Marxist Aesthetics* (New York: Monthly Review Press, 1973), pp. 165–66.

them to combat. Ideological tendencies hardly play a role in their commercial acceptability. Capitalism possesses an amazing ability to absorb even those cultural trends which originally were directed against it. Marx would have been amused, but not surprised, by capitalism's recent success in turning most of the counter culture, apparently so hostile to bourgeois society, into a successful business enterprise. Generation gap, sexual liberation, even global attacks upon traditional society, have all become so much grist for the mill of an economic system whose marvelous adaptability and supreme indifference toward content its young critics naively underestimate.

Yet far more important than this external dependence on social-economic factors is how they determine art and literature *from within*. Here the "ideological" question confronts us with its full force. Not only historical details in literary descriptions and plastic representations, but the entire poetic imagery, the assumed value system, and even the process of artistic formation bear the imprint of the society in which the work originated.

> The historical, social ties of the work of art cannot condition it mechanically or from the outside, but must make up in some way a part of the *sui generis* pleasure which it yields us, and thus must make up a part of the very substance of the work of art as such: its *structural, intellectual* substance.[62]

At the same time, a work of art transcends its age as much as it reflects it. Though Virgil belongs uniquely to the Augustan age and Rembrandt to the Holland of the first Stadthouders, their particular social environment does not explain, much less "necessitate," the *Aeneid* or the *Night Watch*. Great art surpasses its time, surely not by becoming timeless, but by conveying a *lasting* significance to the transitory experiences of its own age. An artistic phase never simply vanishes to make room for the next one the way a theory replaces an ideology. All art holds a mirror up to the society that gave birth to it. The art of bourgeois society is no less "true" than socialist art: it merely reflects a different society. Of course, writers describe the mores of their

62. Galvano della Volpe, *Critique of Taste*, trans. Michael Caesar (London: New Left Books, 1978), p. 127.

age and, to some extent, reflect its prejudices, while artists choose their subjects (portraits, landscapes, still lifes) according to prevailing ideologies. But is what so clearly reflects current ideologies therefore ideological itself? Marx never refers to art as ideological, but most Leninist theorists nevertheless treat it as if it were. Yet art and poetry cannot be ideologies in the same sense as philosophy and religion. Art becomes "ideological" in the sense of "false" only when it ceases to create and simply mirrors the prejudices of its age. At that point it becomes, of course, bad art as well. Artistic "truth," on the other hand, does not consist in a mere reflection of the environment, not even in a correct evaluation of it, but in the achievement of an inner harmony, a balance between form and expression that *relates* to an outside world but never simply mirrors that world. Art "shows" and hence confronts the viewer, the reader, or the hearer with the real without objectively judging it. Althusser therefore rightly distinguishes art from what it reflects. "What art makes us *see*, and therefore gives to us in the form of *'seeing'*, *'perceiving'* and *'feeling'* (which is not the form of *knowing*) is the *ideology* from which it is born, in which it bathes, from which it detaches itself as art, and to which it *alludes*."[63] Indeed, by subjecting them to a wholly autonomous symbolization process, genuine art detaches itself from the ideologies of its age and even of its author. Balzac's oeuvre projects with a great veracity a prerevolutionary society, even though he himself always remained politically conservative.[64] Marx, fully aware of the complexity of aesthetic expression, admired the French novelist all the more for this.

The unique quality of aesthetic symbolization has made some commentators wonder whether art is ideological at all.[65] At the root of this question, however, lies the same lack of historical perspective that characterizes the determinist interpretation. All art, including Greek art and the "communist art" of the future,

63. *Lenin and Philosophy*, p. 222.
64. More so than was realized by Engels who, all too simplistically, presented him as admiring only republican heroes. For a more knowledgeable appraisal, see Peter Demetz, *Marx, Engels and the Poets* (Chicago: University of Chicago Press, 1966), pp. 175–76.
65. Cf. Ernst Fischer, *Art against Ideology* (London: Allen Lane, 1969).

is conditioned by the particular society which gives birth to it. Nor can it ever escape being a mirror, however idealized or distorted, of that society. Bourgeois art and literature, because of the particular function they fulfill in capitalist society, are prevented from revealing their own social position as well as the true condition of the society they reflect. Even their most creative and critical representatives have not succeeded in escaping this distorting effect. So much for the nonideological interpretation. At the same time, no art merely *reflects;* it always also, and primarily, *creates.* Marx, schooled both in the classical and the romantic traditions, was very much aware of this fact. But the mimetic view of art which he nevertheless held, along with most critics of his day, had the unfortunate effect of steering art theories guided by his principles toward an overly simplistic social realism. Art, so it was believed, must *depict* the social conditions in which it was born. Hence, after a short period of hesitation, abstract art in the Soviet Union came to be interpreted as a phenomenon of decadence: profoundly alienated from his society, the modern artist is forced to fall back upon his purely subjective feelings and emotions.[66] In general, Marxist critics have emphasized content over form and have defended "objective veracity" against what they consider to be formalism and subjectivism. In literature their interest has mainly gone to the narrative genres, the epic and the novel, which most directly reflect the social relations of an epoch. Yet their preference often betrays a confusion of aesthetic truth with objective information.

By the end of his life Engels had become aware of the one-sidedness of this trend. In a letter to Franz Mehring (July 14, 1893) he wrote: "We all laid—and were bound to lay—the main emphasis on the derivation of political, juridical, and other ideological notions and of actions arising through the medium of those notions, from basic economic facts. But at the same time

---

66. Trotsky never fell prey to this kind of simplistic interpretation. In his essay on futurism he shares the protest of the Russian artists immediately after the revolution "against the art of petty realists who sponged on life," and defends their movement for a new artistic recreating of life. *Literature and Revolution,* trans. Rose Strunsky (Ann Arbor: University of Michigan Press, 1960), p. 138.

we have on account of the content neglected the formal side—the manner in which these notions, etc., come about" (*Werke* 39: 96; *Sel. Corres.*, pp. 433–34). Earlier, in his letter of October 27, 1890, to Conrad Schmidt, he had stressed that in literature and philosophy the economic factor imposes its influence within the conditions prescribed by the particular area of expression.[67] Until recently, Marxist critics showed less concern for the relative independence of art and literature than the elderly Engels expressed in those retrospective thoughts. The overemphasis of content at the expense of form became nearly universal in Marxist aesthetics. Its first great theoretician, G. V. Plekhanov, features it as a fundamental principle. Though a man of impressive literary erudition and genuine aesthetic perceptiveness, Plekhanov nevertheless spent all his energy exposing the *message* of the works he analyzed. For him they convey above all the social "truth" of their epoch. "The first task of the critic consists in translating the ideas in a work of art from the language of art to the language of sociology, in order to locate what may be called the sociological equivalent of a given literary phenomenon."[68] Plekhanov invokes a host of witnesses—Plato, Plutarch, and Vico among them—in support of the idea that the intellectual labor of society is directed by the existing production relations. Yet even Taine's positivist emphasis on the "milieu" is not narrow enough when it comes to defining the precise *economic* conditions of a particular intellectual development. Only a study of the social-economic origins of that milieu provides access to the promised land of literary "truth." The study of literature consists primarily in the study of class oppositions. In his otherwise knowledgeable essay on drama and painting in eighteenth-

67. Peter Demetz concludes: "It follows, therefore, that the sphere of literature remains basically inaccessible to the concentrated forces of economics. Before the economic impulses can have a formative effect upon the sphere of literature, they must make their way through intermediate levels that do not leave them unchanged; their effect 'takes place within the conditions prescribed by the individual area itself.' No further proof is required that here strict economic determinism is replaced by a complicated conception of a hierarchically structured world that seems to suggest, even though quite remotely, an Aristotelian image of the universe." (Peter Demetz, *Marx, Engels and the Poets*, p. 146.)
68. *Kunst und Literatur* (Berlin: 1955), p. 42.

century France, the Russian critic declares: "Only if we examine this main spring, take into account the class struggle and study its many and various aspects, shall we be able to explain to ourselves at all satisfactorily the 'spiritual' history of civilized society. The 'march of its ideas' reflects the history of the classes and of their 'struggle.' "[69] The more this struggle intensifies, the more directly it effects the entire culture. To Plekhanov all art is class-determined, even though the ruling class may tolerate ideological differences that are unrelated to basic economic interests. Only in an exceptional case does a literary work conflict with the ruling class ideology. Ibsen's dramas directly contradicted the moral ideals of the bourgeoisie, and so did Tchernechevski's novel *What Is to Be Done?*. But such individual efforts reflect the dynamics of a society already in the process of changing its class rule.

Plekhanov absorbs everything into his social-economic theory, even the romantically individualist concept of genius. To him the artistic genius "expresses" the dominant aesthetic traits of his class. His unique significance consists in his ability to capture new social relations, while they are still in the process of being formed.[70] Individual traits that cannot be explained through social-economic factors are of no more significance to the literary critic than the number of fragments into which a missile explodes is to the science of ballistics. "The greater a writer is, the stronger and clearer is the dependence that subordinates the character of his work to the character of his time, and the less personal residual remains."[71] Even the specific impact that a work of art belonging to one epoch exercises upon one belonging to another epoch is entirely determined by social conditions. The different treatment which Homer, Virgil, and the French classical theater give to the same mythical material Plekhanov explains entirely through different social-economic structures. The imitator is as far removed from the model as his own society

69. *Art and Social Life*, trans. A. Rothstein (London, 1958), p. 164.

70. *In Defence of Materialism*, trans. Andrew Rothstein (London: Lawrence, Wishort, 1947), p. 216.

71. Ibid., p. 241.

differs from the one in which that model originated.[72] Hence the "literary" law: the influence of the literature of one country upon that of another is directly proportionate to the similarity between their social systems.

Plekhanov's sociologism may appear atypical. He was, in fact, considerably more moderate in his claims than most later art critics, and resisted the kind of propaganda art promoted by Lenin and imposed by Stalin. For him art still had to make its own imprint regardless of its immediate political effects. Even those who reacted against the purely ideological interpretation of art failed to free it from its undue connection with conceptual truth. Thus socialist realism, inaugurated by Zhdanov in 1934, reduced art to the illustrative function of showing in images what concepts explain. Critics of that period exclusively considered the role of the artist to be that of a social teacher whose techniques had to be simple and accessible to all. Art could only directly reflect the social reality from which it emerged. Any attempt to liberate himself from this role would condemn the artist to inauthenticity. At the root of this primitivism lies the theory of ideological "reflection" which neither Marx nor Engels ever held. Of course, today all Marxist aestheticians (including the Soviet ones) have abandoned the "picture" theory of art. But the cognitive bias of the realist heritage persists. Galvano della Volpe, for instance, attacks the derivative character of art in social realism, but he himself defines poetic "discourse" as an intellectual-rational procedure operating by metaphors that depend on "the same categorical norm as the similarity or sameness which regulates inductive, hypothetical and definitional reasoning."[73] Thus even while deemphasizing the importance of the social content of ideas and while stressing their integration

72. Ibid., pp. 203–04.

73. Galvano della Volpe, *Critique of Taste*, p. 86. Cf. also Terry Eagleton, who writes: "Science gives us conceptual knowledge of a situation; art gives us the experience of that situation, which is equivalent to ideology. But by doing this, it allows us to 'see' the nature of that ideology, and thus begins to move us towards that full understanding of ideology which is scientific knowledge" (*Marxism and Literary Criticism* [London: Metheun, 1976], p. 18).

within the work of art, the Italian critic asserts that only conceptual truth conveys meaning.

Certainly, the study of a work of art requires a historical acquaintance with the intellectual tendencies and sentimental
habits of its age and with the basic structure of its native society.
Neither Pascal nor Racine can be fully appreciated independently of their Jansenist background, nor can the Jansenist
movement itself be properly understood outside the political
situation of the *milieux parlementaires*. But the problem lies in the
use one makes of these valuable principles of literary interpretation. Far too often Marxist critics have assumed the existence of
an *immediate* connection between a particular social system and
the artistic achievements of the same period. Trotsky cautioned
against such easy causal interpretations. "A work of art should,
in the first place, be judged by its own law, that is, by the law of
art. But Marxism alone can explain why and how a given tendency in art has originated in a given period of history."[74] Even
the more modest claim that a social-economic theory can explain
how a given tendency in art has originated in a given period of
history must be qualified. The extent and the mode in which
social developments affect literary trends is an exceedingly complex issue. Most social critics assume that there is one kind of
history, of which the social-economic structure constitutes the
basis. Literary historians have been questioning the concept of a
homogeneous historical development for some time, and recently an entire school has challenged it outright.[75] What evidence is there that cultural cycles run parallel with social ones?
None, according to Fernand Braudel. Even to one who does not

74. *Literature and Revolution*, p. 178.
75. The historian of Italian literature, Francesco De Sanctis, long ago suggested that the notion of literary periods may be intrinsically mistaken. In his
suggestive essays on literary periodization, Claudio Guillén shows how literary
events cannot be directly assimilated to social-political cycles and, hence, how a
search for meaningful connections between a single literary work and an entire
social structure remains fruitless. The tendency to freeze historical processes
into a static set of periods that "domesticate historical change and insert revolutions into a reassuring pattern" is particularly hazardous in the area of literature
and the arts. Here only a dynamic periodology applies. Claudio Guillén, *Literature as System* (Princeton: Princeton University Press, 1971), p. 446.

agree with this extreme, structuralist position it is nevertheless evident that aesthetic movements follow a duration of their own that only reluctantly submits to a synchronization with other historical developments, and never simply coincides with economic phases.

The point of the preceding remarks is not to deny the interaction of social-economic and literary or artistic trends, nor the existence of a general cultural climate that reflects social-economic factors as well as cultural ones, but to question whether this climate is ever unified in, and restricted to, what Goldman calls *une vision‾du monde*—that is, a totality of aspirations, feelings, and ideas that unites the members of a group, usually a class, in opposition to others.[76] A cultural climate normally envelops all educated classes. Moreover, its content, whether we call it the spirit of the age or the ideology of the ruling class, provides no direct insight into the structure or even the content of a work of art. Too many Marxist critics have been satisfied with gathering information which may be useful to the understanding of the social and ideological background of literary works (especially novels), but which provides no adequate basis for distinguishing an authentic work of art from a social document. Lukacs, who in his own way contributed to the misunderstanding, nevertheless remained aware of its existence.

> How many works are offered us which have been repeatedly considered and displayed by the [Marxist] "professionals" because they are extraordinarily important historical documents of past times and because many specialists are inclined to mistake the interest of historical content for the living artistic reality. Thus we must constantly remind ourselves of the unmediated evocation of artistic form. Of course, Sophocles' *Oedipus* provides for the historian of antiquity a wealth of information. It is just as certain, however, that nine-tenths of the later audiences or readers of this drama know little or nothing of such pertinent historical facts and are yet moved very profoundly by its working.[77]

76. Lucien Goldman, *Le Dieu caché*, p. 26.

77. Gyorgy Lukacs, *Über die Besonderheit als Kategorie der Asthetik* (Neuwied and Berlin: Luchterhand Verlag, 1967), trans. Berel Lang in Berel Lang and Forrest Williams, eds., *Marxism and Art* (New York: David McKay, 1972), p. 232.

As Lukacs suggests here, a mere sociohistorical interpretation
fails to fulfill the specific requirement made of the art critic—
namely, to understand the *aesthetic* achievement *as such*. Beyond
the general elements of social content and genre the critic must
analyze the unique individuality of a work of art. He must show
how a particular work has, in a unique way, *aesthetically* assimilated the ideas, trends, cultural concerns—indeed, the entire
social reality—from which it emerges. Furthermore, he must
integrate the aesthetic creation with the whole range of social
experience of which the aesthetic forms an integral part.[78]

Understanding works of art, then, consists primarily in understanding "the indirect relations between those works and
the ideological worlds they inhabit—relations which emerge not
just in 'themes' and 'preoccupations,' but in style, rhythm, image,
quality and . . . form."[79] Rather than reducing the individual
work to a common social denominator, the art critic must show
how it both reflects and opposes the cultural totality of which it
forms a part. For the aesthetic significance of a work of art lies
not in the social information it provides, but in its unique mode
of representation. The genuine artist never merely depicts or
describes: he symbolically transforms a given situation and
thereby moves beyond the sphere of ordinary life. Even the
"realistic" artist *chooses* the expressive details of his description
and, in this process of selective symbolization, creates a distance
between himself and the realities or ideologies in which his art
originates. In doing so, he inevitably becomes a critic, however
unwittingly, of the *given*. This may well constitute the major
difference between genuine literature and ideologies: even if the
writer accepts the ideologies of the ruling class, he inevitably
transforms them in the process of aesthetic symbolization. Such
staunch defenders of the bourgeois establishment as Balzac and
Hugo ended up promoting revolutionary attitudes. Such loyal
members of the Communist party as Eisenstein, Shostakovitch,
and Pasternak repeatedly found themselves in conflict with official doctrine.

78. Frederic Jameson, *Marxism and Form* (Princeton, N.J.: Princeton University Press, 1971), p. 45.
79. Terry Eagleton, *Marxism and Literary Criticism*, p. 6.

Unfortunately, Lukacs himself frequently neglected the very principles he so correctly stated. His lifelong preference for the realistic novel, as well as his insensitivity to any kind of "symbolic" literature (even of such a master as Kafka), betrays a continuing subservience to the kind of social realism from which his own theory should have freed him. The significance of "symbolic"—or nonrealistic—work is clearly other than a mere "admission of defeat" on the part of its author in attempting to bestow meaning upon existing reality. The characters in a novel, however realistically drawn, relate negatively to the society of which they are a part. They represent modern man's effort to reconcile the individual's subjective strivings with a world that no longer possesses an intrinsic meaning of its own. The writer's ability to make his characters symbolize a universal concern, often far removed from the immediate social experience, comprises, according to Lukacs, both the social truth and the essential aesthetic quality of the novel. The critic must reach beyond the content of the work of art to its underlying structure. What claims most of his attention are not the social conflicts which the novelist *describes* or which his characters express, but the specific literary form and the aesthetic structure of the work into which the author translates his characters' awareness of their existential situation.

Indeed, despite the creative innovations in literary criticism of writers like Lukacs, Benjamin, Adorno, and Brecht, one cannot but wonder whether Marxist writers and critics have sufficiently overcome the one-sided emphasis on content observed by Engels. Instead of inciting them to explore new avenues, the social theory of literature merely seems to have distracted them from a serious study of their subject. Of course, mediocrity is not restricted to Marxism, but Marxist literary criticism has produced a large amount of it. Few schools have more readily submitted to the rule of dogmatic a priori assumptions and have less sensitively applied external concepts to literary work. Still, the abundance of poor applications of the social interpretation does not invalidate the method itself.

Conclusion
Culture Reintegrated through Praxis

Marx's critique of culture has proven to be exceedingly complex. It bears on all areas of human activity, and more often than not it overturns received opinion about the motive, structure, and goal of man's social life. In this study I have attempted to follow that critique both in its unstated historical assumptions and its (equally unstated) historical conclusions. I have deliberately abstained from the kind of critical questions that Marx's theory, given its premises, could not raise. Such questions may be legitimate and are, in the end, necessary, since no theory emerges from a vacuum. Thinking, however revolutionary, remains what it was from the beginning of philosophy: a dialogue with other thinking. Yet Marx's theory, so explosive in its practical effects, has seldom received the kind of critical attention it deserves. Instead of prompting sustained reflection and a genuine effort to understand, it has usually provoked immediate refutation or unqualified acceptance. I have therefore restricted the discussion to the kind of internal questions that Marx himself could or should have raised about his theory had he reviewed it in the light of our own age. Yet our investigation has now brought us to a point where the question of the *basis* must be posed *in its entirety.*

Against the increasing tendency of Western culture to isolate the individual subject as the sole source of meaning and value, Marx, both in practice and in theory, placed the *social agent* at the origin of the humanization process. In doing so he broke new ground. To be sure, Descartes's *cogito,* Kant's unity of apperception, Fichte's ego were conceived as transcendental subjects, not as the individual's empirical self-consciousness. Nevertheless, neither they nor any other philosopher of the modern

276

age, with the exception of Hegel, introduced social relatedness into the very heart of consciousness. They added the social dimension to an already constituted individual subject. Marx rejected this supremacy of the ego, transcendental as well as empirical. Individual reflection, the starting point of modern philosophy, rests on a more basic socialization process. The failure to recognize this has reduced that entire philosophy to a self-deceptive ideology oblivious of its own social origins. It has prevented the development of a fundamental theory of society. Social thought had mostly been devoted to the impossible project of showing how essentially self-sufficient subjects can nevertheless build an authentic society. Seldom did it surpass the level of intersubjective cooperation. Marx not only joined Hegel in his attempt to reverse that approach; he also disclosed the particular social conditions which had allowed such individualistic theories to prevail.

The same subject-centered attitude of the moderns explains their inability to develop a genuine philosophy of culture. A self conceived as an individual, self-contained subject is already fully constituted when the cultural process begins. But a process that thus begins *post factum* can possess no more than an accidental significance. To be sure, the intrinsic rapport of the body to an objective world had never been questioned. Yet even those philosophers who did not separate the body from the mind, as the Cartesians did, hardly recognized any corporeal objectivity beyond elementary physical needs and desires. Before Hegel, no one attempted to establish the intrinsic necessity of that higher realm of objective expression in which the social as well as the cultural has its roots. The model of this conception of mental life is a solitary self's dialogue with itself. Objective communication merely sealed an already completed, internal *verbum mentis*. From that perspective, culture, exiled from its native habitat, had to wander aimlessly between the emptiness of a pure subject and the opaqueness of an estranged objectivity.

For Marx, socialization is a primary event that directs simultaneously the highest intellectual achievements and the humblest physical activities. Objectification belongs to the essence of being human, on the level of culture as well as on that of the satisfaction of physiological needs. Both are cultural, both are social, and both are "natural." Through this healthy naturalism Marx abandons the subjectivism of the modern epoch and reintroduces an ideal of integral harmony. Yet Marx fostered no romantic dreams about a return of the Saturnian age. Once man came to control nature, he could no longer accept himself as part of a given cosmos. His relation to nature, then, had to be dialectical. Marx's "naturalism" proposes no return to nature, but a reintegration of all human activity, from high to low, in the social dialectic with nature.

The critical question which then confronts us is whether a social-economic "basis" can adequately support such a total integration. Most of Marx's critics stand ready with a quick and negative answer. If material conditions of production determine the mental superstructure, so they say, the economic reduction of the theory is beyond dispute. The preceding pages should have made it clear that the case cannot be stated this simply. Not the technology of production but the *relations* of production determine the superstructure. Marx distinguishes the material conditions of production from the social structures within which this production takes place. Indeed, he traces all social conflicts back to the opposition between the two. The dynamics of communication that "in the last instance" determine the superstructure cannot be reduced to the mechanics of production. To clear up this misunderstanding, however, is not to eliminate all reductionism. For Marx reduces social interaction itself mostly to economically determined activity, and that, as he informs us repeatedly, depends on "the material conditions of their production" (*MEGA* 1^5: 7; *Coll. Works* 5: 32). It would be unwise to make too much of the term *depends*, for Marx insists that man himself determines the circumstances of this material process as much as they determine him. Nevertheless, when Marx singles out economic production as the basic activity, he decisively restricts the scope of this determination.

Marx's theory displays an undeniable tension between, on the one hand, the primacy of economic activity and, on the other, a dialectical, all-integrating view of man's social existence. To posit the social-economic as the basis of all other aspects of culture shifts emphasis from the interaction of *all* moments needed for a full dialectical integration and moves the theory closer to the very kind of causal dependence which Marx had explicitly rejected in his confrontation with materialism. Clearly this is not what Marx intended. But what did he intend?

As we have seen, the "basic" activity is sociocultural from the start. A social being, man never satisfies elementary needs in a purely physical way. Physical *needs* may be natural, and so are the *means* to satisfy them; but society transforms these needs and their fulfillment into sociocultural symbols. Castles and palaces, banquets and celebrations, fashionable dresses and footwear— what are they but satisfactions of culturally transformed needs? Mainly through Marx we have become aware of the intimate link that joins the highest cultural achievements to the most elementary needs. Yet Marx himself did not consistently uphold his own thesis. He contradicts it when he writes in *The German Ideology* that *first* man satisfies his elementary needs, *then* creates the artificial ones. The creation and fulfillment of artificial needs begins with the first awareness of the elementary ones. Similarly, the hierarchy of base and superstructure conflicts with Marx's more fundamental conception of the organic unity of social life. In the course of this study we have pointed to other, more subtle expressions of an inconsistent socialization, such as Marx's conception of the nature of economic activity.

But even if we interpret the *base* quality of the social-economic to mean no more than a certain priority of the elementary material conditions over all others ("primum vivere . . ."), the question still persists of why they should *remain more basic* than others, once the cultural process has been initiated. Does the very persistence of a dualistic model not reintroduce the schizoid view of culture as a separate sphere?

In asserting the primacy of the economic, Marx legitimated a state of affairs that had in fact prevailed in the industrialized parts of Europe since the late eighteenth century. During that period the theoretical abstractions of the budding science of economics were gradually transformed into a cultural reality. Economic concerns dominated all other aspects of life. Whatever fell outside the system of economic production and distribution became detached from the vital center of social life and isolated within a marginal "cultural" sphere of its own. Man turned into a *homo oeconomicus* too absorbed by purely economic activity to spend vital energy on other matters.

Marx rescued productive labor from its cultural isolation. In his concept of praxis he attempted to reintegrate all facets of culture, the theoretical and aesthetic as well as the practical. But the mode in which he attempted to achieve this integration betrays the particular limitations of the society responsible for the separation. Because economic concerns dominated social relations in the modern age, Marx took them to be the base of praxis itself. To be sure, he *never equated* praxis with economically productive activity, since his aim was precisely to change the dominating role of the purely economic. But he continued to assign to economic production a primary role in the socialization process. Consistent with this position, he defended Ricardo's ruthless promotion of economic production at any cost against Sismondi's humanitarian objections.

> He [Ricardo] wants *production for the sake of production* and this with *good reason.* To assert, as sentimental opponents of Ricardo's did, that production is not the object, is to forget that production for its own sake means nothing but the development of human productive forces, in other words the *development of the richness of human nature as an end in itself.* To oppose the welfare of the individual to this end, as Sismondi does, is to assert that the development of the species must be *arrested* in order to safeguard the welfare of the individual, so that, for instance, no war may be waged in which at all events some individuals perish. Apart from the barrenness of such edifying reflections, they reveal a failure to understand the fact that, although at first the development of the capacities of the *human* species takes place at the cost of the majority of human individuals and even classes, in the end it breaks through this contradiction and coincides with the development of the individual; the higher development of individuality is thus only achieved by a historical process during which individuals are sacrificed, for the interests of the species in the human kingdom, as in the animal and plant kingdoms, always assert themselves at the cost of the interests of individuals, because these interests of the species coincide only with the interests of certain individuals, and it is this

coincidence which constitutes the strength of these individuals. [*Werke* 26²: 111; *TSV* 2: 117–18]

Here Marx speaks the language of classical economy and fully shares its assumption that historical progress unilaterally depends upon the advancement of methods of production. The accumulation of wealth and the improvement of methods for achieving it have now become unconditional demands for securing the well-being of society.

There are other problems. By subordinating theory to productive activity, Marx severely restricted the latter's social scope. All productive activity is, of course, intrinsically social, but as Marx showed in the case of captialism, production that is primarily economic makes the inherently social character of the productive act subordinate to the pursuit of particular and exclusive objectives. Social harmony is simply assumed, and throughout, it is assumed in individual terms.[1] The question, of course, is not whether Marx upheld a social or an individual vision of man. From the very beginning he unambiguously asserted the essentially social nature of man and of his productive activity.

> Thus the *social* character is the general character of the whole movement: just as society itself produces *man as man,* so is society *produced* by him. Activity and enjoyment, both in their content and in their *mode of existence,* are *social: social* activity and *social* enjoyment. The *human* aspect of nature exists only for *social* man. . . . [*MEGA* 1³:116; *Coll. Works* 3: 298]

The *Grundrisse* confirmed this strong statement with an even stronger one: "The human being is in the most literal sense a *zoon politikon,* not merely a gregarious animal, but an animal which can individuate itself only in the midst of society" (*GR* 6; NIC 84). Yet the productive activity which must actualize this socialization remains basically an individual enterprise. "All production is appropriation of nature by the *individual* within and through a definite form of society" (*GR* 9; NIC 87).

From eighteenth-century economists Marx inherited a techni-

---

1. Louis Dumont, *From Mandeville to Marx,* p. 137.

cal, naturalist view of man as productive agent. His attempts to surpass this restrictive concept through his theory of praxis could not entirely succeed, as that praxis itself continued to have its basis in economic activity. Marx firmly rejected the acquisitive model of the classical economists, which reduced the goal of society to an accumulation of individual fortunes, and its activity to a combination of *particular* productive efforts. Yet he did not abandon the economic perspective. The economic relations, singled out from the whole social complex as more fundamental, are inadequate to support the entire social structure. Precisely for that reason, Hegel buttressed them with the more fundamental social institutions of family and state. Isolated from the social totality, economic relations are unable to achieve complete social integration. Of course, such an isolation actually does take place in modern society, and Marx has uniquely contributed to our awareness of it. But his theory failed to overcome it.

The most serious obstacle to full social and cultural integration consists not in the adoption of a particular economic system in preference to another, but in the primary abstraction whereby the economic sphere comes to dominate all others. To overcome this obstacle requires more than changing the conditions of the current systems of production and distribution. It requires eliminating what R. H. Tawney called the "obsession by economic issues." His critique of capitalism applies equally well to Marx's economic approach to society.

> The burden of our civilization is not merely, as many suppose, that the product of industry is ill-distributed, or its conduct tyrannical, or its operation interrupted by embittered disagreements. It is that industry itself has come to hold a position of exclusive predominance among human interests, which no single interest, and least of all the provision of the material means of existence, is fit to occupy. That obsession by economic issues is as local and transitory as it is repulsive and disturbing. To future generations it will appear as pitiable as the obsession of the seventeenth century by religious quarrels appears today; indeed, it is less rational, since the object with which it is concerned is less important.[2]

2. R. H. Tawney, *The Acquisitive Society* (1920), pp. 183–84.

Marx's society continues to be determined by that same concern with production. The elimination of economic class is insufficient to achieve a society both structured and egalitarian. Even a classless society, if it is built on a basis of economic production, cannot free its members from the competition and struggle that it intended to suppress;[3] for social oppositions result more from the combination of economic scarcity and extreme interest attached to productive relations than from the particular mode in which the production takes place. The sad examples of economic conflict and the rise of new classes in allegedly "classless" societies confirm this.

Thus emerges that economization of the political realm which Hannah Arendt denounces: "the role of revolution was no longer to liberate men from the oppression of their fellow men, let alone to found freedom, but to liberate the life process of society from the fetters of scarcity so that it could swell into a stream of abundance. Not freedom but abundance became now the aim of revolution."[4] Yet the one-sidedness of Marx's critique becomes intelligible and hence partly justified if we place it in its historical context. It was one in which the economic question, the spectre of the desperately poor masses, obstructed the road to *social freedom*. The economic question had become *the* single social issue.

Poverty in industrial capitalism was not the direct result of the scarcity or inaccessibility of resources, as it had usually been in precapitalist society, but of a particular mode of exploiting and distributing these resources. Industrialization inaugurated a new system of dependence which, in contrast to earlier forms of "personal" dependence (slavery), was determined by its object. "Personal independence founded on *objective* dependence is the second great form, in which a system of general social metabolism, of universal relations, of all-round needs and capacities is formed for the first time" (*GR* 75; NIC 158). During the period of early industrialism, this system of objective dependence reduced social relations to modes of cooperation for the purpose

3. Werner Stark, *Social Theory and Christian Thought* (London: Routledge and Kegan Paul, 1958), p. 87.

4. Hannah Arendt, *On Revolution* (New York: Viking Press, 1963), p. 58.

of satisfying elementary physical needs. The individual task of physical and economic survival engaged almost all social forces. Marx correctly perceived that a resocialization would require fundamental changes in the production process. Yet when he singled out the economic determinant (so critical to the social structure of his own time) as unqualifiedly "basic" with respect to all other activities, he generalized a historical condition and conferred the status of a universal principle upon a temporary matrix of action.

To deny the universal primacy of the economic is not, however, to declare Marx's critique obsolete. In the current revolutionary modernization of less advanced societies it is hard to conceive that any factor is more important than the economic one. It clearly dominates world politics, and it decisively influences cultural transformations. Still, as more recent developments of advanced industrialized countries have shown, it does not deserve the *permanent* priority in the cultural process which Marx attributed to it. The relation between economics and the rest of culture cannot be adequately understood through a model in which the former always plays a more basic role than the latter.

To be sure, another trend in Marx's thought leads in the opposite direction, where the economic production functions as a temporary means to provide the leisure required for the future aesthetic and cultural emancipation of man.

In fact, the realm of freedom actually begins only where labour which is determined by necessity and mundane considerations ceases; thus in the very nature of things it lies beyond the sphere of actual material production. Just as the savage must wrestle with Nature to satisfy his wants, to maintain and reproduce life, so must civilized man, and he must do so in all social formations and under all possible modes of production. With his development this realm of physical necessity expands as a result of his wants; but, at the same time, the forces of production which satisfy these wants also increase. Freedom in this field can only consist in socialized man, the associated producers, rationally regulating their interchange with Nature, bringing it under their common control, instead of being ruled by it as by the blind forces of Nature; and achieving this with the least expenditure of energy and under conditions most favorable to, and worthy of, their human nature. But it nonetheless still remains a realm of necessity. Beyond it begins that development of human energy which is an end in itself, the true realm of freedom, which, however, can blossom forth only with this realm of necessity as its basis. [*Werke* 25:828; *Cap.* 3:820]

As early as the *Grundrisse*, Marx refers to the saving of labor as the "real economy," and to the time thus saved as "time for higher activity" (*GR* 499; NIC 711–12). But does this ulterior goal justify the present "one-dimensional advance of a process of rationalization"?[5] Indeed, is the future ideal of leisure for culture consistent with a praxis that integrates all activity, transforming the process of production itself into "practice, experimental science, materially creative and objective science" (*GR* 499; NIC 711–12; also *GR* 426; NIC 527)? On the one hand, Marx glorifies productive work as a cultural ideal; on the other, he continues to be fascinated by the ancient ideal of *theoria*.[6]

However, rather than dwelling on this inconsistency, I prefer to draw attention to the primacy of praxis itself. This primacy came to be accepted in the course of the nineteenth century, partly as a result of attitudes created by industrial capitalism. Once considered a divine punishment, work was transformed into a religion in its own right, complete with earthly blessings of wealth and success. Leisure, traditionally considered the ideal goal of life, now deteriorated into a vice. Marx elevated this practical primacy of productive work into the very definition of man, thereby imbuing the practical axiom of the conduct of his age with a theoretical legitimacy.

With Marx's theory of praxis, Western thought reached the final stage of a development in which the intrinsic rationality of the world order has been replaced by a subjective one of man's own being. This development had originated in the nominalist separation of intelligibility from reality. It concluded in a number of modern positions, with vitalist and existentialist philosophies at one end of the spectrum and theories of praxis at the

5. Albrecht Wellmer, *Critical Theory of Society*, p. 109.
6. Hannah Arendt, *Between Past and Future* (New York: Penguin Books, 1977), p. 24.

other. The role of reason thereby changed from a normative to a functional one. In Marxist praxis, reason emerges from the productive act itself as an instrument to further it.[7]

In a praxis that recognizes no standards or rules other than those of methodic action itself, theory ceases to provide criteria for action. Consistency and efficiency emerge to take its place. Henceforth we ask, has something been done in the most effective way? Has it obeyed its own immanent teleology? No higher moral authority exists. No natural bond restricts the appropriating activity, nor does any structure inherent in the mind or in an objective order call for a specific mode of behavior. Even the "given" physical and social worlds provide no *norms,* but merely conditions, means, or at most, limits to this activity. It becomes difficult to conceive how they could in any way enable praxis to do what, according to the Paris Manuscripts, it should do— namely, "produce in accordance with the standard of every species" and "apply everywhere the *inherent standard* to the object" (*MEGA* 1³:89; *Coll. Works* 3:277). The notion of a "right" order of action, as understood in traditional theories of morality and natural law, loses all its meaning. The transforming process itself is the only absolute. Theoretical reason is reduced to a subordinate role. Instead of directing the activity by considerations of ends and means, it merely functions as an instrument of that activity. Henceforth it has lost the right and the means to raise questions of *ultimate* justification.[8]

Does not the universal scope of human thought constantly and inevitably transcend the purely practical level? Indeed, praxis itself requires the presence of *purely* theoretical and wholly disinterested acts. Insofar as all work is a *project,* it presupposes distance, observation, reflection, judgment, and decision. "Consciousness that does not contemplate reality by way of cognition and recognition and that lacks an independent urge is also unable to respond to the needs stemming from that reality."[9] Without some subordination to theory, praxis never attains

7. Max Horkheimer, *The Eclipse of Reason* (New York: Seabury, 1974), p. 3.

8. Compare Leszek Kolakowski, "The Opiate of the Demiurge," in *Toward a Marxist Humanism* (New York: Grove Press, 1968), pp. 118–19.

9. Nathan Rothenstreich, *Basic Problems of Marx's Philosophy* (Indianapolis: Bobbs-Merrill, 1966), p. 135.

the level of the properly human. Even the theoretical part of praxis which some Marxists distinguish so radically from pure theory could not survive without it. For it is precisely the speculative entertainment of ideas which has, in the end, most strongly influenced practical innovation.

Now Marx never questioned the legitimacy of theory as such: his own critique of society was itself a theoretical enterprise. What is at stake is the *priority* of praxis with respect to theory. Unquestionably, theoretical thought often originates in solving practical problems, and praxis constantly reorients and corrects the development of theory. Theoretical activity starts from what Merleau-Ponty called a *practognosie*—the awareness inherent in bodily motions and practical observations. Yet neither this practical origin nor the permanent interference of praxis decides the issue of the autonomy of theory. Mutual impact and interpenetration show that theory and praxis are both constitutive and inseparable elements of overall human activity. But their constant intimate cooperation does not reduce or subordinate one to the other. The meaning conveyed by thinking surpasses in universality the meaning intrinsic *in* action.

Ideas lead a life of their own that survives the practical needs connected with their origin. This allows them to spread far beyond their native soil and to take new roots in societies with very different practical needs. Indeed, the ideological complexes that define the meaning and purpose of a society transcend its practical concerns altogether and direct its praxis more than they are directed by it. When they lose their impact, as when a society moves from a traditional, comprehensive world-view to a secular pluralism, *praxis itself* changes. The alleged priority of praxis is itself an *idea*, and one that has changed the practical life of the modern world.

Having criticized the priority of the economic and the more general priority of praxis in Marx's *theory*, I feel compelled to write a final word in defense of the vision behind it. Beyond the informal theory, still articulated within the sociocultural framework of his own age, lies an elusive but portentous vision of the future. In it the question of priority ceases to occur. Instead, Marx envisions a *total* praxis that reunites theory with practical activity and culture with economic production. In this reintegration of all human activity neither theory nor praxis can claim absolute priority. Each presents one aspect of a total, integrally human activity and, as such, remains *subordinate to the whole*. This applies as much to economically productive activity as it does to poetry and speculative theory. Whether and how such a vision could ever be realized in Western culture remains uncertain after Marx's discussion. I suspect that it might well fall under his own critique of utopian thought. But then, we may wonder whether Marx himself has not truncated his own theory by prematurely dismissing the utopian element which it unquestionably contains and which continues to give it its greatest appeal. In any event, that "vision" escapes my final criticism, which aims, not at the idea of an integrated praxis as such, but at the particular mode in which Marx formulated it. I have restricted my study to Marx's *actual argument*.

Nevertheless, the idea of a fully integrated culture, however utopian it must still appear to us today, deserves serious consideration, independent of the distorting context in which Marx conceived it. Is it not possible to overcome the predicament of our age without returning to the earlier, one-sided, and socially restrictive ideal of contemplation? This study by no means advocates a return to the ancient theoria. Even assuming that it were possible to bracket the entire experience of modernity, it would be extremely undesirable to do so. The dignity and relative autonomy of practical activity, unknown to the ancients and inadequately appreciated in the Middle Ages, have created the very conditions for that universal development of freedom upon which both our private aspirations and our democratic ideals rest. We do not want to abandon them for a return to the education of a small elite which, in its very one-sidedness, itself remains unacquainted with the full scope of human emancipation. Our ideal of culture comprehends all nations and individuals. Marx has considerably contributed to the expansion of the democratic ideal, both through his critique of the past (including that past which we call "modern") and through his anticipation, however timebound and imperfect, of the future. That he has done so may in the end remain his principal merit in the judgment of history.

Index